CliffsNotes®

Praxis® Teaching Reading (5204)

by
Nancy L. Witherell, Ed.D.

Houghton Mifflin Harcourt
Boston • New York

About the Author

Nancy L. Witherell, Ed.D., is a professor at Bridgewater State University in Bridgewater, Massachusetts, where she teaches undergraduate and graduate reading courses. She has presented at numerous state and national conferences, has written a number of books on literacy, and frequently consults as a children's reading teacher.

Editorial

Executive Editor: Greg Tubach

Senior Editor: Christina Stambaugh

Production Editor: Jennifer Freilach

Copy Editor: Pamela Weber-Leaf

Technical Editor: Mary Beth Allen, Ed.D.

Proofreader: Susan Moritz

CliffsNotes® Praxis® Teaching Reading (5204)

Copyright © 2018 by Houghton Mifflin Harcourt Publishing Company

All rights reserved.

Cover image © Shutterstock / Mavrick

Library of Congress Control Number: 2018937300
ISBN: 978-1-328-71552-4 (pbk)

Printed in the United States of America
DOO 10 9 8 7 6 5 4 3 2 1   4500720249

For information about permission to reproduce selections from this book, write to trade.permissions@hmhco.com or to Permissions, Houghton Mifflin Harcourt Publishing Company, 3 Park Avenue, 19th Floor, New York, New York 10016.

www.hmhco.com

Table of Contents

Introduction

Reading is a content area with its own vocabulary, theories, and research—collectively, "the knowledge of what." Yet, reading also includes pedagogy, methodology, instruction, and analysis of reading behaviors—in sum, "the knowledge of how." The main avenue into all other academic content areas, reading is one of the most important skills a child can obtain. Therein lies the importance of having expert teachers of reading in classrooms, and one pathway to this expertise is taking and passing the Praxis Teaching Reading (5204) test. So, let's get you ready for it!

How This Book Is Organized

This book is organized into chapters that will help you prepare for the Praxis (5204). The purpose of each chapter is summarized below:

Chapter 1:
This chapter provides an overview of the test's components, including useful information about test logistics, as well as some study plan recommendations.

Chapters 2–11:
The goal of these chapters is to provide, in concise and clear language, the basic content of reading and reading methodology. These chapters contain the material you will need to know and completely understand in order to pass the Praxis (5204).

Chapter 12:
Chapter 12 offers some tips on test-taking and preparation for the day of the test. It also explains how to use this book's two practice tests to achieve best results on the actual test.

Chapter 13:
Chapter 13 is Practice Test 1, a model practice test that offers 90 selected-response questions and three constructed-response questions. For each selected-response question, the correct answer is provided, along with an answer explanation. Two model answers are given for each constructed-response question.

Chapter 14:
Chapter 14 is Practice Test 2, and it follows the same format as Practice Test 1.

Recalling Information: What Works for You?

Before you begin to study for the test, do a bit of reflection. Think about how you best learn new material. The following questions may help:

- Can you read material and remember it?
- Does highlighting help you to recall information?
- Do note cards help you study?
- Does it help you to record important information and play back the recording, perhaps while you're driving?
- Do game formats, such as matching games, help you to remember definitions?
- Are you tech-savvy and would you, therefore, enjoy an online-game study format?
- Can you study better with music or without?
- Do mnemonic devices help you? (A mnemonic is an abbreviation or word that helps you remember a larger piece of information, such as ROY G BIV for the colors of the rainbow.)

Your answers to these questions will help pinpoint the best way for you to study and learn the information in this book. At this point in your life, you have been going to school for years. You know better than anyone else how you learn best. Use this knowledge to ensure that you are truly ready on the day of the test. When you have studied well, you gain confidence, and that is extremely helpful. Personally, I like to use index cards when I study. This leads to the next topic: the reading and writing connection.

The Reading and Writing Connection

Reading and writing are interdependent processes. What you learn in one process is transferable to the other. When studying, you should take advantage of this interdependence, as it can help you "seal" the information for later recall. When reading, you must sometimes remind yourself to focus on the content of your reading. When writing, you must think and interact with the content. During this thinking stage, you categorize, relate pieces of information to one another, sequence, clarify, and distinguish important ideas from merely interesting ones. While you may not realize that you are performing all of these functions when you read and write, all of this thinking is enormously beneficial. Take advantage of the reading and writing connection, and make a study notebook or note cards as you review the material in this book.

Organizing Notes in a Notebook

There are two ways of organizing notes in a notebook. (When I am preparing for a lecture and taking notes that I must refer to later, I use option two.)

Option One: Linear Method

With this method, organization of notes should begin with the topic label, followed by bulleted information. Start by writing the topic on one line and underlining it. Then, as you read, add the important information underneath. That way, when you study, you can cover the bulleted information so that just the topic name is visible, and try to recall the information that you have covered. After you attempt to recall each topic's information, you may look to see if you were correct.

Option Two: Two-Column Method

With the two-column method, you organize content by drawing a line down a sheet of ruled paper, approximately 2 inches from the left side, dividing the paper into two unequal columns. As you read, write the topic and, perhaps, subtopics, in the left column. In the right, wider column, write and bullet important notes. When you study, use another piece of paper to cover the bulleted points in the right column, and refer to the topics and subtopics in the left column. Try to recall the bulleted information, then check to see if you have recalled correctly.

Organizing Notes on Index or Note Cards

Index or note cards are more cumbersome to store, but they are probably slightly easier to use than a notebook. To take notes on the material covered in this book, 4″-by-6″ index cards would work best. On one side, write the main topic and subtopics. On the other side, write the important information in bulleted form. When you study, refer to the topic and subtopic terms on the front of the card, and try to remember the important information that you detailed on the back. Turn the card over to see if you were right. The advantage of using index or note cards is that you may remove the cards that contain information you feel confident about and study only the ones containing information you are still learning.

Going back to what works for you . . . A young man, I'll call him Adam, a lifetime friend of my 20-something son, asked if he could stay at our cottage for a couple of days because he had to study for an important exam. Adam's exam was in the medical field (he analyzes blood samples for various diseases—a very important and life-saving job). Adam had failed this test the first time he took it, and at $240 a shot, he really wanted to pass this time. Adam showed up at the cottage with over 400 index cards. He had learned that the study approach he used the first time didn't work. His home is very noisy so, aware of the solitude at our summer place (when only I am here; otherwise it's anything but quiet), he asked if he could come and stay for a couple of days to prepare for the test. Adam knew he needed quiet to study. He confessed that he had never used note cards before. A coworker who had passed the exam gave Adam about 300 prepared note cards to help Adam study. Adam found them extremely helpful, so he made about 100 more of his own. As he studied the cards, he would occasionally refer to his 800-page textbook for clarification. Adam was pacing himself. The exam was about a month away, so his study plan was on track. About 6 weeks later, I received a fantastic text that simply said, "I passed." This real-life scenario is why you need to figure out what study approach works for you. You want to pass the test the first time.

How to Prepare for This Book's Practice Tests—Getting Ready for the Real Thing

As mentioned earlier, this book has two practice tests. Each contains 90 selected-response questions (multiple-choice) and three constructed-response questions (essay questions). This setup corresponds to the number of questions on the actual Praxis (5204) you will be taking. The selected-response questions in the practice tests cover all of the test topics. They are set up purposefully, to give you a taste of the real test. The constructed-response section contains three questions that integrate knowledge from the broad categories. Chapter 12, "Test-Taking Strategies," explains how to simulate the real testing experience; be sure to review it as part of your study plan.

Formulating a Study Plan

Before you get started, you need a study plan. Here's a good example:

- First, either register for the test or choose an approximate future date when you plan to take it.
- Open your calendar and plug in windows of study time.
- Reserve 2½ hours of study time for each of the practice tests, perhaps a week before you plan to take the real test. That will allow you sufficient time to review any weak areas.
- Then, go backward in your calendar and plug in windows of study time that lead right up to the practice tests. Be sure to reserve some time to read the "Praxis Study Companion – Teaching Reading (5204)," found at https://www.ets.org/s/praxis/pdf/5204.pdf. The Study Companion contains 22 selected-response practice questions and one sample constructed-response question with three scored sample responses.
- After taking a practice test, allot another hour of study time (1 hour for each practice test) to check your answers and review the answer explanations.
- The week before test day, continue to study. Retake one of the practice tests if you feel this will be helpful.
- If you find it useful to study with other people, form a study group, if possible. If you opt to supplement your preparation with a study group, be sure to maintain your personal study schedule as well.

Chapter 1

Overview of Praxis Teaching Reading (5204)

Test Format

The Praxis Teaching Reading (5204) test measures prospective teachers' knowledge of the basics of reading. Over time, the "what" of teaching reading has remained mostly the same, but the "how" has continually changed with new research or policies. For example, with the passage of the No Child Left Behind Act in 2001, phonics became a focus area, and is therefore emphasized on the test. The content of the Praxis (5204) is arranged as follows:

Note: The subcategories in the table below are the author's take, not the test developer's.

Format of the Test

Content Categories	Subcategories Within the Broad Content	Expected Number of Questions
Emergent Literacy ❑ Oral Language ❑ Concepts of Print	❑ Understanding that oral language and reading are interrelated (relationship of print to speech) ❑ Environmental influences and modeling of standard English ❑ Importance of environmental print and visuals ❑ Book handling skills and print awareness ❑ Letter recognition and print features	15 selected response
Phonological Awareness	❑ Importance of relationship between phonics and phonemic awareness ❑ Progression of phonological awareness ❑ Systematic and explicit instruction and assessment techniques	14 selected response
Alphabetic Principle/Phonics and Word Analysis	❑ Difference between phonological awareness and phonics ❑ Progressive stages and systematic explicit instruction of phonics ❑ Instructional processes and materials	14 selected response

continued

Content Categories	Subcategories Within the Broad Content	Expected Number of Questions
Comprehension and Fluency	❏ Students' background knowledge, cultural and linguistic relationship to comprehension ❏ Systematic and explicit instruction of comprehension and use of multiple strategies ❏ Features, structure, and genres of texts ❏ Writing to support reading comprehension ❏ Choosing appropriate text ❏ Using effective formal and informal assessments ❏ Components of fluency and relationship to comprehension ❏ Fluency instruction and assessment	30 selected response
Vocabulary	❏ Use of context for word identification ❏ Word parts and word relationships ❏ Direct and indirect instruction and selection for direct (explicit) instruction ❏ Grammatical functions' relationship to comprehension ❏ Wide reading and monitoring progress of vocabulary growth	17 selected response
Instructional Processes ❏ Instructional Practices ❏ Curriculum Materials ❏ Assessment	❏ Creating a positive learning environment ❏ Differentiation for ability levels ❏ Knowing a variety of text and how to select appropriate materials ❏ Using technology to enhance instruction and learning ❏ Types of assessment and how to use assessment data to inform instruction and parents	3 constructed response (one for each process category; essay format)

Topics Covered

The primary goal of this book is to help you prepare for and pass the Praxis (5204). Studying the material in this book will also help to increase your knowledge of reading and reading instruction so that you can become an effective teacher of the subject. The more you see and study this information on reading and writing, the more you will be able to understand and recall what you have learned.

The following breakdown of the six Praxis (5204) broad content categories is a preview of the information presented in chapters 2–11 of this book.

Note: You'll find vocabulary terms listed throughout chapters 2–11. As you have learned in your studies, children need multiple exposures to vocabulary words before they "own" them. This holds true for adult learners as well. You'll be exposed repeatedly to vocabulary words and material to help your recall.

Emergent Literacy

Oral Language

The reading teacher is expected to:

- **Know how oral language and reading skills are interdependent and that building skills in one area promotes growth in the other.** The skills of phonemic awareness, vocabulary, fluency, and comprehension begin with oral language. As children learn to read, these skills transfer over into the written word, and vice versa. A child who uses the expression "I'm a lucky duck" will understand its meaning when reading.

- **Know the components of receptive and expressive language and stages of language development.** Language universally develops in a sequence. There are four basic vocabularies: listening, speaking, reading, and writing.

- **Understand that environmental factors influence students' oral language development.** Many elements of home life impact a child's language development. Two specific examples: 1) A child living in a home that is economically disadvantaged will not necessarily come to school having the language skills of a child who has parents who can afford a variety of language-rich experiences. 2) A child who lives in a home environment that fosters and promotes reading and learning experiences will hear a variety of rich language; this vocabulary is likely to become part of the child's listening and speaking vocabulary.

- **Have the ability to model correct language usage and show respect for regional and dialectical variations.** Standard American English is used by professionals. Helping students gain the skills of Standard American English can aid in students' future success. It is the teacher's responsibility to be culturally responsive to speech used by her students, to model Standard American English, and to encourage students' progress in using English grammar.

- **Be familiar with appropriate methods to assess students' oral language development.** Since oral language and reading skills are interdependent, a child's deficiency in oral communication can negatively affect his growth in reading. It is important that teachers recognize when students need additional support for growth in oral language skills.

Concepts of Print

The reading teacher is expected to:

- **Understand the interrelationship between the printed word and the spoken word.** Demonstrate the concepts of print so that the child learns that print consists of spoken words written down, and that those written words contain meaning.

- **Recognize that environmental print, pictures, and symbols are part of literacy and contribute to literacy development.** Environmental print is everywhere, and the majority of children pick up visual symbols at a very young age. Parents of toddlers will point at pictures in books and "read" with one-word utterances such as *dog, clown,* or *apple,* aiding children in recognizing pictures as representations of real objects. Similarly, while riding in a car, children learn environmental print like stop signs, street signs, and fast food symbols. These adventures in print stimulate a child's literacy life.

- **Know methods of modeling one-to-one word correspondence and the directionality of print.** To be able to identify how a word looks, students must be taught to recognize that a written word corresponds with a spoken word. In addition, children must learn to read a book starting at the front cover and proceeding to the back. They must be taught to read text starting at the top of the page and to proceed from left to right, line by line, to the bottom of the page.

- **Understand that influences from a child's environment affect his development of print awareness.** A child starting school who lives in a house where reading and writing are rare begins with a disadvantage in literacy growth compared with a child who has been read to almost daily and has seen reading and writing modeled in the home.

- **Recognize that knowledge of concepts of print includes differentiating words and spaces in print, being able to point to first and last letters in a word, and identifying basic punctuation.** Knowledge of the concepts of print includes knowing the difference between a word and a blank space and being able to identify the beginning and ending of a word. For example, a young child can echo read (say after the teacher) the sentence "The cat ran up a tree." However, the child may simply have the sentence memorized. If the teacher uses a pointer for the child to follow along, the pointer may be on the word *ran* when he has completed "reading" the sentence. This indicates that he does not fully understand the concepts of words, spaces, or end marks.

- **Know various instructional strategies for teaching letter recognition.** Letter recognition should be taught explicitly using hands-on, interactive approaches such as reading alphabet books or poems and highlighting specific letters or making letters from Play-Doh or Wikki Stix. Being able to identify letters by name is an indicator and a predictor of success in reading.

- **Employ observational and other appropriate techniques to assess students' knowledge of print awareness.** There are various ways to assess students' print awareness. Generally, assessments are conducted by observing students' behaviors when interacting with print, using a checklist of specific competencies or skills. In some instances, the observations are implemented through a systematic approach of having students show awareness of particular concepts of print, such as pointing out where one should begin reading. In other instances, anecdotal notes are made regarding students' behaviors during various interactions with print.

Phonological Awareness

The reading teacher is expected to:

- **Know the relationship between phonological awareness and phonemic awareness.** Phonological awareness pertains to a student's awareness of the sound structure of words, such as syllables, rhyming sounds, onsets, and rimes. Phonemic awareness is less broad and focuses on the recognition of different letter sounds in words—the phoneme. Phonemic awareness pertains to the manipulation of sounds only; a student who is phonemically aware may not necessarily know that letters exist. An example of this is a 4-year-old who can isolate /h/ as the sound beginning the word *hat*, yet this child may not know that the sound is represented by the letter "h."

- **Know that there is a relationship between phonemic awareness and the development of decoding and encoding skills.** A child who is phonemically aware can isolate and manipulate sounds in words. The ability to do this provides the foundation for children to learn the letter that corresponds to the sound. This correspondence then aids in the development of decoding (reading words through letter-sound correspondence) and encoding (writing words through letter-sound correspondence).

- **Be familiar with the progression of phonological awareness skills.** This progression includes such things as word awareness, phonemic awareness, awareness of rhymes, alliteration, and syllable sound bites, as well as manipulation of onset and rime sounds.

- **Have awareness of developmental levels for phonological awareness and age ranges of this acquisition.** Phonemic awareness begins prior to school and should be acquired by kindergarten or first grade in the normal sequence of growth. Phonemic awareness activities can be incorporated into classroom activities, but should be intermixed with explicit phonics instruction.

- **Know various instructional strategies to systematically and explicitly teach phonological awareness skills.** The consensus seems to indicate five levels of phonological awareness. To teach systematically, a teacher would teach in this order, beginning with the least complex skill: word awareness, rhyming, segmenting and alliteration, onset and rhyme, blending and segmentation, and finally blending and segmenting individual phonemes.

- **Have an understanding of how to assess beginning readers' phonological awareness.** Most assessments of phonological awareness are based on the analysis of observed reading behaviors. Knowing where a child is on the phonological awareness continuum allows a teacher to teach toward the next skill level. For example, one informal assessment, known as the Yopp-Singer Test of Phoneme Segmentation (easily found with a search), has students segment sounds of spoken words. This assessment allows a teacher to discern whether a child is aware of the different sounds in words; a minimal amount correct on this assessment would indicate that a child is not strong in phonemic awareness.

Alphabetic Principle/Phonics and Word Analysis

The reading teacher is expected to:

- **Know the differences between phonics and phonological awareness.** Phonological awareness is the knowledge that sound structures vary within words and that these sounds can be manipulated in some way. Phonics instruction helps students learn letter-sound correspondences.

- **Understand that readers of all ages progress through developmental stages.** When students learn to decode (read) and encode (write), they go through developmental stages. In the initial stages, most children begin with "pretend" reading and writing. Beginning reading includes memorized stories or stories told from pictures; beginning writing includes pictures, marks, and scribbles that are used to communicate messages.

- **Understand the recommended progression of phonics instruction.** Phonics is taught on a continuum that gets progressively more complex. The progression starts with individual consonant and vowel sounds and segues to blends, digraphs, diphthongs, and so forth. The interrelationship of reading and writing fosters growth in both areas; when instruction is done in one area, it transfers to the other.

- **Know methods to differentiate the instruction between phonetically regular and irregular words.** A significant number of words do not follow phonics generalizations. For example, the word *great* does not. *Great* is pronounced with a long /a/ sound, but the phonics generalization states that when two vowels are together the first one has the long vowel sound—which is true in *beat, treat,* and *meat.* Students need to learn that if they try a generalization in a word and it does not sound correct in the sentence, they must use semantics and syntax to help identify the correct word.

- **Know the two basic types of syllables and the principles for dividing syllables.** There are two basic types of syllables: open and closed. An open syllable ends with a long vowel sound, like the first syllable in *baby*. A closed syllable ends with a consonant, like *bask* in *basket.* Many of the rules that govern how syllables are separated are based on whether the syllables are open or closed.

- **Know methods to explicitly teach both phonics and word analysis to students.** Explicit instruction of phonics and word analysis skills is highly recommended. Word analysis is often referred to as morphemic analysis or structural analysis. When using word analysis skills, students identify word parts and their meaning to aid in word identification.

- **Know techniques to teach the reading and spelling of multisyllabic words.** This represents further development of structural analysis. Students need to learn how to analyze words for reading, but must also understand the rules to add affixes for spelling. For example, to make the word *bike* into *biking,* the final "e" is dropped and "ing" is added.

- **Understand how materials and methods can be used to reinforce spelling rules.** Decodable text, which contains sight words and words that adhere to phonics rules, can reinforce spelling. When students write, decoding can reinforce spelling and can also be used as an assessment for phonics needs.

- **Know a variety of ways to assess phonics and word analysis skills.** This includes formal and informal assessments.

Comprehension and Fluency

Comprehension

The reading teacher is expected to:

- **Understand that students' background knowledge impacts comprehension.** If a student is very familiar with the topic in a text, the reading will be easier and his comprehension higher. On the other hand, if a student has limited knowledge of what is in the text, the opposite occurs: lower comprehension. In this case, teachers can build background knowledge to enhance comprehension. This is exceptionally important with English Language Learners (ELLs) who come from a very different background and culture, and may have limited English vocabulary.

- **Understand the relationship between vocabulary knowledge and comprehension.** If students begin their reading knowing the vocabulary, they are more inclined to comprehend the text. Sometimes it is necessary to explicitly teach vocabulary when the words are unknown and the concepts are difficult. Other times, students can use their background knowledge and context to determine the meanings of unfamiliar words.

- **Know that students' cultural and linguistic background can impact comprehension.** Lack of background knowledge and knowledge of English language vocabulary can impede comprehension. Students have a variety of backgrounds, languages, socioeconomic statuses, learning abilities and disabilities, and attitudes. All of this affects teaching in general, and must be considered in order to provide an optimal learning experience for each student.

- **Know the methods of using systematic and explicit instruction to develop comprehension skills.** Comprehension can be improved using a variety of strategies through metacognitive (thinking about one's own thinking and learning) activities or recognition of text features. A teacher needs to be able to model the necessary tools to aid in students' understanding of text. The tools vary from such activities as visualization strategies to the use of graphic organizers to the teaching of text structures.

- **Know that students need to use multiple strategies to comprehend reading material.** Teachers need to be able to model and help students analyze both fiction and nonfiction texts, which contain various text structures. Reading fiction is different from reading nonfiction (informational) text. Strategies for fiction may include analysis of story elements such as plot and of characters and their motives. In the case of informational text, strategies are needed to teach recognition of text structures, such as compare and contrast, to deepen comprehension. The various strategies that can be employed to enhance reading comprehension do not always work best one at a time. In many cases, students must use a number of strategies in tandem.

- **Be familiar with how language structure in text can impact comprehension.** Language structure has a role in text. Sentences, phrases, and paragraphs are all part of the text structure that leads to understanding. For example, students are taught that a paragraph covers one particular idea or topic and that the next paragraph may add to that information. Also, sentences can have various roles, such as leading a reader into the paragraph or transitioning to the next paragraph.

- **Understand that text features have a purpose and students should know that purpose.** Text features, like headings and subheadings, aid readers in preparing to read a section of text. This in turn aids comprehension. It also brings order to the text, and good text organization is helpful to the reader.

- **Be familiar with different genres and their recognizable text structures.** Genres have criteria that need to be taught to students. For example, a fairytale often begins with "Once upon a time," ends with "They lived happily ever after," and may include magic; a biography is about a person's life; an autobiography is about a person's life and is written by the person; and a mystery has clues and diversions. Various genres need to be read in the classroom and their defining characteristics explained to students.

- **Understand that writing about the text supports reading comprehension.** Written responses to reading can aid with comprehension. When writing, the writer must think about the writing topic, so that in crafting a response, he reviews the subject matter. For example, if a student reads what causes a volcano to erupt, and then has to summarize the information, the student must once again think about what he has learned as he writes.

- **Know a variety of writing styles and how to model techniques to build understanding through this knowledge.** Narrative, expository (informational text), descriptive, and persuasive text, like genres, have certain criteria that distinguish them from one another. When students know the components and expectations of each style, this aids in their reading comprehension of that particular style. For example, students need to know how to recognize persuasive writing and that its purpose is to convince the reader that the author's side or point of view is the "right" side or point of view regarding the topic.

- **Know that interest and ability are important when selecting text for students.** Students need to read texts that are on their instructional level. A fourth grader who reads at a sixth-grade level needs to be given that level text for optimal growth. If he continues in a fourth-grade-level text, there is no opportunity to grow. In addition, texts should be interesting to students, as that motivates them to read. Motivated readers read more, deepen their comprehension, and expand their vocabulary.

- **Know formal and informal methods of assessing comprehension.** Comprehension should be continually monitored. It can be informally assessed with discussions, questions, reading responses, and retellings. Formal methods are usually associated with standardized tests, which some reading programs encompass.

Fluency

The reading teacher is expected to:

- **Know that fluency is the bridge between phonics and comprehension.** When students have passed the stage of decoding words and can read more rapidly, they are on their way to becoming fluent readers. The advantage of reading fluently is that the reader is free to focus on comprehension rather than word identification.

- **Know the components of fluency.** Fluency has four main components: automaticity (automatic word recognition), appropriate rate of reading, accuracy, and prosody (expression and flow). Teachers must be proficient at fostering growth in these areas and assessing them in order to monitor student progress.

- **Know the various strategies to build fluency.** Fluency can be developed through repeated reading via a range of methods, such as Readers' Theater or choral reading. Using smaller pieces of text, students can re-read words and phrases through word sorts or phrase sorts; this re-reading builds fluency. Passages, at the appropriate level, can be read and re-read orally to gain competence in fluency. Choral reading can be used to do this as a collaborative process.

- **Know effective instructional methods to build oral fluency.** A number of instructional strategies can be used during text reading to build fluency. Students can read Readers' Theater scripts aloud as a class. Poems can be practiced through re-reading either individually or chorally to prepare for a performance. For beginning readers, echo reading, in which the teacher reads a line and the students echo the reading while the teacher points to the words, can build fluency. Employing re-reading in a variety of ways increases fluency (and, incidentally, comprehension).

- **Know a variety of informal and formal fluency assessments.** Fluency assessments, whether formal or informal, rely on the components of fluency: accuracy, automaticity, reading rate, and prosody.

Vocabulary

The reading teacher is expected to:

- **Know modeling techniques to show students how to use context to confirm word meaning.** Students need to learn how to identify and pronounce an unknown word, determine its meaning, and so forth as they read independently. Strategies to use context cues need to be taught explicitly and reinforced with guided practice and constant monitoring.

- **Understand the use of structural analysis to aid in word identification and meaning.** Prefixes, suffixes, and word roots all enhance the meaning of vocabulary. Students need to know how to separate word parts to aid in word identification and meaning.

- **Understand that certain words have different relationships.** Specifically, antonyms are words that are opposites, synonyms have similar meanings, and homonyms (or homophones) are words that are pronounced the same, but spelled differently and have different meanings.

- **Know direct and indirect ways of teaching vocabulary.** Research shows that vocabulary should be taught both explicitly and implicitly. When explicitly (directly) teaching vocabulary, teachers should use the same meanings as those used in the text, and clarify the context. Explicit teaching indicates that the teacher is giving the skill to the students in a very systematic way. For example, when teaching the prefix "re," the teacher would say that "re" means to do again in the context of the vocabulary. Implicit teaching is more subtle and exploratory. When using implicit techniques, the teacher may put the following words on the board: *redo, rerun, repost, rework,* and *rebuild.* The goal is for students to discover how the prefix "re" changes the meaning of a word (to do again).

- **Know how to select vocabulary for instruction.** Since classroom time is precious, only appropriate words should be selected for explicit (direct) instruction. For example, if a word and its meaning can be determined by context or word analysis skills, it should not be selected for instruction.

- **Understand that grammatical function and word form affect a word's meaning.** A grammatical function is the role a word or phrase plays in a sentence. That is, some words can act as a noun, a verb, or an adjective. Students need to know that function or word form can affect meaning. The following sentence is a perfect example: "It was not fair that my sister got to go to the fair on this fair day." As this sentence shows, grammatical functions can make words confusing, especially for ELLs.

- **Understand that students need a variety of wide reading and rich contextual support for vocabulary development.** Wide reading increases vocabulary growth. When strategies to identify and understand unknown words in text are modeled and practiced in the classroom, students can apply these to their independent reading, spurring vocabulary growth. When this reading is rich with contextual support, students are able to more easily ascertain the meanings of unknown words.

- **Know a variety of ways to assess and monitor vocabulary knowledge.** Vocabulary knowledge should be monitored in oral speech, reading, writing, and listening; growth in one area affects the other areas.

Instructional Processes

Instructional Practices

The reading teacher is expected to:

- **Create an environment that supports literacy and literacy growth.** The classroom environment should promote a rich and positive visual context that promotes academic, emotional, and social interactions. The environment should be one that respects differences, works patiently with students in need, promotes reading and writing, and motivates readers.

- **Know a variety of ways to differentiate literacy instruction.** Literacy and skill instruction should be differentiated in a number of ways such as instructional leveled groups, tiered responses, and collaborative learning.

Curriculum Material

The reading teacher is expected to:

- **Know the different types and varieties of texts and their purpose in classroom instruction.** Teachers need to know the various text structures and genres, the purpose of each, and how to appropriately use the material for effective teaching.

- **Be able to select instructional material that represents societal diversity.** A variety of multicultural literature is important in any classroom. Student populations with minimal diversity should be able to learn about other cultures through instructional materials. For schools that are diverse, students should see appropriate representation of their respective cultures in texts.

- **Know how to effectively integrate appropriate technology to support literacy instruction and growth.** Technology is now part of nearly every classroom and home. Teachers need to know how to use it to enhance instruction in ways that improve reading and reading comprehension. Teachers should know a variety of apps and programs that can be used to instruct, differentiate, and reinforce curriculum.

Assessment

The reading teacher is expected to:

- **Know how to use a variety of assessments.** Both informal and formal assessments have their place in the classroom. Being able to use different assessments allows a teacher to set specific goals for individual students and set up groups for differentiated instruction. Formal assessments have standardized procedures that must be followed and are norm-referenced (result in percentiles) or criterion-referenced (pinpoint learning areas). Informal assessments allow teachers to evaluate students' needs without using a standardized test. Running records, checklists, and rubrics are some forms of informal assessment. Informal assessments may have some standardization or be part of natural classroom assessment.

- **Know how to use assessment data to drive instruction.** More than one assessment is needed to show measurement of a particular aspect of student growth. Using data from both formal and informal assessments allows teachers to compare results and address the students' greatest needs. Data is analyzed to set goals for learning, and then instruction is put in place to meet those goals. The progress is continually monitored through informal assessments so that instruction can change when goals are met.

- **Be able to communicate a student's reading progress to parents, specialists, and administrators.** Teachers need to be able to communicate effectively when explaining assessments and the results to parents. They should be able to discuss results with specialists and administrators for various reasons.

Answers to Frequently Asked Questions

Q: **How do I register for the test?**

A: You can register for the test online. Go to www.ets.org/praxis/register to see the test sites, test dates, and to register. You must create a "My Praxis" account in order to obtain your admission ticket and, ultimately, your scores.

Q: **What can I expect on test day?**

A: At the test center, you will need to show your admission ticket and a photo ID. Once inside, you will be given the opportunity to see how the test works via a tutorial. There is also a "What to Expect on the Day of Your Test" video at www.ets.org/praxis, which may be helpful.

Q: **Will I take the test on paper or on a computer?**

A: The test is given on a computer; it is not a paper-and-pencil test.

Q: **How long is the test?**

A: Plan to spend 2½–3 hours at the testing center. You will have 2 hours to take the test, plus an additional 30 minutes up front to complete a tutorial. The test is composed of 90 selected-response (multiple-choice) questions and three constructed-response (essay) questions. (*Note:* The test may contain questions that won't count toward your score. This is because the test developers are "testing" some new questions to see if they are valid or reliable.)

Q: **Should I guess?**

A: If you don't know an answer to a question, give it your best guess and move on.

Question Types

There are two question types on the Praxis (5204): selected response and constructed response. These are described in detail below.

Selected-Response Questions

There are 90 selected-response (multiple-choice) questions on the Praxis (5204). Each selected-response question has four answer choices. Questions may ask you to identify a term, analyze classroom instruction built into a classroom scenario, state a concern about one child or a group, or set a goal for students. Select the best answer. Expect to see an "attractive distracter"—one that will be *almost* right—among the answer choices. That is why you need to know the terminology and content in this book!

Constructed-Response Questions

There are three constructed-response (essay) questions on the Praxis (5204). There is one question on a topic from each of the three Instructional Processes categories: Instructional Practices, Curriculum Materials, and Assessment. A constructed-response question may require the addition of some comments that connect the other two broad categories to your explanation. For example, analyzing a running record would necessitate comments on word identification from emergent literacy even if it is an assessment question.

Each constructed-response question has a high score of 3. A score of 3 requires that the response meets the following criteria:

- Answers *all parts* of the question in a way that directly addresses the instructional situation described.
- Shows strong knowledge of concepts, theories, facts, procedures, or methodologies relevant to the question.
- Provides a strong explanation that is well supported by relevant evidence.

A good approach to earning a score of 3 is to answer all of the questions clearly and specifically. Be sure to show that you understand the content of the text. Give a strong explanation, and support it. Proficient writing is expected.

Chapter 2

Oral Language

When you use words to send a message in either speech or writing, you show understanding of new words through **expressive language.** People learn new vocabulary through **receptive language**—words that impart information via listening or reading. In this chapter, you will learn how expressive and receptive language support oral language development and the importance of teaching active listening skills.

Stages of Oral Language Development (Milestones in Language Development)

In the 1950s, linguistics expert Noam Chomsky discovered that all the world's languages had a common developmental structure. Chomsky theorized that language abilities are innate, and the human brain is predisposed to learn language. Studies show that all children go through developmental stages in their language acquisition. Today, Chomsky's doctrine that language is acquired in six sequential stages is widely accepted. Other theorists have suggested developmental stages similar to Chomsky's, focusing on the function of the language—whether it is to demand, question, socialize, and so forth. Language growth progresses in a linear fashion as a child matures, and language development has many milestones associated with chronological age. Study the chart below, and become familiar with how this linear growth occurs.

Chomsky's Six Universal Stages of Oral Language Development Adapted

Stage of Language Development	Description of Language Behaviors
Prelinguistic Stage (Cooing and Babbling)	In the first 12 months, a baby makes noises and gestures as pre-speech to communicate. Sounds might be interpreted as "I'm hungry, tired, wet," and so forth.
Holophrastic Stage (One Word)	Starting at around 10–12 months, a child begins to use one-word communication to express what he wants. (Examples: *mama, dada, baba*)
Two-Word Stage	At around 20 months, a child begins to use two-word phrases to communicate, saying things like "me drink," "daddy out," "no shoe," "no eat." These words can be understood in the context of their use and function—in these cases stating a want.
Telegraphic Stage	At around 2½ to 3 years old (sometimes earlier), children begin to express themselves with shortened speech as in a telegraph, saying things like "me go now," "me get down," "daddy me go car." These phrases send a message in short form.
Intermediate Development Stage	The beginning of this stage is marked by simple sentences. Language structure is usually in place by age 5. For example, a child says "I" instead of "me." Children start school knowing approximately 5,000 words. As children age, their sentences are increasingly complex, and they are learning acceptable pragmatics (expression) in social situations.
Adult Stage	In this stage, speech is refined, strong vocabulary is present, and pragmatics (the way in which the speech is expressed) is as expected.

Strategies for Developing and Expanding Students' Listening and Speaking Skills

Building oral language begins with helping children develop their listening and speaking skills. Hearing begins in the auditory cortex, located in both hemispheres of the brain. The auditory cortex receives signals from the ears and transmits those signals to other parts of the cerebral cortex, which decode the sounds into meaningful words.

Students need to be active listeners by being cognitively aware, understanding what is being said both verbally and nonverbally.

A good listener:

- Focuses on the speaker and does not interrupt the flow of language.
- Looks at the person speaking and gives nonverbal signals that he is listening.
- Shows interest in what is being said.
- Is respectful of the speaker's enthusiasm, concerns, and so forth.

In the classroom, children need to be taught to:

- Know that they listen for different reasons—for example, to get directions, to learn something new, or to hear an opinion—so being a good listener is important.
- Be attentive and mindful of what is being said. They should ask themselves if they understand what they are hearing.
- Look at the speaker.
- Give encouraging nonverbal responses.
- Pay attention to nonverbal cues and gestures from the speaker.
- Listen to gain understanding, and ask questions when appropriate.

To help students learn to be active listeners, teachers should:

- Model good listening behaviors for the class.
- Let students know from the beginning that you will say most things only once, so students must listen.
- Hold students accountable for listening—get their feedback in some way.
- Have students paraphrase what has been said.
- Make time for questions; questions allow you to know what students heard and understood, and if something needs to be clarified.
- Build in activities that allow students to practice their listening skills with each other (for example, have students stand or sit back-to-back and then follow oral directions given by one student to the other or play "Simon says").

Oracy, the ability to express oneself fluently and correctly, is important in the classroom and in life. Students should learn to be good conversationalists. Being able to communicate clearly is an important life skill.

To help students become good conversationalists and speakers, teachers should:

- Model good conversation behaviors.
- Build in less teacher talk; foster more student talk.
- Make students expand on what they are saying; don't accept one- or two-word answers to a question. This is why teachers often say to young children, "Use your words."
- Tell students to look at people when they are talking (and listening).
- Tell students to speak clearly and loudly enough for the listeners to hear.
- Tell students to watch for nonverbal cues from their listeners. These nonverbal cues may help them determine if they have spoken for the appropriate length of time, or if someone is confused.

- Instruct students to take turns talking.
- Ask open-ended questions such as "Do you have experience in this?" "Can you tell me what you are thinking?" "Can you add something more?" Questions like these can encourage reluctant speakers to join the conversation.
- Consider strategies such as using an object that can be passed around like a talking stick or ball that will encourage student participation. When the speaker holds the stick or ball, it means no one else should be talking. The object is passed to a new speaker at the appropriate time.
- Communicate time expectations for oral presentations. If students are giving a class presentation, tell them the amount of time they are allotted, and that they will be timed. Advise them to practice and time themselves at home.

Increasing Vocabulary Through Listening and Speaking: The Impact on Language Development

Listening is one way we receive language and new vocabulary (reading is the other). Speaking involves an expressive vocabulary (as does writing) and allows children to use and apply new language. The listening and speaking vocabularies of your students are directly linked to their reading comprehension and their all-around academic development. The more vocabulary a student knows in the oral realm, the greater his understanding when reading. In addition, having an extensive vocabulary allows students to be precise and accurate in their communication.

The teacher's use of and instruction of high-level vocabulary in the classroom is a fundamental method to get students to use and apply new vocabulary in their own speaking. Not only should the teacher model excellent speech and frequently use high-level vocabulary, but she should give students the opportunity to use this vocabulary in the classroom. Oral vocabulary can be increased through teacher-led activities or via collaborative activities, in which students do most of the talking. (*Note:* Teaching vocabulary for reading and writing is covered in Chapter 6, "Word Analysis Skills.") The listed activities that follow will help engage students in using new speaking vocabulary learned through listening to the teacher and others.

Teacher-led vocabulary activities:

- Instruction of new vocabulary words through discussion and actions.
- Read-alouds using books one or two years above students' reading levels. When new or interesting vocabulary words are used, these words should be discussed and expanded upon.
- Vocabulary words of the week; students are rewarded for using the new words. Words need to be used multiple times in order for students to remember them.
- Turn and Talk: After listening to directions or information containing new vocabulary or concepts, students turn to a partner and talk about what they have just learned.
- Open-ended follow-up questions to foster discussion.
- The Language Experience Approach: The class or group does an activity, such as a baking soda/vinegar volcano explosion. The teacher leads the students in a discussion about what they experienced. Then, the teacher writes, on large chart paper or an interactive whiteboard, what students say about the experience, making sure to include the new vocabulary.

Collaborative activities:

- Prior to reading, have partners look at pictures in the book and discuss with each other what they think is going to happen. Teachers can use the vocabulary to guide students through the pictures, as a way to introduce new words prior to reading.
- Have small groups create a puppet show to foster language use. This can be a retelling of a book students have read, thereby encouraging them to use new vocabulary from the book.
- Have students do a "sketch and tell" in which they draw a part of a story and describe the scene to others.

- Using pictures that represent students' various cultures, have the students tell each other stories inspired by the pictures.

- Have students play games that allow for ample discussion of questions related to the text. For example, divide students into teams and have the teams discuss each answer among themselves prior to announcing it to the class. (Use the talking stick so that more students have a chance to explain the answer to the class.)

Scaffolding Learning for English Language Learners

The teaching ideas introduced thus far in this chapter will be appropriate for more proficient English Language Learners (ELLs), but most ELLs will need repeated oral exposure to new words—they need to see visuals, say the word, see the word, and write the word in a variety of contexts. ELLs have a double learning challenge when it comes to oral language development: They are learning to read and also learning to speak a language that is most likely not spoken at home. The following teaching strategies work better with students who are relatively new to the English language:

- Speak slowly (not loudly) so students can clearly hear your pronunciation.

- If a child is completely new to the English language, initially use telegraphic speech, or what is more commonly called the Total Physical Response (TPR) technique. Telegraphic speech is followed by a sentence using actions, and then the telegraphic speech is repeated. Let's take a scenario where the ELL student must hang up his coat. The teacher says, "Hang coat." The teacher then walks the child toward the classroom coat hooks and says, "You [pointing to child] need to hang your coat [pointing to coat] on the hook [pointing to hook]." Then the teacher repeats "hang coat" as she hangs the coat up for the child or helps the child hang the coat.

- Constantly use visuals to introduce new words and concepts. If students can't understand the language, they will most certainly not be able to understand a definition of a word.

- Ask questions that can be answered with one or two words, or even by pointing.

- Use rebuses (pictures or symbols substituted for words in text) as hints, for example, thumbs-up/thumbs-down pictures for "agree/disagree."

- Use audio reading or computer-assisted reading. Have students listen to talking books or stories on CDs or the computer. Send these resources home, if possible (parents will most likely use these, too).

- Read repetitive books to students (repetitive books repeat the same language or lines several times). Have students repeat the lines with you. Then, using puppets from the story if possible, have children act out the story using words from the book.

- Choose one or two target words that are meaningful to the students and use them multiple times when speaking to the ELL students.

- Do shared reading (an interactive read-aloud often done with a big book). During this experience, point out new words and discuss them; point to pictures in the book that explain the words, using actions when needed.

- Create 30-second action videos or slide shows. For example, when teaching the word *different,* you would show a video or a slide show with four or five slides, each with an item unique to that slide, and the speaker would say what is different.

Cultural Responsiveness

Cultural responsiveness is the ability to be open to, learn from, and relate respectfully to people of all cultures, including your own. To communicate effectively with children and parents of different cultures, a teacher cannot let any type of stereotyping, discrimination, or prejudices interfere with her communication.

In addition, teachers must respect regional and dialectical variations. You are probably familiar with a "Boston accent" and a "southern drawl," but you may not realize how a regional or dialectical variation can morph into the regional "norm." The differences in the sounds of words from region to region result in a range in the number of phonemes in the English language. The number of phonemes ranges in the United States from 40 to 44, but 44 seems to be the most accepted number. Furthermore, words can represent different meanings in different states. Many people think of a soft drink as *soda,* yet in some areas of the U.S., people call any soda a *coke* or *pop.* Another example is the word *cabinet,* which most English speakers would define as a storage area; however, Rhode Islanders typically define this as a milkshake. Such cultural language variations should be accepted in the classroom, although conventional language should always be modeled.

A teacher must be sensitive to a child's home culture and responsive to children's belief systems, cultural traditions, and any language patterns that may interfere with communication. Both verbal and nonverbal communication are essential in connecting with other cultures. When possible, learn about each of your students' cultures, as some cultural differences may cause difficulties in meeting academic expectations. For example, in some cultures, children are taught to look down when speaking to adults; in these groups, intergenerational eye contact is therefore considered disrespectful.

To aid in cultural responsiveness in the classroom:

- Teach students that cultural differences and similarities exist and make the world more interesting.
- Teach students that respectfulness of other cultures is expected in the classroom.
- Nurture a classroom with a safe environment where students feel comfortable and accepted so ELLs will use their new language without fear of making mistakes.
- Teach students that learning a second language can be difficult. Let them know that their help and courtesy in aiding an ELL student in learning new English words are appreciated. ELLs can reciprocate and teach native English speakers some of their words.
- Invite all students to be learners, and show them that their participation is valued and others want to hear their contribution.
- Let students see their respective cultures reflected in classroom visuals (posters), activities (read-alouds), and classroom library books.
- Encourage students to express themselves, and explain cultural expectations when needed.
- Encourage students to analyze and discuss the multiple perspectives of each culture.
- Communicate high expectations to all students.
- Build collaborative activities into your classroom instruction.

To show cultural responsiveness to parents:

- Always respond with respect and understanding.
- Be understanding of language difficulties that might cause unnecessary confusion.
- Stay sensitive if a parent seems frustrated or upset; try to figure out what is happening to cause the frustration.
- When possible, send notices home in the parent's language.
- When conferencing, ask parents questions about their child's learning that may help you in the classroom.

Assessing Oral Language Development: An Overview

For some children, oral language development is assessed prior to students entering school, and is often initiated as a result of a pediatrician referral. Usually when this happens, the child receives early intervention so that any language delay can be remedied prior to the child starting school. Sometimes, lack of oral language progress is not noticed until a child reaches school age or the diagnosed concern may not be remedied, resulting in the child receiving speech therapy in school. In the case of an ELL, the cause of a language delay may be the student's second language rather than a learning disability or an inherent speech problem.

A teacher must always be aware of how a child is using his words. The school system typically provides a checklist for teachers and others to assess where the child is in his oral language development. When a teacher notices lack or misuse of oral language, limited recall of words or ideas, or problems with word retrieval or sentence formation, she should conduct further observation. Some school systems use retellings, role play, and prompts to aid in oral language assessment. There are standardized tests and apps that can be used to aid in assessment. When identifying a child with a potential speech problem or delay, referrals should be made to the district's speech therapist.

Chapter 3

Concepts of Print

You have probably seen a small child "read" a book upside down, but what you might not know is that this scene is actually informative about early developing reading skills. Concepts of print entails a basic understanding of how printed text—books—work. An informal literacy assessment of the concepts of print was first introduced by Marie Clay; it includes a list of expected reading skills for very young children.

Concepts of Print Checklist

Many teachers use a checklist with expected behaviors to assess a child's reading development. This allows teachers to examine exactly what a child knows about print. The concepts of print assessment is an informal literacy assessment used with primary grade students and preschoolers. When checking students' knowledge of concepts of print, a teacher will ask a student if he can show her the following:

- the front and back of the book
- the title of the book
- where the story begins
- a letter, word, and sentence
- where a sentence ends, and the end mark, such as a period or exclamation point
- a space between letters or sentences
- a word by framing it, or tell her how many words are in a selected sentence
- directionality (English print is read from left to right) and top to bottom (return sweep)
- the top and bottom of the page
- uppercase and lowercase letters (recognizing them and matching them)
- a picture versus printed text

This informal assessment provides important information about a child's reading development. A teacher will ask leading questions such as "Can you use two fingers to frame one word?" When children "pretend read," they may say fifteen words while "reading" a seven-word sentence because, although they may follow the print with their fingers, they do not understand what defines a word, or they haven't learned the concept of one-to-one matching between what they say and the words on the page. Teachers can use the concepts of print checklist to show what students know and how much they have learned.

Teaching and Assessing Concepts of Print

The following are examples of ways to teach concepts of print. These are best taught through direct instruction, where teachers tell students what they need to know, model as they explain, and then have students identify.

- **Print features:** The teacher holds up a book and, pointing to the cover, directly states that this is the front of the book and asks students to notice how the pictures are right-side up. The teacher then moves to the title of the book, the beginning pages, and the back of the book, explaining each section. Then, to ensure learning, the teacher has the students apply this information by asking them to identify different parts of the book.
- **Concept of letters:** Using a student's name, the teacher explains that words are composed of letters. For example, the name *Sam* has three letters; together with the class, the teacher counts the number of letters. This is repeated with other names and simple words.

- **Directionality:** As the teacher reads a book, she moves her finger or pointer along the words, going from left to right and return sweeping at the end of the sentence. She also mentions other concepts of print, such as the top and bottom of the page, where a sentence begins and ends, punctuation marks, and so forth.
- **Concept of words:** A teacher takes a simple sentence from a book she is reading to the class, such as "The boy put on his new coat." After writing each word on an index card, she shows the students the sequenced sentence. She then tells them that there is one word on each card. They count the seven words together. The teacher explains that when writing sentences, you leave a space between words so the reader can tell where a word begins and ends. Volunteers in the class point to where each word begins and ends.

Teaching Recognition of Uppercase and Lowercase Letters

The best predictor of reading success corresponds to a student's ability to recognize uppercase (capital) and lowercase letters. If the student can recognize the letter "t," then when a teacher states that "t" says /t/, the child is on his way to learning letter sounds. He already knows the name of the letter, as compared to a child who is learning the name of "t" and the sound at the same time. Some educators feel that lowercase letters should be taught first, as reading entails more lowercase letters than uppercase letters.

Strategies to Teach Letter Recognition

Teaching letter recognition should be fun and engaging. Here are a few strategies you can try:

- **Direct instruction:** Write the letters "Bb" on a card, and state that these are the uppercase letter "B" and the lowercase letter "b." Show them that the name *Ben*, written for children to see, starts with the uppercase letter "B." And the word *box*, written, begins with the lowercase letter "b."
- **Find the letters:** Tell students that Freddie Fox came into the classroom last night and hid big and small letter "f's." Show students what the uppercase and lowercase (big and small) letter "f's" look like, and have them find the letters hidden in the room.
- **Letter tracing:** When teaching a letter, show students both the uppercase and the lowercase letter, and have letters for students to trace. You can also use letters cut from sandpaper and have students do a "rubbing" as they say the letter name.
- **Cut and paste:** After explicitly teaching a letter, have students cut out images of the letter from magazines and glue them to a piece of paper labeled with the letter.

Assessing Concepts of Print: An Overview

Teachers use informal assessments to guide instruction and to show growth. Using the concepts of print is essential in assessing emergent readers. A few months ago, as my college students were working with their second-grade book buddies, a new student arrived and needed a college book buddy. I decided to administer an informal reading inventory with this second grader (an evaluation instrument with grade-level word lists and passages that, when administered, gives an idea of a student's reading level). I began by asking the young girl to read the pre-primer (before grade 1) list of words. She could recognize only the word *no*. Then, to see if she could grasp words better in context, I asked her to read the pre-primer–level passage. She could not begin. I immediately switched to a concepts of print criterion—recognizing letters. The young girl could recognize four letters by name. Two of the letters were in her name. The little information that I gleaned from this assessment came with a wealth of knowledge about this child's reading. Using the concepts of print allows teachers to assess what reading behaviors a nonreader or emergent reader possesses, and offers a starting point for the teacher that will show growth in the emergent reader.

Chapter 4

Phonological and Phonemic Awareness

Phonological awareness is considered the crux of beginning reading. Recognizing sounds in words and then eventually being able to associate a letter or letters with those sounds are beginning steps in "breaking the code." Phonological awareness, while a content category on the Praxis (5204), can be considered an umbrella term covering phonemic awareness and phonics. Where phonemic awareness focuses on letter sounds, phonological awareness includes being able to segment syllables and identify rhyming sounds. This chapter's focus is on phonemic awareness; phonics is covered in detail in Chapter 5.

How to teach phonics is most likely one of the most controversial issues in reading instruction. Research points to the superiority of explicit instruction, which can be reinforced in a variety of ways. Yet, research has shown that prior to learning phonics, students need to have phonemic awareness, the ability to distinguish and manipulate sounds in words. When a child can isolate the sounds of /h/, /a/, and /t/ in *hat* when shown the written word, it's easier for the child to make a single sound connection to the letter that represents the sound. This aids students in learning the letter-sound correspondences. Teachers use a variety of techniques to help students gain this knowledge.

Phonemic Awareness

Phonemic awareness is the ability to hear, isolate, and manipulate individual speech sounds. It is important to remember that phonemic awareness refers only to sound; it is an auditory process. In phonics, children learn that there is a sound-letter correspondence—they learn which letters represent the speech sounds. *Children do not need to know that letters exist to have phonemic awareness.* Since a phoneme is defined as a single unit of sound, children may be asked to manipulate or count sounds; this activity does not involve seeing or naming the actual letter or letters—just isolating and counting the sounds. For instance, the word *bat* has three letters and three sounds: /b/, /a/, and /t/. (*Note:* Sounds in reading are designated by the / / symbols.) In comparison, the word *back* has four letters, but it still has only three sounds: /b/, /a/, and /k/. A child who is phonemically aware should be able to understand that each of these words has three sounds. This same child does not need to name the letters, but he must be able to hear and identify separate sounds. If a question on the Praxis (5204) refers to letters, then the topic is most likely phonics. If the question or scenario does not involve letters, but instead refers to beginning, ending, or middle sounds, the topic is most likely phonemic awareness. It may be helpful to remember that a child can show you that he is phonemically aware even if his eyes are closed. Pictures may be used in a phonemic awareness activity, but no letters are involved.

As mentioned earlier, phonological awareness encompasses more than phonemic awareness; it also includes being able to separate and count syllables and to recognize rhyming sounds. Usually phonemic awareness activities are designed for very young children, up to second grade, and focus on speech sounds.

The Role of Phonemic Awareness in Learning to Read and Write

Phonemic awareness is extremely important. Research has shown that students who have phonemic awareness are more ready to learn to read than those who do not. Being phonemically aware supports a student in "breaking the code" because this knowledge provides the foundation for learning phonics. Being able to isolate a sound in a word, such as the /g/ or /o/ in *go*, paves the way to one-on-one correspondence from sound to letter.

Vocabulary Worth Knowing and Understanding

Elkonin boxes: Boxes drawn on a piece of paper, so that children can place a token in an individual box for each sound they hear in a word. This activity helps to build and assess phonemic awareness.

grapheme: A visual representation of a single sound, usually a letter or group of letters. For example, "t" says one sound, /t/; "gh" says one sound, /f/. Another example is the "igh" in *high.*

morpheme: The smallest unit of sound that has meaning. For example, the word *rebook* contains two morphemes: the prefix *re-* and the root *book.* The meaning of the word *rebook,* therefore, is a combination of the meanings of its two morphemes.

phoneme: A single unit of sound.

phonemic awareness: The ability to identify, isolate, and manipulate sounds in a language.

phonological awareness: A broad understanding that encompasses letter sounds as well as syllables, rhymes, onsets, and rimes. Some experts also include phonics under the phonological awareness umbrella.

syllable: The part of a word that contains one vowel sound. For example, in the word *eating* there are two syllables, even though there are three vowels (*eat/ing*).

Check Your Understanding

Read each of the following scenarios and determine whether or not they involve phonemic awareness. Explain your answers.

1. A teacher shows Sarah a group of pictures and asks her to pick out the pictures that begin with /h/.
2. A teacher shows Jerome the letter "b" and asks him what picture begins with this letter.
3. Mrs. Welter says the word *cat* and asks her students to put a token in an Elkonin box for each sound they hear.

Answers:

1. Yes, there are no letters involved—just pictures and sound.
2. No, this is not phonemic awareness; it is phonics. This is teaching letter-sound correspondence.
3. Yes, this is checking phoneme segmentation; no letters are involved.

Continuum of Phonemic Awareness

Levels of phonemic awareness overlap one another, and understanding this structure aids teachers in planning a student's next steps. Although it is difficult to distinguish precise degrees of difficulty, the easiest level is considered to be phoneme segmentation—separating sounds; the most difficult level is phoneme substitution—more specifically, being able to substitute the medial phoneme (middle vowel sound). The point to remember is that as a phonemic awareness activity becomes more difficult, the child participating in the activity becomes more phonemically aware, and therefore is getting ready or is ready for phonics instruction. (Often in kindergarten and first-grade classrooms, this happens simultaneously, as the teacher provides instruction on letter identification as it relates to sound, but the child needs to understand the concept of sound and sound blending.)

Levels of Phonemic Awareness

Note: The terminology used below can also be found in the booklet "Put Reading First," a publication developed by the National Institute for Literacy (https://lincs.ed.gov/publications/pdf/PRFbooklet.pdf).

Level of Phonemic Awareness	Description
phoneme isolation	Recognizing an individual sound in a word. For example, a child can tell the teacher the first sound in the word *luck*. This is considered the easiest skill in phonemic awareness.
phoneme identity	Identifying a spoken sound in different words. For example, a child can recognize that /d/ is the same sound in *duck, dark,* and *dot*.
phoneme categorization	Identifying a variant sound. For example, a child can identify that the /f/ sound in *fun* is different from the /b/ sound in *bug* and *bike*.
phoneme blending	Being able to hear individual sounds and blend them together to make a word. A child can listen to a group of phonemes (sounds) and combine the phonemes—blend them together—to say the word. For example, if a child is given the sounds /h/, /i/, and /t/ separately and in order, the child will say the word *hit*.
phoneme segmentation	Being able to hear a word and distinguish the individual sounds within the word. For example, a child is told the word *bug,* and can say /b/, /u/, and /g/, and also state that there are three sounds.
phoneme deletion	Recognizing a smaller word within a word when a sound is taken away. For example, when told the word *stall* and asked what word is left when the /s/ is taken away, the child would answer *tall*.
phoneme substitution	Substituting one phoneme for another. A child is told the word *cat* and asked to change the /a/ to /u/, and the child says *cut*. This is considered the most difficult skill in phonemic awareness.

Strategies for Teaching Phonemic Awareness

In general, any letter-sound activity or a listening game involving letters and sounds will aid children in becoming phonemically aware. The following are examples of activities that can be used to teach, and at the same time assess, children's phonemic awareness.

- **Phoneme isolation:** The teacher says a word and asks the student to say the first, middle, or ending sound. The teacher might say the word *hat* and ask the student to isolate and say just the beginning sound.

- **Phoneme identification:** Students are asked to tell which sounds are the same. The teacher might ask a question like "Which words begin with the same sound when I say *bike, can, boat, mouse*?"

- **Phonemic categorization:** The teacher asks the student to identify a different sound. The teacher might say, "I am going to say three words. Tell me what word ends differently from the other two: *tall, bat, fall*."

- **Phoneme blending:** The teacher says the sounds /p/, /i/, and /g/, and stretches them out as she speaks. She has the students point to different spots on their other arm in order to put the sounds together. Beginning at the top, the /p/ is said at the upper arm, they glide down to the elbow and say /i/, and then say the /g/ sound at the hand level. The teacher asks the students to do this again, faster, and then has them identify the word as *pig*.

- **Phoneme segmentation:** The teacher uses Elkonin boxes and gives students tokens. When the teacher says a word, the students put a token in a box for each sound they hear. For the word *pen*, three boxes would each have a token. For the word *make*, the answer would be the same.

- **Phoneme substitution:** The teacher says, "Listen carefully to the word *cup*," and she stretches out the word. She then asks, "What does the word become when we replace the /u/ with the short /a/ sound?"

Check Your Understanding

Read the following scenarios and identify whether or not each is considered a phonemic awareness activity. Explain your answers.

1. A teacher shows a student a chart of pictures that all begin with the /b/ sound. She has the student name what the picture represents, such as a bag, and then say what letter the word begins with.
2. A student listens to the teacher as she says the word *dog*. The student is to tell the teacher what sound he hears in the middle of the word.
3. A teacher stretches out the sounds /n/, /o/, and /t/, and students have to identify the word being said.

Answers:
1. No. Because the teacher asks for a letter name, the activity is phonics; it involves letter-sound correspondence.
2. Yes. This is phoneme isolation.
3. Yes. This is phoneme blending.

Assessing Phonemic Awareness: An Overview

Phonemic awareness is usually assessed informally. It can be evaluated naturally during regular classroom instruction. For example, after discussing a sound such as /p/, and modeling how to select items or pictures that begin with /p/, a teacher can then check students' understanding through a reinforcement activity. An activity as simple as giving the students pictures of a tent, pan, pen, bunny, pants, flower, and paper and having them select the pictures that begin with the /p/ sound provides a teacher solid information about students' beginning phonemic awareness. There is a free assessment, easily found via an online search, called the Yopp-Singer Test of Phoneme Segmentation. With the Yopp-Singer assessment, a student is assessed individually to see if he can segment various words. When assessing, the teacher must consider levels of phonemic awareness.

Chapter 5

Phonics and the Alphabetic Principle

The Alphabetic Principle

The alphabetic principle dictates that specific letters and sounds correspond to one another. This principle is known by a variety of names: phonics, breaking the code, sound-symbol correspondence, and letter-sound correspondence. If you see any of these terms on the exam, remember that each refers to phonics. In the classroom, the alphabetic principle is discussed in terms of a child's decoding skills.

Vocabulary Worth Knowing and Understanding

alphabetic principle: There is a predictable correspondence between a letter and a sound.

consonant blend/consonant cluster: When two or more consonants appear together and each consonant can be heard in sequence, there is a consonant blend. When there are three consonants together, they are called a consonant cluster. Examples: _blow, stream, bust_.

digraph: Two letters that represent one sound. For example, the "ai" in _pail_ is a vowel digraph, making a long /a/ sound; the "ph" in the word _digraph_ is a consonant digraph, making an /f/ sound (a nice way to remember the definition). Note the digraphs in these words: _steal, piece, trout, phone, shift, change_. Consonant digraphs: "th," "wh," "sh," "ch," "ph," and "ng." Vowel digraphs: "oo," "ou," "ow," "oe," "oo," "ue," "ey," "ay," "oy," "oi," "au," "aw," "ai," "ay," "ee," "ea," "ie," and "ei." (These vowel digraphs are often taught with the following chant: "When two vowels do the walking, the first one does the talking.")

diphthong: Two vowels that, when spoken together, make a glided sound (for example, "oi" in _oil_, "ou" in _ouch_).

grapheme: Written text that represents one phoneme. For example, "b," "oa," and "t" are the three graphemes in the word _boat_.

morpheme: The smallest unit of sound that contains meaning. For example, the word _bag_ is a morpheme. Adding an "s" to the end of it makes it plural and, therefore, gives it another meaning; _bags_ is called a bonded morpheme.

onset: The initial consonant of a syllable (for example, the "b" in _big_).

phoneme: The smallest unit of sound (for example, /b/ or /o/).

phonics generalization: A rule that governs letter sounds under specific conditions. For example, a silent "e" makes the preceding vowel long; when a "c" is followed by an "i" or "e," it makes the soft sound, as in _city;_ when a "c" is followed by an "a," "o," or "u," it makes the hard sound, as in _cake_.

phonological awareness: Knowledge of letter sounds as well as of syllables, rhymes, onsets, and rimes. It is the awareness of the sound structure in words.

rime: The part of the syllable that follows the initial consonant and begins with a vowel (for example, the "ig" in _big_).

systematic phonics: Teaching phonics in a systematic manner from part to whole, letter sound to word.

word family: A group of words with the same spelling pattern: _tug, bug, hug, chug,_ and _shrug_. The words in a word family don't just rhyme—they also have the same spelling pattern. In contrast, _through, shoe,_ and _boo_ rhyme, but they are not a word family.

Common Phonics Generalizations

Before learning the general phonics rules, students should have an understanding of long vowel sounds and short vowel sounds. In a long vowel sound, the vowel says its name (for example, "a" in *cake,* "e" in *be,* "i" in *bike,* "o" in *tow,* and "u" in *unit*). In a short vowel sound, the vowel does not say its name (for example, "a" in *cap,* "e" in *bet,* "i" in *lip,* "o" in *hot,* and "u" in *cut*).

Students should also be aware of silent consonants and the schwa sound. Students must be taught that some words include silent letters. These letters appear in the written word, but do not have a sound when the word is read. Some common patterns with silent letters besides the silent "e" discussed in the VCe rule are the "k" in *know,* the "w" in "wr" in *write,* the "gh" in *night,* the "b" in *climb,* and the "t" in *listen.*

The schwa sound is a reduced vowel sound that sounds like "uh." It occurs in the unaccented syllable. Any vowel can make the schwa sound; it is represented by an upside-down "e" (ə). Examples of words with the schwa sound include *amazing, item, pencil, money, syrup,* and *syringe.*

The following table contains some very basic rules that can be taught to elementary school students. There are exceptions to many of these rules, but the ones listed here are fairly predictable.

Some General Phonics Rules

Sound	Rule	Examples
CVC	When a single vowel comes between two consonants, that vowel is usually short.	*mud, bat, stuck*
VCe	When "e" is the final vowel in a word, the preceding vowel is usually long and the "e" is silent.	*home, make, like*
Closed syllable—VC	When a single vowel is at the beginning of a word, it is usually short.	*am, is, up*
Open syllable—CV	When a syllable ends with a vowel, the vowel sound is usually long.	*ba/by, ta/ble*
CVVC	When two vowels are adjacent, usually the first vowel says its name and the second vowel is silent. (***Remember:*** When two vowels do the walking, the first one does the talking.)	*goat, pail, beat*
"y" as a vowel	When "y" is acting as a vowel at the end of a one-syllable word, it usually has the sound of a long /i/. When "y" is acting as a vowel at the end of a two-syllable word, it usually has the sound of a long /e/.	*fly, try* *candy, silly, happy*
"r"-controlled	When "r" follows a vowel, it controls and changes the sound of the vowel.	*car, fir, murky*
Hard and soft "g" and "c"	When "g" is followed by an "a," "o," or "u," or is the last letter of a word, it has the hard sound. When "c" is followed by an "a," "o," or "u," or is the last letter of a word, it also has the hard sound. When "g" is followed by an "e," "i," or "y," it has a soft sound, /j/. When "c" is followed by an "e," "i," or "y," it has a soft sound, /s/.	hard: *garage, gate, good, got, guilty, gum, frog, leg; cat, cake, coat, cold, cut, cuddly, sac* soft: *general, angel, giraffe, engine, gym; cell, space, citrus, rice, cyclops, icy*

Strategies to Promote Letter-Sound Correspondence

Research has shown that phonics should be taught explicitly, through direct instruction. In direct instruction, information is clearly communicated via a process of explaining, showing, and then having the students apply their new knowledge. A teacher teaching the letter "m" would show the letter, say that the letter is "m" and that it says /m/, and inform students that words like *man, map,* and *money* start with /m/ because they start with the letter "m." In contrast, implicit instruction is indirect. In this case, the teacher reverses the instruction. She would say and show the words *man, map,* and *money,* and then ask students what sound the words begin with. After the students responded that the words start with the /m/ sound, the teacher would ask what letter the words start with, and finally ask, "So what sound does the letter 'm' make?" Explicit instruction states essential information, whereas implicit instruction entails a bit more exploration for students. Although explicit instruction is the best way to teach phonics to young or struggling readers, both implicit and explicit processes help students learn the letter-sound relationships and how to use those to figure out new words. The following table shows activities that teachers can use to reinforce letter sounds once they have taught students these sounds.

Letter-Sound Correspondence Activities

Activity	Description
Find the letter	Direct students to find something in the room that begins with the sound of the letter "f" and place a cut-out letter "f" on the item.
Beanbag toss	Have a student throw a beanbag onto a mat displaying the letters of the alphabet. If the beanbag lands on the letter "p," for example, the child says /p/.
Make a word (short vowel sounds)	Use word cards with the letters that are to be taught or reinforced to make words. In the case of short /a/, the letters "a," "n," "f," "m," "c," and "p" can be used to make a four-word word family. Stress the short /a/ sound while building these words. Give students a card with "an" and say the sound. Then have students put the "f" in front of the "an" and ask what that says. Continue through *man, can,* and *pan.* (This can be adapted to any sound.)
Make a word (long vowel sounds)	Explain to students that when words have the pattern of vowel, consonant, and then "e," (VCe), the "e" is silent and the vowel says its name. Then explicitly show some VCe-patterned words, and say some examples. Take a short vowel word and change it to a long vowel word by adding an "e" to the end. Word pairs such as *can/cane, fat/fate,* and *con/cone* can be used to explicitly teach the difference. Eventually, students are encouraged to read the word pairs and tell you why the vowel makes the long sound.
Bossy "r" ("r"-controlled sounds)	Explain to students that when a vowel is followed by the letter "r," the "r" becomes the "boss" and changes the sound of the vowel. Use the "make a word" lesson format and add the letter "r" to reinforce how the "r" becomes boss and changes the sound. For example, the following word pairs can be used: *cat/cart, fist/first, hut/hurt,* and *pot/port.*

Instructional Sequence of Phonics

Phonics instruction should progress from the easiest to what is considered more difficult. In the overall instruction, the progression starts with phonemic awareness, goes into phonics, and then into the more complex structural analysis. Although the sequence of letters taught in phonics may vary, there are commonalities, such as beginning with initial one-consonant phoneme sounds before teaching blends, and teaching short and long vowel sounds prior to vowel digraphs and diphthongs. Many systematic phonics programs use the following sequence:

1. Consonant sounds
2. Short vowel sounds
3. Combination of consonant sounds with short vowel sounds
4. Consonant blends
5. Long vowel sounds: digraphs (two vowels together)

6. Long vowel sounds: silent "e" rule
7. Consonant digraphs
8. Variant vowels and diphthongs
9. Silent letters and consonant digraphs
10. Inflectional endings

Once students have mastered the above letter-sound correspondences, they can begin to use structural analysis to decode new words, expanding their reading vocabulary. Using structural analysis allows readers to use roots and affixes to discern word meaning and pronunciation.

Differentiating Phonetically Regular and Irregular Words

Many English words do not follow phonics generalizations, and not all words can be identified through decoding, thereby causing difficulties for many English Language Learners (ELLs). For example, a teacher instructs, "When two vowels do the walking, the first one does the talking," and then asks a student to read a text that contains the word *field*. The student reads, "The farmer planted seeds in the *filed*." Although the student is following the phonics generalization, the rule doesn't work in this case. If the student is reading for meaning, he would realize *filed* is not the right word. Students need strategies to differentiate regular words (those pronounced in accordance with a phonics generalization) from irregular words (those that don't follow any phonics rules). Some strategies to aid students in this differentiation are as follows:

- Teach students to use cueing systems, semantics, syntax, and phonics to figure out an unknown word.
- Focus on semantics (the context in the surrounding text) to identify the word.
- Provide students multiple exposures to frequently used phonetically irregular words so that they learn to know the words by sight, increasing the automaticity of their reading.
- Consider making a word bank with index cards for students to study phonetically irregular words.
- When possible, teach a word family or team of phonetically irregular words, such as *field, yield,* and *shield*.
- Instruct students to be mindful of what they are reading and to use metacognition to ensure that their reading makes sense. Advise students to ask themselves, "Does this make sense?" as they read.

Promoting Automatic Word Recognition and High-Frequency Sight Words

Sight words are words that readers automatically recognize. High-frequency words are the most commonly used words in printed English. Why is it important for a reader to be able to recognize high-frequency words by sight? A child with a large bank of sight words that he automatically recognizes is able to read the text more fluently, thereby concentrating on comprehension while reading. The focus of the reading can be on meaning instead of decoding words—and allow for easier decoding of harder words. On the other hand, if a child has to decode several words in each sentence, this detracts from his focus on comprehension. In addition, knowing words by sight aids in reading speed.

Vocabulary Worth Knowing and Understanding

automatic word recognition: The ability to recognize words quickly, effortlessly, and automatically.

high-frequency words: Words that are frequently used in reading and writing. Examples include *a, the, she, he, they, as,* and *it.*

sight words: Words that readers recognize automatically, and therefore can read immediately, with no decoding necessary. Sight words cannot easily be decoded. There are two traditional lists of sight words: Dolch Sight Words and Fry Sight Words. Both are easily found online and contain words that have been proven to be in print frequently.

word wall: A board or wall that features isolated words that students are learning, usually presented in alphabetical order. New words are added weekly, and all words can be practiced on a regular basis, with whole group and small group activities.

Techniques for Teaching Automatic Word Recognition

The best method for aiding children in automatic word recognition is repeated exposure to the words being taught. Repetition and reinforcement are important. There are multiple ways to employ repetition and reinforcement to aid in automatic word recognition:

- Use books with predictable and decodable text that offers repeated phrases.
- When reading with the child, point out the targeted sight words he must learn.
- Identify, model, and reinforce sight words during paired and assisted reading.
- Utilize repeated reading with sentences and phrases that include the targeted words.
- Create a word wall to ask game-like questions so that students select targeted sight words. For example, "I am thinking of a word that rhymes with *Jim*." (*him*). This needs to be done often to reinforce the word.
- Try game formats such as bingo, in which children "cover" the words they are learning. The students write the given words on a blank bingo card. Once the card is ready, the teacher calls a word, which they cover on their card when recognized.

Instructional Strategies for Developing and Reinforcing Students' Phonics Skills

Reinforcing developing readers and writers while they read is also effective methodology. When talking about reinforcing children's skills in using phonics, the focus is on how a child uses phonics to both read and write.

As a child begins developing literacy skills, the teacher should encourage the child to sound out words when reading and writing. For example, a child is trying to read the sentence "The dog barked at the cat in the tree." He comes to the word *barked,* stops, and looks up to the teacher to say the word. Effective reinforcement of phonics dictates that she does not say the word, but instead guides the child to decode the word. This approach will aid in reinforcing what the child knows about sounding out words and using phonics or context to help figure out a new word. So, when the child looks up, there are a number of guiding questions the teacher can ask depending on the word itself: "What sound does the word begin with?" "What sound does the word end with?" "Can you tell me the sound in the middle?" "What vowel do you see?" "What do you see after the vowel?" "Do you remember what happens when an 'r' follows the vowel?" "Can you chunk the word and read a part of it?" Or, using context to aid in figuring out the word, the teacher may ask, "What does a dog usually do when it sees a cat?" Then, "Yes, how can you tell that is the word *barked*?" Although you would want to minimize your questioning, these types of guided questions allow the teacher to reinforce phonics skills. When a student begins to use phonics, the teacher needs to be aware of the student's developmental need in order to help him progress independently, giving him a vehicle to eventually be able to decode unknown words independently. For example, a student reads a book about football, and stops when he comes to the word *tackle*. Instead of saying the word for the student, the teacher may tell him to cover the "le" and say the word. Once the student says "tack," the teacher may ask what word is used in football that begins with "tack." In this way, the teacher shows the student how to chunk words for pronunciation and to use context to aid in decoding and recognizing words.

Activities aiding in the development of phonics skills:

- **Letter manipulation:** Have students look at a group of letters, such as "p," "r," "t," and "a." Guide the students to form the following words: *pat, tap, at, part, art, tar,* and *par.* Emphasize how the vowel sound changes when the vowel is followed by "r."

- **Chunking:** Have students practice chunking—separating parts of words to see if they can read the word. For example, give students the word *worker,* have them cover up the "er," and ask if they can read the first sound of the word. Practice this with numerous words.

- **Analogy strategy:** Have students compare a word with other words that have the same letter pattern. When using onset and rimes, similarities can be found. Once students know the consonant sounds, they can use the analogy strategy to identify unknown words. For example, working with the rime "ike" from the word *bike,* students can use the analogy strategy to decode *hike* and *like.*

Some techniques for reinforcing phonics skills:

- Ask students for the beginning and ending sounds of the targeted word.

- Ask students what vowel is in the word, and what sound the vowel makes in the word.

- Remind students of any phonics generalizations that may help, such as "I see the word ends with an 'e.' What sound does that make the vowel say?" Or "Two vowels are together; what does that mean?" Be sure to explicitly explain any generalization the child cannot remember.

- Chunk the word and ask if the child can recognize a part of the word.

- Use word family comparisons or the analogy strategy, such as stating to the child "I have seen you read this word [writing down *butter*], but the new word begins with 'sh,' so what would it be?"

No matter what technique is being utilized, the child needs to use metacognition and think about whether what is being read makes sense.

Assessing Phonics Skills: An Overview

Phonics skills can be assessed both formally and informally. Most school districts have a phonics assessment that has students read words as the teacher codes how the words are read. The students' knowledge of the letter-sound correspondence can then be analyzed, and students can be grouped for instruction. A running record (see Chapter 9) is another vehicle used to assess students' phonics and word identification skills. In a running record, teachers code the student's reading errors and evaluate them to see if any particular letter sounds are pronounced incorrectly, or if a particular phonics rule is not being used. For example, if a child is reading words such as *like, cake,* and *cute* with short vowel sounds, instruction on the silent "e" rule is necessary (VCe). In addition, teachers can assess phonics through student writing samples by analyzing which sounds and phonics rules the student is applying in his writing.

Chapter 6

Word Analysis Skills

A word analysis skill refers to any of a number of ways in which readers analyze unknown words. Word analysis is often used in conjunction with structural analysis, which will be described in detail later in this chapter. Word analysis includes such skills as using phonics to decode words, being able to chunk words into parts (syllables), and being able to recognize meanings of these parts. However, word analysis is broader than structural analysis, as students also analyze at the letter level. In other words, when an emergent reader is decoding the word *bat,* the reader is first isolating each letter and sound and eventually blending them together. Word or structural analysis also looks at the structure of the word. Consider the word *baker.* Students are taught that one definition of the suffix *-er* is "one who does." In this case a baker is one who bakes. In essence, in structural analysis, students focus on the structure of the word and identify known word parts, such as prefixes, suffixes, base words, and letter patterns. Of course, letter patterns can themselves be found in prefixes, suffixes, and base words, but analyzing words by common letter patterns aids students in phonics, spelling, meaning, and word retention. What is important to recognize is that students have a range of means to analyze unknown words, ultimately enabling them to encode new words in their reading.

Methods of Teaching Word Analysis Skills

There are several methods for teaching students word analysis skills. A few of them are described here:

Making word families: Teaching word analysis at the letter level. The teacher gives students a group of letters, such as "b," "c," "f," "m," "p," "a," and "t," in order to work with the spelling pattern "at." Working with the students, the teacher models the process and then has the students apply their learning. To start, the "at" may be on one card, with the other letters on separate cards. The teacher begins by combining cards to make the word *cat* and saying a sentence like "I saw the cat up in the tree." Next, the teacher makes the word *mat* and recites a sentence: "I bought a new yoga mat yesterday." Then, the teacher has students analyze the words by asking "What sound did both of these words end with?" After helping students determine the sound of "at," the teacher has the students make the following words: *bat, fat,* and *pat* and form a sentence with each. As the students make the word, the teacher supports their word analysis by asking which two letters make the "at" sound. Teaching students to analyze words when building word families will lead them to greater success in the next activity: word sorts.

Word sorts: Students are given a group of words to sort into various categories. A word sort can be a free sort or guided sort. Here are examples of each:

- **Free sort:** The teacher tells the students to sort the words any way they wish, and to note their criteria for sorting. Students may sort words by beginning sounds, ending sounds, rhymes, parts of speech, and so forth.
- **Guided sort:** The teacher directs the students to sort into particular phonetic categories, such as the "at," "ing," and "ake" rimes. Then, the category is changed and the teacher directs students to group words that begin with the same consonant blend, such as *brat, bring,* and *brake.*

Take apart: Students build a word, take it apart, and build it again as they study the word's formation.

Blending wheel or T-scope: Different onsets can be matched to the same rimes as one another, or to different ones, to make a new word. A rime, such as "ab," is written on a cardstock paper. A slider with beginning consonants is pulled through two slots to show one word. The rime "ab" can have a slider with the consonants "c," "d," "f," "g," "l," "n," and "t." As the student pulls on the slider, he says each newly made word (*cab, dab, fab, gab, lab, nab,* and *tab*). Tablet apps can be used in a similar fashion.

Word walls: Word walls can be used to build categories of words, such as word families, words with the same number of syllables, and words with beginning/ending consonant blends.

Structural Analysis: Multisyllabic Words and Syllabication

Structural analysis is part of the continuum of learning to read that begins with phonemic awareness and continues with phonics (the alphabetic principle). This analysis should be incorporated into the word-study curriculum beginning in third or fourth grade. Structural analysis focuses on teaching children to look at words through word parts and their meanings (that is, root words, syllables, and affixes), which aid in identifying and understanding unknown words. This section focuses on multisyllabic words and syllabication rules to assist in identifying the root word.

Vocabulary Worth Knowing and Understanding

closed syllable: A syllable that ends with a consonant (CVC pattern) and usually has a short vowel sound. Examples: *mas/ter* and *but/ler*.

multisyllabic words: Words with more than one syllable; these can often be challenging to readers.

open syllable: A syllable that ends with a vowel (CV or V pattern) that usually has a long vowel sound. Examples: *ba/by* and *a/way*.

structural analysis: The ability to look at words and analyze them through word parts and their meanings.

syllabication: The act of dividing words into syllables.

Syllabication Principles

Reminders: A syllable contains one vowel sound, an affix is a prefix or suffix that carries meaning, and a root word also contains meaning.

Every syllable contains a vowel sound. Knowing where to break words into syllables can help with identifying different parts of a word and in discerning the word's pronunciation through accented and unaccented syllables.

The following are the basic syllabication rules—but remember, language rules often have exceptions. These rules stem from the six basic syllable types: open, closed, "r"-controlled, VCe, vowel teams (digraphs and diphthongs), and consonant-le.

- When two consonants are consecutive, with a vowel before and after, the word is divided between the two consonants. Examples: *but/ton, muf/fin, mar/ket, bas/ket*. The first syllable is usually accented.
- If there is only one consonant between two vowels, divide the word after the first vowel. Examples: *ta/ken, bi/son, de/clare, fu/tile*. The first syllable is usually accented.
- When dividing words into syllables, keep consonant blends and digraphs together. Examples: *to/geth/er, ful/crum, mi/grate, friend/ship*.
- Vowel digraphs and diphthongs are never separated. Examples: *beat/er, oil/er, joy/ous*.
- The consonant-le portion at the end of a word has its own syllable. Examples: *ba/gle, man/tle, fid/dle*. The consonant-le syllable is unaccented.
- VCe makes its own syllable, usually at the end of the word. Examples: *com/plete, graph/ite*.
- Affixes have their own syllable or syllables. Examples: *re/make, cook/ing, in/ter/lock, pre/tend/ing*. The root word is usually accented.
- Separate individual parts of a compound word into syllables only if the part in question contains more than one syllable. Examples: *grass/hop/per, fin/ger/nails, house/keep/er*.

Check Your Understanding

Divide the following into syllables per the basic syllabication rules. Note that some of these words follow more than one rule.

1. graphite
2. tablespoon
3. pealing
4. transatlantic
5. pattern
6. subtle
7. cashew
8. casino

Answers:

1. *graph/ite* (digraph *ph* together or *ite* VCe)
2. *ta/ble/spoon* (open syllable, *ble*)
3. *peal/ing* (one vowel sound)
4. *trans/at/lan/tic* (VC pattern, separate between two consonants)
5. *pat/tern* (separate between two consonants)
6. *sub/tle* (consonant-le)
7. *cash/ew* (blend)
8. *ca/si/no* (CV pattern; one vowel sound)

Methods of Teaching Structural Analysis

Structural analysis is taught by using word parts and teaching similarities in meanings between words that have the same base word, root, or affix. Students need to understand that base words, roots, suffixes, and prefixes have meaning, and that affixes can change the meaning of an original root or base word. Structural analysis instruction can be directed in a variety of ways:

- Teach the meaning of the base words, roots, and affixes.
- When reading a book aloud or working with a group, discuss words with roots and affixes.
- Explicitly show how affixes can change word meanings (for example, *like, unlike, dislike, likeable*).
- In a game format, build words using different roots and affixes.
- Make a "word tree" by building onto the root word. Cite derivatives, how they may change from the original spelling, and how word parts can change the meaning. For example, the root *port*, which means "to carry," has these derivatives: *deport, import, portable, portage, deportation, importation, important*, and so forth.

Working with Homographs and Their Pronunciation

Homographs are words that are spelled the same, but have multiple meanings and may not be pronounced the same (examples: *fair, bow, desert, minute*). Teachers often talk about words with multiple meanings. In the case of homographs, the focus is on words that are spelled the same, may sound different, and have different meanings. Some common homographs found at the elementary school level include *lead, wind, live,* and *desert*.

It is best to teach homographs in context, when a more common meaning is expected. However, the following mini-lesson may also prove helpful:

1. Give the definition of *homograph,* and tell students you will work with some examples.

2. Introduce the words one at a time. (Example: *Wind* means fast-blowing air.)

3. Use the word in a sentence. (Example: The *wind* blew my hat off my head.)

4. Introduce the second word. (Example: *Wind* means to make tighter, or twist.)

5. Use the second word in a sentence. (Example: The man had to *wind* the clock.)

6. Discuss how the two words are spelled the same, but sound different and have different meanings. Explain that when a student is reading, he may have to re-read and use the context to ensure that he has the correct pronunciation to correspond with the meaning in the sentence.

7. Share other examples, such as *lead, live,* and *minute.*

Inventive Spelling

In inventive spelling, young children attempt to write words as they hear the sounds in each word. For example, a young child might write *bg* for *big* as he identifies the beginning and ending sounds of the word. Inventive spelling is considered acceptable until about third grade, when children should know the skills needed for traditional spelling (although students in the older grades may use inventive spelling as a placeholder in the drafting stage of writing). The idea behind inventive spelling is to allow children to concentrate on the content of what they want to say, and not the mechanics of the writing.

Inventive spelling is also used as a tool to assess a child's phonics skills. In encoding, the reader thinks of the letter sound (phoneme) and writes the corresponding letter or letters (grapheme). In decoding, the reader reads the written letter (grapheme) and says the sound (phoneme). If a child consistently writes a letter or letter pattern incorrectly, the error should trigger a specific phonics lesson. For example, suppose a child writes *I lik mi new bik. It maks me happe.* The spelling errors can be analyzed and the teacher can set goals for the child. In this example, the child might need to learn the VCe rule and that "y" says the /e/ sound at the end of a two-syllable word.

Look carefully at the following sample written with inventive spelling. Search for any patterns in the spelling or phonics generalizations the child may have used.

> *I wnt to the stor wth Mom to gt bred.*
>
> **Analysis:** It is clear that the child knows the following: the fact that sentences begin with a capital letter and end with a period; consonant sounds; and *Mom* and *to* as sight words. On the other hand, the child does not yet know that all words should have a vowel, the "r"-controlled rule, or the proper spelling of *store* using the VCe rule.

Let's try this one:

> *me lik yu vere muh yu gd techr*
>
> **Analysis:** This child has some understanding that vowels belong in words, and has a strong comprehension of consonant sounds. On the other hand, the child does not know the VCe rule (*lik* to *like*), the "er" spelling pattern (as in *teacher*), or that the /e/ sound at the end of a word is usually spelled with "y" (*very,* not *vere*).

This next practice analysis is from a young child at the end of second grade. Look for what the child knows and still needs to learn.

> *Wher going to camp at my house With the hole cub Scouts because We have the bigest yard.*
>
> **Analysis:** This child has a good understanding of common spelling errors and the correct use of tenses. He also understands that a sentence begins with a capital letter, "wh" sounds like /w/, and sentences end with a period. On the other hand, the child overuses capital letters (as in *With* and *We*), but this may be because

both words start with "w" (like the word at the beginning of the sentence) or because the uppercase and lowercase "w's" look so similar. He may not know contractions (*Wher* should be *We're*) or homophones (*hole* should be *whole*). He has some understanding that *Cub Scouts* is a proper noun and should be capitalized.

Developmental Stages of Writing

A few years back, I walked over to the writing center in a preschool where a 4-year-old had just finished "writing" his postcard. I took a few seconds to admire the scribbled lines across the index card, and asked the child if he would read it to me—and, of course, he did, rattling on and on! (This also showed me that the young boy understood that print has meaning.) As you will see by the developmental stages of writing detailed in the table below, there is a continuum of growth, and that is what is important for the Praxis (5204).

When children learn to speak, you hear the stages: first the cooing, then the babbling, and later the one- or two-word statement. A parallel type of development occurs in writing. A child begins writing with scribbles, which may be abstract pictures, or a scramble of letters that makes no sense—to an adult. But if you asked that child what he wrote, you could be given quite a bit of information. Eventually the scribbles become recognizable drawings, as children usually draw before they write. Teachers should encourage a child to draw as much detail as possible so they can see what the child has envisioned.

Developmental Stages of Writing

Developmental Stage	Description
Prephonemic Stage (some call this the scribbling stage)	The child writes with scribbles and drawings. Sometimes, some of the scribbles can be identified as letters, as the child "pretends" to write.
Early Phonemic Stage (some call this letter-like symbols and/or strings of letters)	The child begins writing with a beginning or ending sound. He might label a picture, such as a "b" for bunny; copy letters from print sources, such as STOP; or write "sentences" with letters or letter combinations representing words. (Example: *IPB* for *I play basketball.*)
Letter-Name Stage (some call this the Beginning Sounds Emerge Stage)	Usually, the child uses the beginning and ending letters to represent a word. (Example: *BL* for *ball.*)
Transitional Stage	The child uses beginning and ending letters and may not include a vowel or all vowels, but does use other letters in the word. He uses inventive spelling. In general, this stage is easier for an adult to read. (Example: *Mi bik iS brKn* for *My bike is broken.*)
Conventional Writing Stage	The child now writes the majority of words with conventional spelling. Most experts say that inventive spelling should end around third grade, by which time conventional spelling of common words should be expected on all final drafts in writing.

Adapted from http://www.mecfny.org/wp-content/uploads/2015/06/StagesofWritinghandout.pdf

Developmental Stages of Spelling

There are a few models for the developmental stages of spelling. The one presented here seems to be the most prevalent; it was derived from the research of Charles Read and Edmund Henderson in the early 1970s. This model has five stages (some models have as many as eight) and shows progress from preschool to the conventional writing stage and covers development for most elementary students. Reading specialists Bear, Invernizzi, Templeton, and Johnston add two more stages for advanced and older students: syllable and affixes spelling, and derivational relations spelling. In both of these stages, as the complex stage names indicate, students are becoming sophisticated spellers.

Developmental Stages of Spelling

Developmental Stage	Description
Precommunicative Stage	The child uses letters to spell words, but there is no order, and no words are recognizable. (Example: *XPQTRD*)
Semiphonetic Stage	The child sometimes uses single letters to spell, and sometimes uses a couple of consonant letters. (Example: *I rD b* for *I ride my bike.*)
Phonetic Stage	The child recognizes some words but not others; however, he can understand these words if he reads them phonetically. The child uses inventive spelling for some words. (Example: *My brthr is bigr thn me* for *My brother is bigger than me.*)
Transitional Stage	The child spells an increasing number of words with conventional spelling, but still uses some inventive spelling; he may attempt to use spelling rules, but cannot yet properly apply them. The child usually recognizes that words have vowels. (Example: *I hurd my rite hand yesterdy* for *I hurt my right hand yesterday.*)
Correct Stage or Conventional Stage	The child uses conventional spelling, but may make some errors with irregular or unfamiliar words.

Spelling Strategies

Teaching common orthographic patterns is considered the best way to teach spelling to young learners. (Back to roots here: *ortho* is derived from the Greek root *ortho,* meaning "correct," and *graphos* means "writing.") Children must be able to use common orthographic patterns to aid in their spelling.

In the early grades, both phonics and spelling are taught with onset and rimes and word family combinations. Children work with word families such as *cat, mat, hat* and *cut, hut, rut.* As the children advance in their spelling, the onset and rime patterns become more complex: *clock, mock, dock* and *night, fight, light.* Teaching word families exposes children to common orthographic patterns and strengthens their recall for spelling these words correctly. The reading and writing connection also plays a part in this, as generalizations in phonics aid in spelling. So when a child learns to spell word families using the analogy strategy, a child can read a word that was not on the original "spelling list." Although there are usually exceptions to most generalizations and rules, common spelling rules do help as a guide to correct spelling and should certainly be taught. You may remember many of the following common spelling rules from when you were in elementary school.

Common Spelling Rules

- Write "i" before "e," except after "c," unless it sounds like the long /ā/ as in *neighbor* and *weigh.* (Examples: *belief, thief, sleigh*)
- If a one-syllable word ends in a single consonant, double the consonant when adding a suffix that begins with a vowel, such as *-ed, -ing,* or *-er.* (Examples: *bat→batted, batting, batter*)
- When a word ends with a silent "e," drop the "e" before adding a suffix that begins with a vowel, such as *-ed, -ing,* or *-er.* (Examples: *bike→biked, biking, biker*)
- If a word ends with an "e" and the suffix begins with a consonant, keep the "e." (Examples: *safe→safely, hope→hopeless*)
- To make most nouns and verbs plural, add an "s." (Examples: *mats, locks, caps*)
- When "y" is at the end of a word, if a vowel comes before the "y," just add "s" to make the word plural. (Examples: *boys, toys*)
- When a "y" is at the end of the word, if a consonant comes before the "y," change the "y" to "i" and add "es" (or change the "y" to "i" before adding any suffix except one that begins with "i"). (Examples: *candy→candies, lady→ladies, happy→happiness*)

- If a word ends in "ch," "s," "sh," or "x," add "es" to make the word plural. (Examples: *witches, dresses, dishes, lynxes*)
- For words that end in "f," change the "f" to a "v" and add "es" to make the word plural. (Examples: *wolf→wolves, loaf→loaves*)

Suggestions for Teaching Spelling

- Rely heavily on onset and rimes (what we commonly call "word families").
- Have children work with other common word patterns using the common spelling rules (listed above).
- Use mini-lessons prior to writing in order to teach common orthographic patterns. For example, teaching the rule of dropping the "e" and adding "ing" to present tense words.
- Teach spelling through word study, using common spelling words. For example, have students "make words" by manipulating letters into the pattern, or adherence to the rule, they are learning. For example, when teaching the "at" word family, give the students the letters "a," "t," "b," "f," "h," and "m." They can then rearrange the letters and make the words *bat, fat, hat,* and *mat.*
- Teach spelling through writing as children polish their writing piece to its final draft. Also, assess all your students' writing to see which spelling rules most children are not using correctly, and provide some directed lessons and practice on the particular rules or patterns where improvement is needed.
- Use word sorts. For example, give students nine words, three ending in "it," three ending in "at," and three ending in "et." Then have the students sort and say the words. This aids students in recognizing common word patterns.
- Play spelling games. For example, have groups write words ending in "ack" to see which group can write the most words. This will reinforce the rules or patterns students are learning.
- Use a word wall for support while playing thinking games, such as "I'm thinking of a word on the wall that begins with 'm' and rhymes with *night*" (*might*).

Assessing Word Analysis Skills: An Overview

Word analysis skills, like phonics, are assessed through oral readings, running record analysis, and student writing. A teacher listens to determine whether a student can recognize parts of words or can chunk words to aid in word identification. For example, if the word *doghouse* is in the text and is unknown to the child, the teacher should discern whether the child separates it into two words to aid in the correct pronunciation. If the child does not, the teacher should instruct him on this method. Teachers also analyze student writing samples to see if students are using phonics skills to write words correctly and if they are utilizing word parts such as syllables and/ or affixes correctly in their writing.

Chapter 7

Reading Comprehension

Comprehension, the goal of reading, refers to the reader's ability to make meaning from text. A reader's comprehension can be significantly influenced by outside factors. Viewing literacy from a linguistic, sociological, cultural, cognitive, and psychological perspective, teachers understand the reader as a "whole child." How a child is brought up, where a child is brought up, the child's experiences, economic status, cognitive abilities, and attitude—all of these can contribute to whether the child is a struggling, grade-level, or advanced reader. Each of these factors influences the child's growth as a reader in different ways.

Understanding Literacy Through Linguistic, Sociological, Cultural, Cognitive, and Psychological Influences

The five literary influences are described in detail below.

Linguistic Influences

In the broad sense, linguistics is the study of language. There are four different types of vocabulary: speaking, listening, reading, and writing. How many times have you gone to write a word and changed it because you were not sure of its spelling? That is because like all literate adults, your speaking vocabulary is still larger than your writing vocabulary. Children enter school with different levels of vocabulary. Some students are stronger in oral language (or reading, writing, or listening) than others. Students with strong oral language skills encounter fewer unknown vocabulary words in their reading than do students with weak oral language skills.

Students' oral language experiences can affect their reading and writing in a variety of ways. When a child is raised in a language-rich environment, he is exposed to more vocabulary and a higher level of vocabulary. With multiple exposures to a word, the child learns the word at a deeper level. For example, a *square* is usually thought of as a four-sided figure with all sides of equal length, but then multiple meanings become apparent with more exposure to the word, such as *square* means not cool, a carpenter's square, or the center of town. Some students may come from homes where the vocabulary used is not broad or repeatable, television may consume family time, and few activities may be offered that encourage language use. On the other hand, there are students whose parents use and explain new vocabulary whenever possible, discuss daily news and events to broaden language and concepts, and focus on experiences that will immerse their child in a new lexicon.

Generally speaking, for an English Language Learner (ELL), the effects of a second language being spoken at home are easily understood, as the language itself is new. With a native English speaker, the child's language experiences have less impact, and the child's need may be less noticeable. Some native English speakers come from homes where the parents do not speak English. In some states, that child is given ELL status nonetheless. Further expanding the range of language abilities in the classroom are children born with a language processing disorder, delaying their language development; such a disorder can also affect their growth in reading and writing. All of this is crucial because, as discussed in Chapter 2, "Oral Language," when children are exposed to and know a great deal of oral language, it highly impacts their reading.

Sociological Influences

Sociological influences include the child's economic status and his school district's level of affluence and culture. Both are described here.

- **Economic status:** Money buys food and healthcare, enriching experiences, and a lot more. When students are well fed and healthy, they can learn more easily. If a child comes from a home that can afford books, family field trips, and other luxuries, the child comes to school with a more than adequate background knowledge of book-handling skills, and with vocabulary gained from those experiences. In addition, being dressed to a "peer norm" can boost his confidence, which can aid his academic performance.

- **School district:** Inequality between school districts exists. The economic level of the district and the culture within the district or classroom affect learning. School districts with strong preschool intervention programs aid in setting up disadvantaged children to be more successful in school. A district can enhance learning by providing the best possible supplies, traditional and technological learning materials, learning environment, school opportunities, teacher-pupil ratio, teacher professional development, and so forth. A well-run economically advantaged school district can make a difference in a child's learning. In addition, a district without as many funds but with creative and impassioned leaders can also make a difference.

Cultural Influences

Cultural influences can also impact literacy growth in children. The following have significant impact:

- **Class and race:** Class and race can either confer or limit privilege. Cultural beliefs strongly influence family culture and children's attitudes toward learning. If parents value learning, they will support their children in their studies and ensure they attend school.
- **Language and dialect:** The educational concerns for ELLs have been discussed, but parents who speak another language may not be aware of what school districts offer, and therefore, important advantages, such as early intervention, can be missed. Culturally and regionally influenced dialect can impact reading and writing. For example, if a young child is brought up saying "you" (as in "It's you problem.") instead of "your," the child assumes this speech is the acceptable norm. Standardized tests do not take dialect into consideration. Students will often write the way they speak, and certain dialects do not follow traditional English.
- **Customs and traditions:** Being familiar with a culture aids in background knowledge and often deeper understanding when reading a story rooted in that culture. Since prior knowledge influences how we build meaning from a text, the more a child has been immersed in a culture, the greater the comprehension will be when reading about that culture. A child from China will most likely construct deeper meaning from a story set in China than someone who has never been there.
- **Family culture:** Family and peers have a culture that influences learning. Family culture encompasses family habits, rules, beliefs, roles, activities, and other areas of family life. Examples include reading to children, bed time, and family rules. A tired child does not learn well, and a child who does not have polite behavior modeled at home may be more likely to be impolite at school, affecting his learning and perhaps that of others.
- **Values:** Families that value education will be more likely to support children's learning as well as their habits that encourage learning.

Cognitive Influences

Cognitive influences include the ability to think, reason, and understand. The pace of children's development is widely divergent and cognitive processing matures with growth. A very young child thinks he can hide behind a thin pole, while a 6-year-old understands this is not possible. Cognitive development in each of the following areas affects learning:

- **Information processing:** The ability of a child to understand and categorize information.
- **Perceptual skills:** The ability to develop a mental image, or to see similarities and differences in objects.
- **Language processing:** The ability to receive information with correct understanding and then express it verbally.
- **Visual information processing:** The ability to make sense of images taken in by the eye.
- **Auditory processing:** The brain's ability to interpret and understand information that is heard.
- **Working memory:** The ability to store and decipher information temporarily.
- **Attention span:** The amount of time a person can concentrate on the task at hand; this usually lengthens with age.

Psychological Influences

The mind-set of the learner and the perspectives the learner has regarding a wide range of areas vary with each individual, and significantly affect learning. Some of these psychological factors that can impact learning are:

- **Biases:** Having a bias against an idea or value can influence learning.

- **Motivation:** The goals, interests, and needs of a student can motivate him to try harder to succeed at a particular task, or can deter that success.

- **Attitude:** A student's position or feeling about learning. A "bad" attitude toward learning can negatively affect student growth, whereas a positive attitude toward learning enhances the learning experience and growth.

- **Self-esteem:** How a child feels about himself can affect his ability to learn.

- **Self-efficacy:** How a person views himself impacts how he approaches goals and challenges. In the area of literacy, a child who believes he is a good reader is more apt to become one. A child who views himself as a nonreader may have more difficulty learning to read.

- **Emotional conditions:** At some point in their lives, some students may undergo trauma that makes conditions in their life not conducive to learning. There are myriad reasons for a child to be upset, such as divorce, misunderstandings, punishment at home, violence in the house, death in the family, loss of a pet, or simply a bad morning due to being late for the school bus. On the other hand, teachers expect the excitement of an upcoming vacation period or holiday to impact learning and strive to make the impact minimal. Teachers need to be aware that emotions impact learning and behavior. Some school districts have a code for when a young child goes to school in the morning after the police were forced to visit their home during the night. A nonprofit organization calls the school and asks that the teacher be informed that the child needs "extra care" that day.

- **Level of learning activity and scaffolding:** Teachers use assessment to guide instruction. A child needs to be given materials and tasks that match his ability. If a child is given a book to read that is at his frustration level, the teacher can scaffold by preteaching vocabulary and building background. If a child is frustrated and not well supported, he may develop attitudes and feelings that can impede learning.

- **Reaction to teachers:** Sometimes a child's emotional reaction to particular teachers can interfere with learning. For example, a child may react negatively to a teacher for no known reason. Perhaps the teacher reminds him of someone else with whom he has had a conflict, or the teacher's manner may not mesh well with the child's personality.

- **Environmental factors:** External noise or commotion can cause stress, disturbing the learning process.

The Interactive Model of Reading

Readers bring different elements of knowledge to what they read. The interactive model of reading states that a reader interacts with the text and constructs meaning as he reads. The meaning that is constructed is highly influenced by prior knowledge. As students read, they absorb the author's words and construct meaning from prior knowledge and experiences. The linguistic, sociological, cultural, cognitive, and psychological influences discussed in the previous section all impact what the reader brings to the text. In a scenario where a 6-year-old in Guam is reading *Snowy Day* by Ezra Keats, much more background building would be needed than for a 6-year-old in Alaska reading this book. On the other hand, if the 6-year-old from Guam moved to Alaska and then read a story about sea cucumbers, the Alaskan student's comprehension would be impacted, while the Guamanian could be perfectly comfortable with the story. If background building was not done, the Alaskan child would be wondering why a green cucumber grows in the sea, and if it could be eaten. On the other hand, the young Guamanian, now in Alaska, would remember fondly dodging these elongated, blackish sea creatures when swimming in the shallow waters in Guam. As you can see from this scenario, prior knowledge gleaned from experiences can impact reading comprehension.

Scaffolding reading experiences should be conducted via a three-tiered reading lesson: pre-reading, during reading, and post-reading. The lesson before reading may include activating prior knowledge, building background, teaching selected vocabulary, and predicting. This scaffolding allows students to begin the reading with enough preparation to fully comprehend the text. Students should be taught to activate their prior knowledge before reading any book, as thinking about the topic prior to reading has been shown to increase comprehension.

During-reading lessons include purpose setting and reading mode. Purpose setting gives students a focus for reading, such as telling students to read to see if their predictions come true. Mode of reading defines how the students will read (partner, silently, and so forth).

Post-reading usually includes discussion questions and reader response. Discussion questions should be text dependent and help students derive deeper meaning from the text. Reader response reinforces what students have learned in the text.

Vocabulary Worth Knowing and Understanding

building background: When a teacher directly teaches, or has students work with materials that will increase their relevant knowledge, before reading a particular text. For example, if students read a text on the art of weaving, the teacher might share some artistic samples or have students weave from a shoe box loom.

interactive model of reading: This model posits that a reader comes to the text with prior knowledge and concepts that allow him to construct meaning while reading. This is influenced by the context of the reading, the text itself, and what the reader brings to the text from prior knowledge.

metacognition: Thinking about thinking. (Is the reader thinking about his understanding of the text as he reads?)

prior knowledge: The knowledge and beliefs that a reader brings to the text.

schema: A mental concept or generalization. This includes the concept of prior knowledge, but is much broader. For example, we all have a mental concept of a chair and that a chair is something we sit on—a recliner, a rocking chair, a desk chair, and so on. Our schema allows us to think in general categories.

transactional theory of reading: This theory is the basis for the understanding that when readers read, because of prior knowledge they can interact with the text and construct meaning. Louise Rosenblatt, who proposed the theory, found that a transaction occurs between reader and text, and that the reader constructs meaning through background knowledge and personal notions, making each reader's understanding unique.

Literal, Inferential, and Evaluative (Critical) Comprehension

Literal, inferential, and evaluative comprehension refer to the type of thinking needed to read and understand a text. The following passage will be used to explain these three terms.

> Kayla and Sarah were going to the beach. Kayla was a really good swimmer. Sarah was afraid of the water, but she wanted to be with her friend so she did not tell Kayla that she could not swim. When they got to the beach, Kayla ran into the water and yelled for Sarah to follow. Sarah put her feet in the water, but said she didn't want to get her whole body wet. Kayla yelled again, "Come on in!" Sarah said she wasn't feeling well, and sat down on the towel while Kayla went swimming. When Kayla got out of the water, Sarah said that now she felt fine, and the girls went for a walk down the beach.

Literal Comprehension

Literal comprehension means understanding what is explicitly stated in the text. This is sometimes called "reading by the line," and is text-dependent because the reader must read and refer to the text to state the fact. For example, the passage explicitly states that Kayla and Sarah were going to the beach. So, if the question is asked, "Where are Sarah and Kayla going?" the answer is literal and can be found directly stated in the text: "the beach." Literal questions are considered the easiest to answer, as they require minimal thinking. Consider the question "Who went swimming?" Again, this is a literal question with a "right there" answer; the text states, "Kayla went swimming." Literal questions are text-dependent.

Inferential Comprehension

Inferential comprehension means understanding what is inferred or implied in the text. This is sometimes called "reading between the lines" because the idea or statement is not directly visible. Inference questions are considered text-dependent because information from the text must be used to answer them. To answer an inference question, the reader must take what the author states and what he, the reader, already knows in order to make the proper inference. When answering inference questions, a reader must use prior knowledge and schema along with text information to get the correct answer. Using the above passage, one inference question might be "How did Sarah feel about going to the beach?" The answer depends on the reader's interpretation of the text—what the text says and what the reader, through prior experiences, thinks is happening. The answer could be "Sarah is excited because she will be with her friend." Or "Sarah is uncomfortable because Kayla probably thinks she likes to swim." Another inference question could be "Did Sarah really not feel well? Explain your answer." Again, answers may vary, depending on the reader's background and cognitive abilities. Someone with a literal interpretation may say, "Yes, because she went and sat on the towel." Others who are reading between the lines may say, "No, she was hiding the fact that she is afraid of the water," or "No, she didn't want Kayla to know that she couldn't swim, and she felt fine when Kayla came out of the water." Inference questions are also text-dependent.

Evaluative Comprehension

Evaluative comprehension entails making a judgment about what is said in the text or about the text, such as when the reader has an opinion, a favorite, or a dislike. In some way, the reader is placing a value on what is being said. The reader needs to both know the facts and have some sense of opinion, value, or background about the experience being evaluated. Using the above passage, one evaluative question might be "Was it fair of Sarah not to tell Kayla that she was afraid of the water?" Some might answer yes, as Sarah wanted to be with her friend. Others might say it was not fair because Kayla should have been able to play in the water with the friend she brought to the beach. Another evaluative question might be "In your opinion, was it right of Sarah to lie to her friend?" Some might say, "No, she should have been honest and said she was afraid of the water." Others might say, "Yes, being afraid of the water is embarrassing." Evaluative questions may not be text-dependent; being able to answer these questions takes critical comprehension.

Author's Note: Although the Praxis (5204) objectives do not refer directly to the evaluative comprehension question type, since it is not always text-dependent, you should be able to recognize it if you come across one. There is one type of question referred to as *scriptal* in the *No Child Left Behind* booklet. This is a "beyond the line" question, which means a child can answer the question without having read the text. Two examples of a scriptal question using the above passage are "What do you like to do at the beach?" and "Tell me about a time you have been at the beach." These questions help children make a connection to the passage, but a teacher cannot use them to evaluate the child's comprehension of the reading material. Scriptal questions are not text-dependent.

Check Your Understanding

Read the passage below and the six questions that follow. Identify each question as asking for literal, inferential, or evaluative thinking.

Noah rushed into the classroom, promising himself he would never be so stupid again. He had just walked by Ava, and had wanted to ask her to hang out after school. She was standing there talking to her friends. So, he snuck up and playfully pinched her arm. She turned around and stuck her tongue out at him, and her friends laughed. He just foolishly grinned, and then took off fast. Man, did he feel like an idiot.

1. Why did Noah pinch Ava's arm?
2. Was it right of Noah to pinch Ava?
3. Why did Ava stick out her tongue at Noah?

4. How did Noah feel?
5. Do you think it was a good idea for Ava to stick out her tongue? Explain.
6. What did Ava's friends do when she stuck her tongue out at Noah?

Answers:
1. Inferential
2. Evaluative
3. Inferential
4. Literal
5. Evaluative
6. Literal

Independent Reading

Independent reading refers to students reading apart from the teacher, in or outside of school. Many primary classrooms have color-coded baskets so that students can choose their "just right" books for independent reading. A good independent book is at the student's instructional level, in which the student knows 90% to 94% of the words in the book. This allows the student to read comfortably, yet gain new vocabulary. Fostering independent reading is important because:

- independent reading encourages wide reading, thereby building vocabulary, fluency, and comprehension.
- it develops interest in reading, and reinforces reading as a habit.
- it allows students more time to practice their reading skills.
- it allows students to be exposed to a variety of topics.
- reading more books helps build background through both content and gained vocabulary for more complicated books.

Vocabulary's Impact on Comprehension

There is no doubt that vocabulary impacts comprehension. The effect of children's large listening and speaking vocabularies was discussed in the Chapter 2 (see the "Increasing Vocabulary Through Listening and Speaking: The Impact on Language Development" section, p. 17). When children have knowledge of words that they encounter in text they are reading, the text is easier for them to understand. Try the following sentence: "The men moved the davenport into the large bedroom." Most people have probably never heard of a *davenport*. Reading the sentence, you get the idea that it is large (since it took more than one man to move it); from context, you probably glean that it is a type of furniture—maybe a bureau, since it is being placed in the bedroom. *Davenport* is actually an old-fashioned word for *couch*. As you can see, having a wide knowledge of vocabulary enhances comprehension. It is important that students not only have knowledge of words, but also depth of meaning. The dictionary definition describes a davenport as a "large sofa usually used for sleeping," which gives even deeper meaning to the sentence. Teachers need to teach students when the "gist" of a definition is enough or when they need to know more about the word to comprehend the text.

The Reading and Writing Connection

Connections between the reading and writing processes should be clearly explained to students, so as to aid in their understanding of the importance of each process. Connections include:

- Readers decode when they read a word, and they encode when they write.
- Reading can be used to reinforce word identification skills that enable word spelling for the students. These skills include the development of word families that expand the students' writing vocabulary. (Example of a word family: *rank, crank, blank, lank,* and *bank.*)

46

- The more children read, the better they write.
- Texts become "mentor texts" or models for student writing.
- Studying the author's craft in a particular text aids students in using this same technique in their own writing.
- Students learn as they read; this knowledge is transferred to their writing, giving them something to write about.
- Reading various genres and text structures aids students in writing; conversely, writing various text structures and genres builds understanding in reading.
- An avid reader knows that writers read and re-read their work. When children write and revise, they must continually read over what they have written. So, they are getting more practice reading as they write.
- Writers and readers bring their own interpretation to the text as they construct meaning.

Ways to Promote the Reading and Writing Connection

Teachers can help their students make the reading and writing connection in a number of ways:

- Have students study informational and fictional text structures in both their reading and writing. Being able to identify a particular text structure in a text allows students to carry that into their writing.
- Use genre studies, in which students are immersed in a particular genre to learn its characteristics; then, have the students complete a writing assignment in that genre.
- Use mentor texts to show students the author's craft. For example, if the class is working on metaphors, share samples of metaphoric writing and analyze them with your students.
- Create classroom publications to allow students to both write their own texts and read those of their peers.
- Give students a writing assignment that focuses on a specific audience; for example, have them write directions for young children.

Promoting Reading Comprehension Through Written Responses

Reader response is often a follow-up activity that teachers may assign after students' reading or as they are interacting with the text. Responses may be oral, such as a group conversation in which children discuss the reading, or written. A written reader response should be engaging—anything from writing a postcard from the story setting to making a brochure sharing something gleaned from an informational text. A reader response needs to be engaging, academic, and authentic.

When demonstrating comprehension through written responses, the student should ensure that his response is closely connected to the event or information from the text. For example, if students are studying volcanoes, it's fun and informative to do the baking soda/vinegar experiment, and it does help students remember that a volcano erupts. But this is not a reader response, as it doesn't use the concepts and vocabulary within the text. This experience will be enhanced if students follow up the experiment with a written response, such as drawing a diagram of a volcano and writing an explanation of why the volcano erupts. This will result in a deeper understanding and promote better recall; plus, learning could be easily assessed. When responding during the reading, readers may make annotations on the edge of the text, or post thoughts on sticky notes. These notations can then be used to support discussion about the text.

Reasons to use written reader responses to promote comprehension:

- Written responses to reading take advantage of the reading/writing connection.
- When thinking about a written response, the reader must consider evidence in the text, think about what the text said, and re-read it; this deepens understanding.
- When writing a response, the reader must think about the text, events, and information as he is writing, which also deepens his understanding.

- A writer needs to re-read and analyze his own written response, and the way it relates to the text.

- The writing assignment can give students the opportunity to ask questions or give opinions, depending on the nature of the reader response.

- Written responses allow readers to use new vocabulary and show understanding of the meaning and usage of the new words.

- Written responses allow the teacher to discuss interpretations privately with students, and "unpack" thinking for better assessment of students' understanding.

Common reader responses in written format:

- Write journal responses: These can be anything pertinent to the text, such as a summary, a character description, an answer to a teacher's question, or what may be in the main character's diary. In the case of during-reading reader responses, notations are used.

- Write a letter to the character, perhaps giving advice.

- Choose five vocabulary words from the chapter (or book) that you can use in writing about a key event in the chapter (or book).

- Create a postcard from one of the characters.

- Explain how the character changes in the chapter (or book).

- Write three important facts from the text.

- Draw a cartoon about the text and include dialogue.

- Write a summary of events, containing facts and information from the text.

- Use graphic organizers for various purposes (story mapping, predictions, character analysis, and so forth).

- Write answers to inferential text-dependent questions.

- Make predictions: Pre-reading—what you think will happen and why you think it will happen; during reading—what clues you have and how they affect your prediction; post-reading—what actually happened and why the prediction was right or wrong.

- Perform Readers' Theater skits written to retell a story.

- Create a learning log (a written journal that contains facts and concepts learned from the text).

- Create diagrams with labels and explanations.

- Write a book report and include a "Why you should read" section.

- Write a book review with a critique.

- Create a podcast in which fellow students write out the script and read to record.

- Do a cloze activity (filling in the blanks) or writer's frame—used mainly with younger children or struggling readers.

- Create a flap book or accordion book according to a teacher's preselected criteria.

- Do compare-and-contrast writing: character, theme, animal, and so forth.

- Write a poem—any genre of poetry that invites a well-thought-out response.

Assessing Reading Comprehension: An Overview

Reading comprehension can be assessed using a variety of methods. For example, natural classroom assessment is conducted by evaluating students' performance when answering literal, inferential, or evaluative questions; analyzing students' reader responses; and through a monitored discussion of text information or events. Comprehension can be assessed through students' retellings and summaries. Reading comprehension is often assessed via standardized tests in which students read a passage and answer questions. A similar format is used in informal reading inventories, which indicate students' approximate reading levels by evaluating the students' accuracy and comprehension.

Understanding and Promoting Reading a Variety of Genres

A genre is a category of literary work, characterized by similarities in form, content, and writing technique or formulas. Genres are further identified through specific literary devices; for example, a mystery has clues leading up to the solution, and a fairy tale typically begins with "Once upon a time" and ends with "They lived happily ever after." Genres can be defined very broadly, transcending book type such as a biography or romance novel. A website may be considered a genre because each is a specific writing/reading product. Over time, new genres have emerged, such as nonfiction mixed with fiction and, thanks to advances in technology, graphic media mixed with printed text.

Things to consider when teaching genre:

- There are different genres written for different purposes.
- Students need to be exposed to a variety of genres—each of them multiple times.
- Teachers use mentor texts (texts that model good genre writing) to teach genres and writing.
- Teachers should identify and discuss the uniqueness of each genre.
- Genre knowledge helps readers predict the information that will be presented, how it will be portrayed, and navigate the text for needed information.
- Different genres can require different reading styles and speeds.
- Knowing characteristics of a particular genre will aid in writing in the genre.
- Authors choose the genre that will best fulfill their writing purpose.
- Authors can use genre to influence the reader (for example, the persuasive genre) or to decide what to include or not include in a person's biography.
- Exposure to one genre can influence the reader's comprehension of another. For example, pairing a historical fiction work with an informational text about the same time period provides students a much deeper understanding of both texts.

Students can be taught genre in one of two ways: explicit teaching or inquiry learning. In explicit teaching, the teacher names and explains the genre, such as biography, a story of someone's life. The teacher reads or assigns biographies to be read, discusses the characteristics of biographies, and has students apply that knowledge by writing a short biography. With inquiry learning, the whole class reads books from the same genre, such as memoir. Guided by their teacher, students discuss the common characteristics of the genre (in the case of memoir, a written memory of an actual event or series of events). Students apply this new knowledge by thinking about their own past and writing a short memoir of an event in their life.

Common genres and their characteristics are detailed in the following table. Not all genres are listed, but popular text genres used in classrooms are included.

> **HINT:** You don't need to memorize the following table for the Praxis (5204), but do familiarize yourself with these genres, know that authors use different genres for different purposes, and understand that genre study is important in teaching both reading and writing.

Common Genres and Characteristics

Genre	Characteristics
Realistic fiction	Story that could actually take place. Examples include romance, satire, drama, action/adventure, horror, thriller, tragedy, and so forth.
Historical fiction	Fictional characters and a true historical setting.
Mystery	Involves some sort of wrongdoing. The genre ordinarily has clues that can lead the reader to the solution.
Fantasy	Involves occurrences and/or creatures that do not exist. The genre ordinarily includes strange and imaginary characters.
Fairy tale	Usually begins with "Once upon a time…" and ends with "They lived happily ever after." The genre frequently includes magic.
Myth	Story told as if it were fact; explains a natural phenomenon and teaches a lesson.
Fable	An imaginary short story that has a moral. The genre ordinarily has two to three animals as the main characters.
Legend	Story that may be based on fact. When the story alludes to a historical truth, it includes imaginary events as well as heroes whose great deeds are exaggerated.
Tall tale	Story that is exaggerated with humor. Examples include heroes who can perform the impossible.
Poetry	Verse format; there are a multitude of subgenres within this genre. Examples include couplets, free verse, haiku, concrete, diamante, and so forth.
Graphic novel	Written with pictures and dialogue.
Expository (nonfiction)	True information, usually focused on a topic or theme.
Narrative	A story that may or may not be fact-based.
Personal narrative (nonfiction)	Fact-based written memoir. This is ordinarily an essay-like piece about an incident that occurred in the writer's life.
Persuasive	Contains convincing and believable statements that are meant to persuade the reader to agree with the author's viewpoint.
How-to	Practical advice. The genre ordinarily consists of directions on how to create or assemble a product or an explanation about how to perform a task.
Biography/autobiography	Writings about a person's life, events, important incidents, inventions, and so forth. In the case of an autobiography, the author is writing about herself.
Descriptive text within genres	A structure within genres. No matter the content, the genre includes very detailed text that carefully describes a person, place, thing, or event. The text ordinarily contains specifically chosen adjectives and uses attributes such as qualities, characteristics, and parts.

Selecting Literature to Promote Reading Growth

To promote reading growth, teachers should consider a number of areas. Four factors are discussed here: instructional reading level, developmental needs, fluency, and reader interest. First, teachers should consider each student's instructional or "just right" reading level. The "just right" level is defined as when the student can read 90%–94% of the text correctly (89% and below is too difficult; 95% and above is too easy). These percentages are guidelines to help teachers place students at reading levels that are optimal for their reading growth. In addition, students should be showing adequate comprehension at the instructional level. Students need to be challenged in order to become better readers. Vygotsky explains in his zone of proximal development theory that there is a range in learning in which students should be placed. If the information or task is too easy, the student is not learning. If the information or task is too difficult, the student is not learning adequately. In his theory, Vygotsky states that the learner needs to be at a place where he has more to learn with guidance from an expert. So, if a student reads a beginning grade-2-level book at 92% accuracy, he has a bit more to learn at that level. When the percentage increases to more than 95%, the student needs a higher-level book to continue growing as a reader (provided that he can comprehend what he is reading). Second, when selecting texts, teachers should consider the student's developmental needs. Some students have better word recognition than comprehension, so although they can score at a higher reading level through word recognition, they may not understand what is being read. Third, teachers should pay close attention to each reader's fluency. If a student reads too slowly and without expression, repetitive books at his reading level might be the best fit. Finally, reader interest is also important when selecting texts. The more a student is interested in a subject, the more likely his attitude toward reading about it will be positive.

Reading Stances

Louise Rosenblatt, the creator of the transactional theory of reading, stated that the stance (purpose/position) of reading can be characterized in two different ways: aesthetic and efferent. With the aesthetic stance, the reader is reading for pleasure, be it a fiction or nonfiction book, and there is no outside pressure to perform. With the efferent stance, the reader is reading for information, most likely to apply in some situation after the reading (such as when a teacher assigns a text to be read along with follow-up questions to be answered). In reality, most reading incorporates elements of both stances.

Selecting Texts for Multiple Levels of Reading

Classrooms should have an abundance of books in different genres. Selecting texts for students can be challenging, especially if the range of reading levels in the classroom is large. This section provides some guidelines for text selection, as well as some important vocabulary terms.

Vocabulary Worth Knowing and Understanding

author study: A unit lesson that gives students the opportunity to delve deeply into an author's life and body of work. When a class does an author study, the students will be inspired to read as many books written by the author as they can.

leveled text sets: Texts at a particular grade level. In primary classrooms, sets are often organized in different colored baskets, and students are directed to the basket that contains their "just right" reading level.

series books: Books that have the same characters and often the same setting in time, but vary the problem and solution. They usually have the same author.

text sets: Can be books on the same content area, written by the same author, or from the same genre, but may represent different reading levels.

Books for Emergent Readers or Early Readers (Usually Grades K–1)

For emergent and developing readers, decodable books (using phonetically regular words) and predictable books are utilized in the classroom. Decodable texts are used because they contain words that follow a regular phonetic pattern and students can decode the words. Repeated readings of these books increase fluency. Predictable books, which encompass a number of different genres, ordinarily follow some predictable pattern. Books can be predictable because they rhyme, they follow a known sequence, they repeat certain phrases, they have a particular text structure, they include songs children have heard, or they have other similar characteristics. Books in this category make it easier for emergent and developing readers to predict what their text says before they read it, aiding in their understanding and enjoyment of the book. Readers may also begin to memorize the repetitive materials, thereby increasing their vocabulary.

When teachers work with these books, they are modeling for young children various book handling and text skills, as discussed in Chapter 3, "Concepts of Print." These concepts include the following:

- Books communicate meaning through pictures and the printed word.
- Pictures tell what is happening in the story, and have meaning, give hints (inferences), and so forth.
- Words in the book are used to tell stories or to present facts about topics.

Types of predictable books used in classrooms:
- **Cumulative sequence:** The story builds on a pattern. It starts with one person, place, thing, or event. Each time a new person, place, thing, or event is introduced, all the previous ones are repeated, Old MacDonald's Farm being a prime example.
- **Chain or circular story:** The story's ending leads back to the beginning. Such as planting a seed which grows into a plant and then eventually makes its own seed.
- **Familiar or known sequence:** The story is built on a common, recognizable concept or sequence, such as the alphabet, days of the week, months of the year, and so forth. Any alphabet book follows this pattern.
- **Pattern stories:** The book's scenes, events, or episodes are repeated, often with some variation. For example, the story of the Little Red Hen who keeps asking characters to help her make bread is a pattern story.
- **Question and answer:** A question is repeated throughout the story, such as "Mama, do you love me?"
- **Repetitive sentence or phrase:** Text, such as "The sky is falling," is repeated throughout the story.
- **Repetitive rhyme:** A rhyme, rhythm, or a refrain, such as "It was too [big, or hot, or difficult]," is repeated throughout the story.
- **Songs:** A familiar song that repeats sentences and phrases, such as "The wheels on the bus go 'round and 'round," appears as a refrain throughout the story or book.

Books for Early Readers (Usually Grades 1–2)

Early readers need less repetition and more practice with the cueing systems. The three main cueing systems are phonics, semantics, and syntax. Very simple books, such as those with picture cues, are best. The books may be fiction or nonfiction, but they should include vocabulary that can be decoded using semantics and context.

Transitional or Developing Readers (Usually Grades 2–3)

Transitional readers can read "just right" books fairly easily, and are practicing their word attack strategies as they read. Transitional readers are beginning to rely less on picture cues, if they have done so in the past. They do well with simple series book sets, author studies with books at the students' instructional reading level, and simple chapter books.

Fluent Readers

Fluent readers are ready for challenges. Their reading pace is solid and at grade level or above. They understand how text works, how to apply word attack skills and strategies, have a large bank of sight words, and read independently with minimal guidance. Fluent readers can read longer passages of texts, and utilize strategies that enable them to understand more complex text.

Author's Note: No matter what grade or reading stage a child is in, the "just right" or instructional level of the child must be considered. Instructional level means the child can read the text with 90%–94% accuracy, and this is the best context for teaching students new strategies or processes for making meaning of text.

Types of Reading

Children's comprehension may be impacted by *how* they read. The following list details different types of reading, or what is referred to as reading modes. It begins with reading that is somewhat dependent on the teacher; as the list progresses, the reading is less teacher-dependent.

- **Shared reading:** The teacher has a book and points to the words while reading. The story is re-read, and children begin to chime in and read along.
- **Computer-assisted reading:** Students listen to a story on a tablet or computer. In some cases, the student can click on words for meaning to aid in their comprehension.
- **Echo reading:** The teacher reads a line, the children read the same line as if echoing her, the teacher reads the next line, the children read that line, and so forth.
- **Choral reading:** Children read aloud together. A teacher can use choral reading with a small group and a simple text to ensure that all children in the class are engaged in the reading; groups of children can also practice reading together, independent of the teacher.
- **Partner reading:** Children are paired and each child takes a turn reading a predetermined section to his peer. The children help each other out and discuss the reading.
- **Sustained silent reading:** Children read independently and will most likely discuss the reading at group time.

Reading Comprehension Strategies for Fiction Texts

Reading comprehension strategies are tools that readers use to help them understand the text. These strategies can be employed before, during, and after reading; many use metacognition, in which the reader self-monitors as he constructs meaning. Metacognition, introduced in Chapter 7, "Reading Comprehension," is thinking about thinking. When using metacognition, students think about what they are reading and understanding. Metacognitive strategies encourage students to ask themselves questions like:

- Am I reading the word right? If not, what can I try?
- Does this make sense? If not, do I need to re-read? Is there something on the page that will help me understand?
- Am I reading too fast? Too slow?

Students should use metacognition when reading both fiction and nonfiction, as it allows them to self-monitor their understanding of the text. This, in turn, encourages student to use "fix-up" strategies. Fix-up strategies are helpful when a reader realizes after his initial reading that he does not understand the text; fix-up during re-reading may involve asking for clarification, looking back, reading ahead, and so forth. In addition to the fix-up strategy, many comprehension strategies that focus on fiction can also be used with nonfiction. A few of these are included here:

- **Setting a purpose:** When a student sets a purpose for reading, whether for pleasure or to acquire specific information from the text, he can focus on the task.
- **Activating prior knowledge:** Students must be taught to think, prior to their reading, of what they know about the content of a text in order to incorporate this new knowledge. If students are going to read about someone who is at a city park, they should think about what they know about parks. This allows them to approach the reading with the correct mind-set for understanding. Semantic webs are often used for group brainstorming. (A semantic web is a diagram with a word in a middle bubble and lines branching out from it on which to write brainstorming ideas.) As students add their knowledge to a semantic web, the teacher can use this as an informal assessment by gauging how much prior knowledge students have on a topic. Let's say a student reads the sentence "The car slid off the icy road into the snow bank." If the student has no concept of a "snow bank," then he might picture a car having crashed into a financial institution that is covered with snow. As you can see, it is advantageous to determine whether students' knowledge prior to reading is erroneous or inadequate.

- **Building background:** Teachers must be sure to build background only on necessary topics without telling students what is happening in the text. The practice has aroused some controversy around the amount of time it requires, and on claims of teachers providing so much background that students don't need to read the text. Although teachers shouldn't overdo, adequate and correct background knowledge aids in reading comprehension. When a teacher builds background or has students do a research-type activity to look up needed background knowledge, the stage is being set for deeper comprehension. This is especially important for English Language Learners (ELLs), who may be confused because of cultural differences.

- **Teaching vocabulary:** Explicit teaching of confusing vocabulary prior to the students' reading aids them in comprehending the text. (Vocabulary is covered in detail in Chapter 10.)

- **Making predictions:** When students make predictions about what is going to happen in a particular text, it allows them to infer, and motivates their reading. Predictions must be based on evidence from the text, and not be off-the-wall guesses. Students' predictions rely on inferential comprehension of the text. In making good predictions, students are forced to use information from the text, along with their prior knowledge about the situation in the text, to infer what might happen. They can make predictions before starting a book by looking at the cover or reading the book jacket. Teachers may have students stop at specific pages in the book and make predictions, using text clues to help confirm or adjust those predictions, and perhaps make new predictions.

- **Visualizing:** Often referred to as "making a movie in your mind," visualizing is a great strategy in which students create mental images of the events in a text to help themselves "see" what is happening. When a book includes a lot of action or a detailed description of a scene, if students create a picture in their minds, it helps them "see" and understand what the author is saying. In addition, visualizing can aid in recall of text information. *Tip:* When taking the Praxis (5204), you will be reading classroom scenarios. Use the visualization strategy to "see" what is happening in the classroom. This will help you select the correct answer.

- **Questioning:** When students ask questions as they read, it helps them to interact with the text and gain a deeper understanding. For example, a question may focus on a character's motive, such as "Why is the stepmother so mean to Cinderella?" When a student asks questions like this, it makes him think about the text—the stepmother was jealous, Cinderella was more beautiful than her stepsisters, the stepmother wanted to ensure that she retained control over the family inheritance, and so forth. Questioning the text, or the author's purpose, often leads students to predictions and inferences that help to improve their comprehension.

- **Clarifying:** Clarifying is used to monitor understanding. With clarifying, students learn to recognize when something in the text does not make sense to them. If they don't understand a part of the reading, then they stop and use other comprehension strategies, most likely the fix-up strategies mentioned previously.

- **Summarizing:** When students are asked to summarize a book, they must determine what information is important and then recall that information. In order to do this well, students must learn to concisely restate ideas as they recall information. Graphic organizers may help students learn how to summarize. Students can summarize sections of text and/or the whole text.

- **Synthesizing:** Students must synthesize information, connecting new information to what they already know. Doing so can make them think more deeply about what is happening in a text. This thinking process allows students to reevaluate what they think is happening to determine whether new information alters that perception.

- **Making connections:** When students make personal connections to a text, it deepens understanding and aids in recall. Making such connections entails the use of background knowledge and schema. These connections are categorized into three types.
  - **Text to self:** Connections made between the student and the student's personal background and experiences. (Example: My mom cleans ashes out of our fireplace, just like Cinderella.)
  - **Text to text:** Connections made between the text currently being read and a text the student has read previously. (Example: Snow White was kind to animals, just like Cinderella.)
  - **Text to world:** Connections made between the text being read and something that has occurred or is occurring in the world. (Example: There is a prince in the story, and England currently has a few princes.)

- **Inferring:** When students infer from their reading, they form the best guess about what is happening in the story by using evidence from the text and their background knowledge. That evidence can be from context cues or pictures, but in some way, the students draw conclusions about what is happening or, in the case of a prediction, what is about to happen. Sometimes it can be as simple as "The mother of the three girls was yelling for them to come over to her." The student can infer from this sentence that the girls are actually sisters, as the text says "the mother of," and his background knowledge should tell him that this makes the girls sisters. So, when the next sentence states "The sisters ran to see what their mother wanted," it is clear that *sisters* refers to the three girls. This is probably one of the most important comprehension strategies a student reader can use.

- **Picture walk:** For young students who are having problems with comprehension, or are just learning comprehension strategies, a picture walk is often used. Before reading the text, the students and the teacher will "walk" through the text, discussing pictures and the information the pictures convey about what is happening in the book. The picture walk provides students a preview and a mental map of where the story is going.

Reading Comprehension Strategies for Nonfiction Texts

Reading fiction and nonfiction text requires two different skill sets, although many of the same comprehension strategies can be used to foster understanding. Young children grow up to be much more familiar with fictional stories, but they do not have as much exposure to informational text. Because of this, around fourth grade, when children begin to read more nonfiction texts, it is often much harder for them to understand the structure. The Common Core requires that students in earlier grades be exposed to a great deal of informational text, and the amount increases in higher grade levels. The following are recommended strategies and techniques to use with nonfiction texts:

- **Use a KWL chart:** A KWL chart helps to activate students' prior knowledge when reading informational text. The chart is divided into three columns, and can be addressed by individual students, by a small group, or by a whole class. The K and W columns of the chart are completed during pre-reading. The K stands for "What I Know," and the W stands for "What I Want to Learn." The K column involves brainstorming and using prior knowledge of the topic to be read. The elements of the W column build anticipation and motivation for the reading, as students list things they are hoping to learn about the topic. (*Note:* The L column, "What I Learned," is completed during reading or post-reading and is a great vehicle for summarizing and recalling information learned.)

- **Preview text:** Prior to reading a nonfiction text, students should look at the bolded headings, italicized words, and bolded words or phrases; analyze pictures; and glean pertinent information from graphs and diagrams. Taking these steps before they read the text provides students an overview of the text and aids in their comprehension and their recall of the material in the text.

- **Determine the author's purpose:** An author's motive for writing a fiction or nonfiction text is called the "author's purpose." Texts can be written to entertain, inform, teach, persuade, or convince. Frequently, nonfiction texts are written to inform. Signal words and phrases may hint at the author's purpose for that particular section (for example, *let me explain, to illustrate my point, comparing this to*). Authors can use a variety of text structures to relay information.

- **Identify the text type:** There are three major types of nonfiction: informational, descriptive, and persuasive. If students can recognize the text type, it will help them identify the author's purpose.
  - **Informational text:** Written to inform readers about a particular topic. This text might include numerous facts, pros and cons, definitions, conclusions, and summaries. These may sometimes be found compiled in a how-to book or similar work.
  - **Descriptive text:** Written to give a picture of what is being talked about. This text may include descriptive details such as location and background information.
  - **Persuasive text:** Written to convince the reader to agree with the author's opinion on a topic. The text is meant to convey that the author's position on the issue is the best. This text may include qualities, activities, advertisement-like statements, and repetition of strong points.

- **Identify the text structure:** Text structure, described in detail in the chart below, is the organizational structure of a text. This may refer to the overall structure of a book, sections within books, or paragraphs within sections. Often, one text structure is embedded in another. The author chooses the particular text structure that fits her purpose and conveys what she wants the reader to learn. For example, an author writes a book on alligators to inform the reader about alligators. But an author writes a book on both alligators and crocodiles in order to compare and contrast the two animals. The reader's understanding is aided when knowing that text structures underlie what is important to learn from the text.

- **Learn content area vocabulary:** Words in particular content areas have definitions that correspond to that content, sometimes called domain-specific vocabulary. A simple example of this can occur when discussing growing plants and the vegetable "squash" is introduced. Another definition of "squash" is to crush something. Yet, "squash" is also an indoor game using rackets and a ball.

Nonfiction (Informational) Text Structures

Nonfiction text is often called informational or expository text. When students get to fourth grade, they are required to read a great deal of informational text. Often at this stage, they have problems with comprehension because they may not have been taught the strategies needed, or may have had scant experience reading informational text. One strategy that aids in the understanding of informational text is to first identify the text structure. Text structure is important for comprehension because it lays the foundation for deciphering what is important in the text. For example, if the text structure is sequential, the author wants the reader to remember the order of events. Many times, authors will embed one text structure within another.

Teaching students how to recognize different types of text structure can be done by pointing out when various text structures occur in a text. In addition, modeling a particular text structure and then having students write in that text structure allows them to use a specific text structure for the intended purpose. The following chart provides pertinent information about the main nonfiction text structures.

Informational Text Structures

Type of Text Structure	Description and Selected Signal Words	Author's Purpose	Example
Description or descriptive	Descriptive text can be included in fiction or nonfiction. Descriptive text, no matter the content, is very detailed and carefully describes a person, place, thing, or event. It contains specifically chosen adjectives and clear details. Signal words: *also, then, as, another, furthermore, a few, likewise, besides, several, many, in addition*	The author uses this description when details are important; these details can deepen understanding of what is being discussed.	The Eiffel Tower in Paris is 1,063 feet tall, and has an antenna at the very top. If the antenna were removed, the tower would be 984 feet tall.
Chronological (or sequential)	Chronological text structure must be written in the correct order, which can be arranged by occurrence of events, size, importance, and so forth. This may be a series of events that leads up to a conclusion. Signal words: ordinal numbers (*first, second*, and so forth), *next, until, while, last, soon, then, after, now, immediately, during, before*	This text structure is used when order is important, such as with historical events, scientific cycles, directions, or some form of ranking.	First, you open the car door. Then, you step in with your feet. Next, you sit on the seat.

Type of Text Structure	Description and Selected Signal Words	Author's Purpose	Example
Compare/contrast	Compare/contrast describes similarities and differences between two or more events, places, characters, objects, or concepts. Signal words: *however, but, yet, instead of, even though, on the other hand, on the contrary, despite, still, in comparison*	Authors use compare/contrast for a variety of purposes. It may be used in the persuasive genre to show weaknesses in an opposing view. It may be used to compare current and past societies, and so forth.	Apples and oranges are more alike than the saying would imply. They both have skin, even though the orange has thick skin and the apple, thin. They both are fruits and have small seeds. Despite the fact that an apple is red and an orange is, well, orange, they still have similarities.
Problem/solution	The author goes into detail to describe a particular problem, and counters that problem with the solution, solutions, or proposed solutions. Signal words: *one reason, to solve, a solution, the problem is, it was recommended, as a result, so that, something was wrong, this is a concern, now*	Authors use this text structure to inform readers of problems or possible problems in any area.	The people of Cleveland have been concerned because traffic has increased dramatically in the last 10 years. Many of the busy roads do not have sidewalks, and children and adults cannot walk safely. The town council applied for state grants, and a number of the busy roads now have sidewalks.
Cause/effect	The cause of the problem is given; what resulted from the problem is the effect. (The cause is the action; the effect is the result.) There can be several reasons identified as the cause, and there can also be several resulting effects. Signal words: *for this reason, in order to, as a result, because, consequently, so that, therefore, on account of, thus*	Authors use cause and effect to show a relationship between two or more occurrences. In persuasive text, the author can select the information pertinent to her own bias.	Susan has to study for the Praxis (5204) because she is taking it on Saturday. For this reason, she is not going out to dinner with us tonight and will not be playing in the volleyball game on Saturday.
Enumeration	Enumeration is a list, usually elaborated on, that connects particular information. Enumeration does not need to be in any necessary order. Signal words: *also, then, as, another, likewise, furthermore, a few, besides, several, many, some, in addition*	Authors use enumeration when it is necessary to "list" and elaborate on facts, items, subcategories, important events, people, etc.	There are many flowering bulbs that bloom in the spring. Daffodils, which are usually yellow, make a nice spring garden. Also, hyacinths bloom about the same time and add color. Finally, crocuses bloom very early and are low to the ground.
Question-and-answer	As the structure's name sounds, the text is written first with a question and then with the answer. Signal words: *what, why, when, where, who, how, how many, in this instance, refers to, the conclusion, one may conclude, in this case, it could be that*	Authors use question-and-answer when they want to get straight to the point and make sure the reader has a clear understanding of the material.	Why do we have daylight saving time? The idea is to get the most out of the daylight and use less energy. This started around World War I to save money during wartime.

Main Idea and Supporting Details

Being able to recognize the main idea is fundamental to comprehending text. The main idea of a text is the central thought or overarching topic of the passage, conveying what the passage is mostly about. Supporting details are facts, examples, reasons, or causes that corroborate the main idea; they may provide background information. It is through the identification of the main idea and supporting details that readers are able to summarize and review what is being said in the text.

Students need to be taught:
- The definition of main idea and supporting details.
- That supporting details relate back to the main idea and provide more information about the main idea.
- That the first sentence, the topic sentence, is often the main idea.
- That the main idea is the important idea, and the details support what is being said about the main idea.
- That some examples or facts provided about the main idea are often interesting, but not important.
- How distinguishing what is important from what is merely interesting enables the reader to state the main idea and important supporting details.

Close Reading and Comprehension

A close reading is an analysis of a short text that is thoughtful, critical, and focuses on details. This analysis provides the reader a deeper understanding of the text as he thoroughly investigates it for form, purpose, craft, language, meanings, and so forth.

Close reading involves:
- short text or passages
- minimal to no pre-reading activities (that is, activation of prior knowledge, building background, and teaching vocabulary)
- analyzing the short text for form, purpose, craft, language, meanings, ideas, concepts, and so forth
- text analysis strategies
- inference skills
- re-reading for deeper meaning and annotations (to write thoughts and comments)
- examination of text graphics and text features
- returning to any areas that can be confusing
- answering text-dependent questions
- collaborative discussion

Usually, close reading entails at least three readings, each with a specific purpose. The text is first read to determine the general meaning of what is being read. The second is to examine how the author uses language and text organization. The third reading is to identify themes and make connections with other known texts. Students are taught to use close reading to gain skills that will make them independent, competent readers who can analyze text and answer text-dependent questions while grasping the deeper meaning of the text. As students learn to employ close-reading skills, they will be able to read and understand more complex text.

Using Evidence from the Text to Support Predictions, Opinions, and Conclusions

It is important for students to use evidence from the text in their predictions, opinions, and conclusions because doing so enables teachers to see that the students have read and understood the text. Techniques for using text-based evidence are presented below.

Supporting Predictions

Students use information from the text to make sound predictions. When students do not use information from the text, their prediction can become a wild guess. Using predictions is a good way to familiarize students with the concept of inference skills and create support for text-dependent discussions. When predicting, the reader is making an educated guess as to what might happen next. This can be a very abstract concept for young children. With young students, the teacher begins making predictions by using specially selected pictures as text (such as a glass on the edge of a table). As she shows pictures to a class or group, she asks, "What do you think is going to happen?" After the children answer, the teacher then asks, "What did you see that made you think that would happen?" This teaches children at an early age that predictions need to be supported.

Students then learn how to predict from text in the same way, but are asked "What did you read that led you to make the prediction?" Traditional graphic organizers for predictions have two columns: one for "What I predict" and one for "What happened." However, if the teacher is using support-based answers, the graphic organizer should have three columns: "What I predict," "What evidence did I have," and "What happened." In addition, students are often given the opportunity to change their predictions as they read and gather more information. This allows them to use evidence from the text to make a more accurate prediction of what is happening in the text.

Supporting Opinions

A fact is something that is correct and true. On the other hand, an opinion states what someone believes, a judgment, or a way of thinking about something. When students offer an opinion or make a claim, they need to be able to provide reasons to support the opinion or claim. They should be able to state what fact in the text gave them their idea, then explain how the text supports the idea. By offering a supported opinion, students learn to analyze text and think about what the author is saying.

Supporting Conclusions

A conclusion is an idea, a judgment, or a decision that is reached by reasoning. As do opinions, reasoning must be sound in order for the reasoner to arrive at an appropriate conclusion. As students read, they use inference to construct meaning, and draw conclusions about what is being read. Students need to be able to support their conclusions with evidence from the text. Consider the following text:

> Amelia and Autumn went into the convenience store to pick up milk while their mother waited in the car. Amelia ran down the aisles looking for where the milk was kept. She bumped into a big man and a packaged headset fell out from under his coat. The man quickly put it back and Amelia found Autumn in line holding the milk. Amelia and Autumn turned as the security alarm went off at the door.

Reading this scenario, most likely the reader has drawn a conclusion: the big man was stealing a headset from the store, therefore the man is a thief. We need to look at evidence in the text that allows us to come to this probable conclusion: a packaged headset fell, it was under the man's coat, and the security alarm sounded as the man left the store. Readers synthesize information from the text and from prior knowledge to draw a conclusion. Students must analyze details in a text to draw conclusions.

Assessing Reading Comprehension Across Genres and Text Types: An Overview

Comprehension can be assessed in an oral or written format. Summarization is often used for assessing and when working across genres, the details included are important. If students are reading a compare-and-contrast text structure, they should be able to give both sides of what the author is comparing. If reading a cause-and-effect text structure, students should be able to identify the cause and the effect. This can be done through oral discussion or a herringbone type of graphic organizer. Graphic organizers can also be used to aid students in determining main ideas and details. Text-dependent, inferential questions allow teachers to assess whether a child can go deeper than the literal meaning of the text.

Chapter 9

Reading Fluency and Assessing Accuracy

Fluency entails more than just reading accurately and quickly, although that is the basic premise. A thorough definition of fluency also includes reading with expression, to show understanding.

Understanding Fluency

Fluency is considered the bridge to comprehension. A fluent reader reads at grade-level reading rate, with expression, and with most words being accurate. Practicing reading contributes greatly to developing fluent reading. When students read and re-read, they develop accuracy and comprehension. Part of fluency is reading with expression, or prosody. This starts as early as kindergarten when students mimic what and how the teacher reads. Students begin to use the power of expression to convey meaning. For example, think of the word *no* and how it can be expressed in numerous ways to convey different meanings. How does *no* sound when a parent is frustrated? When someone is surprised? When someone is joking? When someone says, "No, not happening." Although they include the same word, each of these scenarios has a tone and an expression that tell the listener more than just the word. In these cases, the expression used imparts an understanding of the word's contextual meaning. A similar process happens during reading. A child who reads accurately, with the right expression (surprise, joy, sadness, irritation), at the expected grade-level reading rate, can be designated as a fluent reader.

Vocabulary Worth Knowing and Understanding

accuracy: The percentage of words read correctly.

error: Although not a part of fluency per se, error indicates a misread word, usually called a miscue.

prosody: The expression and intonation used in oral reading.

rate: The speed of reading, counted as words per minute (WPM) or words correct per minute (WCPM).

Reading Rate

Reading rate is the number of words read per minute and, in some assessments, the number of words read correctly per minute. Although the ability to read fast is not essential to becoming an effective reader, reading at an appropriate speed can aid in comprehension. If a child has to stop and decode frequently, he is unable to focus properly on comprehension because of the effort he must put into decoding. Knowing a huge bank of sight words also supports fluency. Having an idea of a child's reading rate helps a teacher monitor progress.

Reading rates do not need to be memorized, but understanding the basics is important:

The basics:

- Silent reading rates are usually faster than oral reading rates. The exception is first grade, where many students subvocalize (so they are basically reading aloud), resulting in comparable speeds for their oral reading and silent reading.
- The average silent reading rate for first-grade students is around 60 WPM by the end of the year.
- The average silent reading rate for sixth-grade students is around 190 WPM, although rate is influenced by text and purpose.
- The average increase is 25 to 30 WPM each year.
- Fluent readers can concentrate on comprehending the text and don't have to worry about decoding.

Fluency Activities

Fluency can be taught in numerous fun and creative ways. Fluency activities should incorporate repetition. Teachers structure their lessons to include reasons for students to re-read text so that word recognition is reinforced. In this way, students increase their sight word knowledge.

Fluency Activities

Activity	Description
Word sorts	Using word cards with selected words, students do a guided sort. Students may sort in ways that highlight the word meaning as they continually re-read words to select the correct ones. For example, students may sort *bacon, baby, beef,* and *butterfly* as words that begin with the letter "b." Then, the teacher may ask the students to sort the words into food and living things, so the new sort would now show the words *bacon* and *beef* in one pile and *baby* and *butterfly* in another. Changing the parameters of the sort forces students to re-read the words as they re-categorize. For example, with just a single pile of words, students may be guided to sort in the following succession: ❏ select the words that are nouns ❏ select the words that show action (verbs) ❏ select the words that are past tense (certain verbs) ❏ select the words that describe (adjectives and adverbs) Students are re-reading the words, reorganizing the pile, and thinking about the word's meaning each time they do a new sort.
Echo reading	Using a text that students can see, the teacher reads a line and has the students repeat it out loud. With this activity, she models reading rate and expression. The students then "echo" her modeling.
Readers' Theater	This activity is typically a classroom favorite. Students are assigned characters in a story and parts they are to read, similar to a "read like a character" activity. Since Readers' Theater is eventually "performed" in front of others, students must re-read the text in order to practice saying their lines correctly and with the correct expression.
Choral reading	In choral reading, children are divided into groups to practice a poem or short piece of text. They re-read and work together, reading in unison and with expression. When the teacher deems them ready, the group chorally reads in front of the class. In addition, small groups of beginning or transitional readers can read short pieces of text together in reading groups and then discuss. This ensures that all students participate in the reading.
Wide reading and re-reading	Frequent reading aids children in developing fluency. Wide reading has students reading a large number of books in a variety of genres. For beginning readers, this would include predictable and repetitive books. When children re-read a book, they improve their reading rate, as they are familiar with the book. Re-reading the words in the book allows the child to read at a faster rate.
Recorded reading	Students record themselves reading, listen to the recording, and then read again, trying to fix errors they detected in their recorded reading.
Timed readings	This works well with older students. A student times himself as he reads a selected piece, and then graphs the amount of time it took for him to read. Then the student times the reading as he re-reads and graphs the second reading, then repeats the process with a third reading. The student can tell by the slope of the graph that his time is improving with each re-read.

Activity	Description
Computer-assisted reading	A computer may be used to increase fluency in a variety of ways: ❑ A student can read along orally as the computer reads. ❑ In some computer programs, the student can click on unknown words and hear the pronunciation. ❑ Some programs will move the text at a set speed, so a student is forced to read faster in order to read every line.

Assessment of Accuracy: Running Records

Running records are informal assessments that allow teachers to assess children's reading level, accuracy, and rate (if desired) in a natural setting. A teacher will sit next to a child who is reading his book. As the child reads orally, the teacher looks at the words and codes what the child says as he reads (see "Coding a Running Record," below). After the child reads, the teacher analyzes the miscues to set future goals for him. If a Praxis (5204) question presents a running record, you should be able to analyze it in order to best design the child's subsequent instruction. The main purpose of a running record is to assess word identification skills, although a running record may indicate that a child is using context to identify an unknown word. In this case, a running record may provide a hint of a child's understanding, but it is an evaluation of word and letter-sound accuracy, not comprehension. Therefore, the assigned instructional level indicates word recognition.

Coding a Running Record

Familiarize yourself with coding marks by reviewing the chart below. Coding is standardized to enable teachers to read and analyze any child's running record. The chart lists the main codes that are used for miscues. If a child repeats a word—that is, he makes what is called a repetition—it is not counted as an error. If a child makes an error and then corrects himself while reading, this is called a self-correction and also is <u>not</u> considered an error.

Items to Be Coded	Coding (What the Teacher Writes)
Correct word	Makes a checkmark

Substitutes another word for a word in the text	Writes incorrect word over the correct word.
	    Reader says: **dram**
	    Text states: dream

Omits a word	Draws a line
	    Reader says: ——
	    Text states: horse

Inserts a word	Uses a caret (^) and writes word inserted
	                                  red
	    Reader says: ^
	    Text states: jump into the car

Is told a word	The child tries to pronounce the word, but gives up. The teacher may say the word, or tell the child to read on.
	    Reader says: **mo-mo**
	    Text states: The lion headed up the mountain.

Self-correction	SC (not counted as an error)
	    Reader says: **shine SC**
	    Text says: The sun shone brightly.

Repetition	R (not counted as an error)
	    Reader says: **crashed R**
	    Text says: The waves crashed against the rocks.

Analyzing the Running Record

In order to analyze a running record, teachers must be able to translate the coding. In this analysis, the three cueing systems (phonics, semantics, and syntax) are essential for pinpointing a child's strengths and weaknesses. In addition, when analyzing a running record, it is extremely important to look for patterns in what the child gets correct, and in what he gets incorrect, as well as the underlying issue of the miscue. For example, the coding on a running record may show that a child is saying the initial part of the word correctly, but missing the ending. This pattern usually signifies the child is not reading through the word. If a child gets a particular item incorrect only once, it is not necessarily a sign of weakness.

Phonology (Visual) Errors

Phonology errors are mistakes made with letter-sound correspondence and word pronunciation. Things to think about include the following: Are the child's mistakes due to errors in how the word is said? Is there a pattern to the errors? Some common phonology error patterns that may be found in running records are:

- **phonemes:** Letter sounds—initial, medial, and/or final.
- **affixes:** Prefixes or suffixes. Examples: *re-* as in *return, rewrite, redo; -ing* as in *bending, licking, ducking.*
- **diphthongs:** Blending vowel sounds for words with "oy," "oi," "ou," and so forth. Examples: *ouch, boy, oil.*
- **digraphs:** Two vowels or consonants together that make one sound. Examples: *beat, pail* (vowels); *tough, graph* (consonants).
- **compound words:** Two words combined to form a new word. Examples: *lighthouse, shoebox.*
- **homophones:** Words that have the same sound and might confuse meaning. Examples: *hear, here; byte, bite.*
- **multisyllabic words:** Words with more than one syllable. Examples: *mountainous, important.*
- **sight words:** Frequently used words that readers should memorize. Examples: *was, the, in, they, saw.*

Semantics (Meaning) Errors

Semantic errors occur when a reader incorrectly reads a word and replaces it with a word that does not make sense in the sentence. Things to think about include the following: Are the child's mistakes due to not knowing a word's meaning? Does the child frequently make word errors that render a sentence nonsensical? For example, a child might read the sentence "The bird flew into its nest" as "The bird found into its nest." This makes no sense, and thereby it is a semantic error. Following are some of the main semantic errors that readers make:

- **Context cues:** Using the known words within the text to identify unknown words. There are two types of context cue errors:
  - Error from not using context cues: The child makes an error that makes absolutely no sense with respect to the sentence or paragraph.

    Example: The child reads, "He rode the blue *bunk*," but the text states, "He rode the blue *bike*."

    In this case, the child is not using metacognition; he is not aware of whether or not he understands what he is reading. Metacognition is defined as thinking about thinking. The child does pick up the visual cue of "b" and says that letter phonically, but just replaces it with a word that begins with that sound.

  - Error from using context cues but not phonics: The child makes a miscue, but it still makes sense in the sentence or paragraph. In this case, the error is not considered terrible, but if it happens too often it could confuse the child.

    Example: The child reads, "The little girl held the *bunny* in her lap," but the text states, "The little girl held the *baby* in her lap."

    In this case, the teacher recognizes that although there is a phonological error, the child is using semantic (meaning) cues and metacognition, as holding a bunny makes sense, but it is an error that will interrupt comprehension.

- **Synonyms:** Words that mean the same.

    Examples: The child reads *home* for *house, feeling sad* for *feeling blue, sloppy* for *messy.*

- **Omission:** The child omits words from the text. There are two types of omission errors:

    - Omission with meaning change: A word is left out, and the meaning is changed.

        Example: The child reads, "The mosquito itched, and I stopped to scratch it," but the text states, "The mosquito *bite* itched, and I stopped to scratch it."

    - Omission without meaning change: A word is left out, but what is read basically retains the same meaning as in the text.

        Example: The child reads, "The skirt went down past the girl's ankles," but the book states, "The *long* skirt went down past the girl's ankles."

- **Self-monitoring:** The child recognizes that he has made an error in either phonics, semantics, or syntax—all of which are tied to meaning. If the child does a lot of self-correcting, then he is self-monitoring because he realizes—once again using metacognition—that what he has just read doesn't make sense. This pattern could be considered a strength.

    Example: The child reads, "We had fried cherries for supper." Then he corrects *cherries* to *chicken,* as that makes more sense in the context. If the child does not make this change, he is not self-monitoring (checking his understanding).

Syntax (Structure) Errors

Syntax entails using the structure of language to aid in identifying unknown words. The structure of language is usually well known to a child by age 5. So, when reading, unless there is a local or cultural dialect, children should be able to recognize when a syntactic error has been made. Syntactic errors include using the wrong tense, the wrong part of speech, an incorrect pronoun, and so on.

    Example: The child reads, "The bird *fly* to its nest," but the text states, "The bird *flew* to its nest."

Determining Strengths and Weaknesses

When analyzing a running record, teachers not only analyze the error patterns, they also look at what a child is doing correctly, as a running record can tell us both the strengths and weaknesses in a child's reading behaviors. Teachers analyze the use of the three cueing systems—phonics, semantics, and syntax— to see what a child is doing wrong and what he is doing well. In the case of the previous example, saying *fly* instead of *flew* gives the teacher more information than the use of an incorrect word. The error shows that the child is using phonics for the initial phonemes, as "fl" begins both the correct and incorrect words. The error also shows that the child is using semantics, as the miscue is similar in meaning to the correct word.

Running Record Analysis

This section will give a short running record example and an analysis. In the following running record, the words that have miscues are in italics. In the record, the dash between the student-read words means a second syllable. The text is the plain print, with the words missed in italics. The student miscues, as the child read the words, are in bold.

Running Record Example

>   **walk-ed**   **tap-ed**
> Matt and Emma had *walked* to the park with their mother. Matt *tapped* Emma on the shoulder and
>
>   **turn-ed**
> said, "Look," as he *turned* his head to face behind them. To Emma's surprise, there was a puppy
>
> following them.
>
>   **yell-ed**
> "Here, puppy, here," *yelled* Emma as she stopped to let the puppy catch up. When Emma bent down,
>
>   **lick-ed**
> the little puppy *licked* her hand.
>
>   **holler-ed**
> All of a sudden, a little boy came running from around the bush and *hollered* with delight, "I found
>
>   **clip-ed**
> him! I found him!" He *clipped* a leash on the puppy's collar, thanked Emma for finding his puppy,
>
> and headed back the way he came.
>
>   **grin-ed**   **sh-sh d**
> Matt and Emma *grinned* at each other and *shrugged* their shoulders.   (117 words)

Analysis

Note: This analysis has been written as an essay question response.

    The code marks on this running record show both a strength and a weakness for this child.

    This child has strong word-identification skills in the area of phonology. The child did not make any errors in identifying individual or cluster letter sounds, even in the words that received miscues. The child was able to pronounce without trouble the majority of the words in the passage, including the following multisyllabic words: *shoulder, surprise, following, sudden, running,* and *around.* Words with errors, such as *walked* and *tapped,* had their base words pronounced correctly.

    This child shows a weakness in the pronunciation of the suffix "-ed." The student made nine errors, and in eight of them, he pronounced the "-ed" as a second syllable. The child was able to read *thanked* correctly, possibly due to the frequent use of the word *thanked.* The child also correctly read the word *headed,* as the "-ed" is correct as a second syllable in this particular word. The child needs instruction on the pronunciations of the suffix "-ed." The child needs to learn that "-ed" has three pronunciations: (1) as a /d/ as in *played,* (2) as a /t/ as in *kicked,* and (3) as an "id" sound, as in *headed,* which he read correctly in this passage. The child did not correctly read the words *walked, tapped, turned, yelled, licked, hollered, clipped, grinned,* and *shrugged.* All of these words, with the exception of *shrugged,* showed a miscue with "-ed" pronunciations.

Reading Level

Running records can also be used to tell whether a text is too easy, too hard, or "just right" for a child. This is determined by the percentage of words read correctly. The expected reading level percentages are defined as follows:

    Independent: 95%–100% correct (This text is easy for the child.)

    Instructional: 90%–94% correct (This text is considered the "just right" level for learning to read.)

    Frustration: 89% or below correct (This text is too hard, and is not the optimal learning level for the child.)

In the running record on this page, there are 117 words and nine errors. That means the student read 108 out of 117 words correctly, or $\frac{108}{117} = 0.92$ or 92%. Therefore, the percentage correct in this running record was 92%, which means this text is in the child's instructional or "just right" level.

Reading Speed

A running record can also be used to time readers. Reading speed can be assessed by timing the reader for 1 minute. When 1 minute is up, make a mark on the word the reader stopped at. Then count the number of words the reader read in that 1-minute time period to get his word-per-minute rate.

Check Your Understanding

For practice, try analyzing the running record below. The idea at this point is not to write an essay-style response, but to analyze. Look for a strength and a weakness, and be able to state what the child needs to work on (that is, set a goal). Again, the words with the miscues are in italics to help you with this practice; what the child said is in bold. See if your analysis matches the suggested analysis.

---

                                                      cooting

Mia and her friends were playing hide and seek in Mia's backyard. Sarah was *counting* down from

          ran   **enug**

ten as everyone *scattered* to hide. Mia ran past a small tree, not wide *enough* to hide her. She looked

                barl SC   ————

behind the trash *barrel*, but Julia was *already* there. Another friend was behind the car. Mia was

          nervous   ————   **numb SC**   **foond**

getting a bit *worried*. Sarah had *just* said the *number* three and Mia still hadn't *found* the place she

                             carton

wanted to hide. Then Mia saw the *container* that hid the hose. She ran quickly and hid behind it,

as Sarah ran over to look behind the car. Mia knew she was safe!   (104 words)

Suggested Analysis:

There is often not one correct analysis of a running record, even if you are asked to name just one strength or one weakness. What is important is what you determine to be the child's goals, and how you support that finding.

A strength may be one of the following, as long as your answer is supported.

- Sight words: The child was able to read fluently because sight words such as *the, was, there,* and *then* were correct. This enabled the child to focus on meaning.
- Reading for meaning: Although the child made errors, there were two self-corrections. The miscues (*ran* for *scattered, nervous* for *worried,* and *carton* for *container*) did not alter the sentence meaning. Finally, although two words were omitted (*already* and *just*), the sentences made sense without them.

A weakness may be one of the following, as long as your answer is supported.

- Vowel pairs: Three out of eight miscues were made with words that contain the "ou" vowel pair: *counting, enough,* and *found.* In *counting* and *found,* the "ou" is a diphthong, and in *enough* it is a digraph. The child needs to know that "ou" has more than one sound, and words with this vowel pair need to be corrected if they don't make sense in the reading.
- Multisyllabic words: Of the eight miscues and two self-corrections, eight of the words have more than one syllable. The child needs to learn how to chunk a word into parts to assist in reading the complete word.

What level (independent, instructional, or frustration) is this text for the child's reading? There were eight miscues out of 104 words, meaning the student read 96 words correctly, or $\frac{96}{104} = 0.92$; therefore, the child read with 92% accuracy. This means that this text was on the instructional, or "just right," level for the child according to word accuracy.

Assessing Reading Fluency and Accuracy: An Overview

A student's fluency is often assessed by using an adaptation of the running record assessment. When assessing fluency, a timing device is also used, as fluency incorporates rate of reading as well as automaticity. DIBELS is a well-known formal assessment of fluency and is used in schools nationwide. In addition, fluency is informally assessed through rubrics. Teachers listen to a child read and then rate the reader on the following aspects of his reading behaviors: attention to meaning, smoothness, expression, reading rate, and pace.

Chapter 10

Vocabulary

As an adult, when you read this sentence it appears that your understanding is automatic. Now, read the following sentence:

The guitarist's fado was enjoyable as we finished our dinner.

The word *fado* probably brought you to a stop. But, because you automatically use your cueing systems, you have an idea of the word's definition. Using phonics skills, you can most likely make an educated guess regarding pronunciation of the word. Next, using syntax, you can probably determine that the word is a noun. Finally, using the context information in the sentence—the semantics—you will most likely decide that *fado* is some type of a song, since substituting "The guitarist's song" for "The guitarist's fado" makes sense in the sentence.

You now have a good idea of the meaning of the complete sentence because you utilized the three main cueing systems: phonics, syntax, and semantics. With respect to pragmatics (expression), the tone of the sentence is as gentle as the background music it references. All of these cueing systems aided you in constructing meaning. (In case you are curious, a *fado* is a Portuguese folk song.) Children use cueing systems in the same way. As a teacher, you must model strategies and ask guiding questions to help your students use these systems.

The Cueing Systems: Phonics, Syntax, and Semantics

Cueing systems are signals that readers use to aid in figuring out unknown words. There are three main cueing systems: phonics, syntax, and semantics. Some teaching includes a fourth system: pragmatics.

- **Phonics:** A correspondence between letters and sounds.
- **Syntax:** The structure of the language.
- **Semantics:** Meaning; how words relate to form meaning.
- **Pragmatics:** The way in which expression can provide meaning to language.

Strategies for Using Context Cues

Context cues refer to the words surrounding an unknown word. The context cue could be just one or two words, a phrase, sentences, illustrations, etc., that would contribute to determining word meaning. It is important that children learn to use context cues to identity unknown words. Some children pick this skill up naturally, while others need teacher modeling and guidance.

Children learn most of their vocabulary words through wide reading. Wide reading entails reading a great number of books on a variety of topics. Using the cueing systems, children are able to determine the definitions of unknown words. They use phonics to try to sound the words out. Then they attempt to define the words through context—by what the sentence (or pictures) tells them. Finally, they use syntax; for example, they will read "a house" instead of "a houses" because they understand the structure of our language. Consider the following scenarios:

A first-grade student does not recognize the word *bus* when he sees the following sentence in a book: "The children rode a bus to school." First, the student tries to sound out *bus,* but gives it the long /u/ sound, and the sentence doesn't make sense. Re-reading the sentence, the student realizes that *bus* is something the children rode to school, so then he pronounces it correctly. Although the word ends in "s," the student knows the word is not *buses* because it is preceded by the word *a,* indicating that the next word is singular.

A fifth-grade student does not recognize the word *originals* in the following sentence in a book about Vincent van Gogh: "Although there are thousands of copies of van Gogh's art, the majority of originals are now in museums." First, the student tries to sound the word out. Using phonics, the student gets the *or,* but says "gin" with a long /i/ sound, and leaves off the "s." Realizing what he read does not make sense, the student goes back to the beginning of the sentence. Once he re-reads "thousands of copies," he realizes, through semantics, that the author must be using the word *original.* Finally, as the student re-reads the rest of the sentence, he also sees that *originals* is plural and corrects his miscue.

Strategic readers use context cues continually and, therefore, increase their vocabulary through wide reading. To help readers become strategic in using context cues, four ideas are presented here: teacher modeling, guiding questions, cloze procedure, and using root words or base words to gain word knowledge.

Teacher Modeling

The teacher's role is teaching students, through modeling and thinking out loud, how to use context to figure out unknown words. Think-alouds, often used in classrooms, allow teachers to model their thinking and are useful in teaching how to use context cues. When modeling the use of context cues, a teacher orally states how she figures out the meaning of unknown words when she is reading a text. The teacher explains that the word is new to her, but there is something in the text that will help to determine the word's meaning. She then points out the context that helped her learn the new word. This modeling is repeated a few times during read-alouds and shared reading. Eventually, the teacher begins to ask the students for help in determining the meaning of an "unknown" word.

Guiding Questions

Questioning can also assist students in learning these words. The following are questions that students can ask themselves, or that teachers can ask to guide students in deciphering unknown words.

Guided questions for developing readers: (The unknown word is indicated in italics.)

- Can you make out the beginning sound? The ending sound? The middle sound?

  Example: The hat *blew* in the wind and went on the grass. (/bl-oo/)

- Read past the word you don't know, and see if you can figure out what it is.

  Example: The dog *jumped* up and barked loudly. (The word *up* should help the student figure out *jumped*.)

- Chunk the word to see if you can figure it out.

  Example: He went *upstairs* to get his new truck. (Cover *up* to read *stairs;* cover *stairs* to read *up*.)

- Are there any pictures on the page that could help you think of what the word is?

  Example: The sentence reads, "There are cookies on the *table*." The picture shows a plate of cookies on a table; therefore, the child can look at the picture and see the cookies and the table.

- Are there words in the sentence that could help you figure out the unknown word?

  Example: The sentence reads, "The *monkey* ate the banana." The sentence refers to a living thing eating a banana; through semantics, the child would realize it must be a monkey.

- Does the unknown word have a particular function?

  Example: The sentence reads, "The *alarm* buzzed and woke up the girl." The reader does not know the word *alarm,* but from the context of something that buzzed and woke up the girl, he realizes that the word must be *alarm.*

Questions for intermediate readers:

The following questions aid readers in identifying the word and using context to determine meaning. (The unknown word is indicated in italics.)

- Are there any parts of the word for which you recognize the meaning? Such as in the following example, what does *hemi* mean? What does *sphere* mean?

  Example: The guide pointed to the northern *hemisphere*. (*hemi* = half; *sphere* = ball)

- Do any words in the sentence give you a hint of what the word may mean? (If not, try to guess what would make sense; if needed, go to a dictionary after reading.)

  Example: The buttons on the *remote* won't change the channels. (*change channels → remote*)

- Can you categorize or group the word with other things or animals?

  Example: I need pencils, paper, and *crayons* for school. (school supplies → *pencils, paper → crayons*)

- Does the sentence contain a problem and/or solution?

  Example: The young boy needed *glue* to fix his broken plane. (*fix broken plane → glue*)

- Is there a definition in the sentence? (A definition is often given in the form of an appositive.)

  Example: My *cosmetologist,* a hairdresser, is the nicest person. (A *hairdresser* is a type of *cosmetologist.*)

- Can you identify something that directs you toward something opposite?

  Example: That island is so small to have such a *gigantic* mountain. (*small → gigantic*)

- Can you tell what the unknown word does?

  Example: The *telephone* kept ringing and ringing. (A *telephone* rings.)

- Are there familiar cues that can help you figure out the new word?

  Example: The huge dog, a German *shepherd,* tried to jump onto my lap! (*dog, German → leads to shepherd*)

Cloze Procedure

A cloze activity uses a blank space in place of a word. This allows the reader to read the sentence or passage and use context to determine what word or words would make sense in the blank. The cloze procedure forces the reader to use the surrounding context; when guided by the teacher, students learn how context may help them determine the meaning of unknown words. For example, the teacher could write the following sentence on the whiteboard:

Taylor took the lunch count to the _____ for the teacher.

The teacher would then have the students read the sentence and fill in the blank. A discussion would be held as to why they answered "office" (or "cafeteria"). What hints or clues did they find in the sentence to get to the correct word? Then the discussion would lead into how strategic readers do this when they come across an unknown word in their reading.

Using Root Words or Base Words to Gain Word Knowledge

Although the terms *root word* and *base word* are often used interchangeably, technically, they are different. A base word is a standalone word that may have affixes added (*bike → biker*). A root word carries meaning, although it may be a standalone word. A root word may be dependent on affixes for more precise meaning such as *port* and *portable.* The root word *port* is a standalone word, but it conveys a different meaning when the suffix "able" is added. According to *The Literacy Dictionary: The Vocabulary of Reading and Writing* (Harris, 1995), root words may be base words like *alter* in *altercation,* or word pieces that must be connected or bound to another word, such as *liter* in *literature.* Some resources will identify the word *alter* as a base word, and *liter* (as in *literature*) as a root word. Knowing the meanings of root and base words enables readers to recognize small parts of a larger word, helping them to identify and understand unknown words.

Etymology, the history of words, plays an important part in structural analysis. Students learn that words come from Greek or Latin beginnings, and contain meanings similar to their original use. Etymology can be useful in elementary and early childhood classrooms as a tool for word study—helping students to remember new words and expand their vocabulary.

It is helpful for students to know some very general etymologies of Greek and Latin roots to aid them in discerning whether a word has a root. For example, the Latin root *cent* means "one hundred," and knowing this aids in understanding such words as *centipede* and *century.* Yet, this would not help in understanding the word *scent,* because in this case *scent* is a base word itself and has no connection to the Latin root *cent,* although it does contain *cent.* Additionally, compound words are usually composed of two base words, such as *snowman, baseball,* and *keyboard,* and can be analyzed by structure.

There are two basic methods used to teach the use of root and base word meanings. First, the teacher can use "think-alouds," as discussed earlier, this time focusing on words containing roots. For example, a teacher writes the following sentence on the whiteboard: "The car slowed as it drove over rough terrain." The teacher explains that "terr" means "earth or land," and, therefore, the car must have been driving over some bumpy land.

The second basic method involves having students deduce the meaning through a list of words. For example, the following words would be written on the whiteboard: *triangle, tricycle, triple,* and *trio.* The teacher would then ask the definition of each word, and students would recognize that each definition contains the word *three.* The teacher would then ask what word part was common in all of these words, and guide the students to discover that *tri* means "three."

There are numerous sites online that list Latin and Greek words, their meanings, and their word derivatives. (Simply search "common root words.") The following chart is a very small sample of common roots.

Examples of Latin and Greek Root Words

Latin Root Words		
Root	**Meaning**	**Derivatives**
aqua	water	*aquarium, aquamarine, aquatic*
fract	to break	*fracture, fraction*
port	to carry	*portable, airport*
multi	many	*multitude, multiply, multiuse*
rupt	to break	*rupture, corrupt, bankrupt*
Greek Root Words		
Root	**Meaning**	**Derivatives**
morph	form, shape	*morpheme, metamorphosis, amorphous*
phon	sound	*homophone, phonics, telephone, phonograph*
graph	writing	*graphics, photograph*
dia	across, through	*diagonal, diameter, diagnosis*
logy	study of	*biology, psychology*

Using Affixes

Affixes have their own meaning and, like root words, also can come from Greek or Latin roots, such as the Latin *inter,* which means "between," or the Greek *hemi,* which means "half." The chart that follows lists common affixes used at the elementary level and their meanings. (Search "common affixes" to find numerous charts online.)

Common Affixes

Common Prefixes

Prefix	Meaning	Examples
re-	to do again	*remake, redo, rewrite*
pre-	before	*prefix, preview, prewriting*
un-	not	*unlike, unnecessary, unkind*
in-, im-	not	*impossible, improbable, inconsistent*

Common Suffixes

Suffix	Meaning	Examples
-able	to be done	*comfortable, manageable, accomplishable*
-er	one who	*baker, worker, writer*
-less	without	*guiltless, fruitless, fearless*
-ness	state or condition of	*happiness, fondness, likeness*

Explicit Teaching of Targeted Vocabulary Words

There are numerous variations on how to explicitly teach vocabulary. The commonalities are as follows:

- The word must be visible (that is, on a word card, chart, or whiteboard).
- Either the students can try to pronounce the word or the teacher can say the word, but the correct pronunciation must be given.
- The word must be used in context so that readers can learn to use context. The context in which the word is used should provide the same meaning as in the text. For example, when teaching the word *bank,* as in the *bank of a creek,* the teacher should use a sentence like "He slid down the *bank* of the creek into the water." (not "He took money out of the *bank*.").
- Students should be exposed to new words multiple times in multiple contexts so that they will "own" the word.
- Reinforcement—students should practice using the word in context through writing, speaking, and games.

Selecting Vocabulary to Be Taught

Words that will be taught need to be selected using the following criteria. They:

- Should be central to concepts within the text.
- Should not be defined within the text. (Informational texts are an exception, as the concepts need to be discussed.)
- Should occur in the text in a way in which the meaning cannot be discerned from the context.
- Will most likely be seen in other texts; they are not isolated, oddly used words.

Education authors Isabel Beck, Margaret McKeown, and Linda Kucan developed a relatively easy strategy for selecting targeted vocabulary. Their three-tier method of selection is recommended by the Common Core State Standards. This method is described in the following table. *Note:* Beck, McKeown, and Kucan recommend that only Tiers 2 and 3 be explicitly taught vocabulary. The selection criteria listed below shows that Tiers 2 and 3 are the best words to be explicitly taught. Tier 1 words could be taught to beginning readers for word recognition purposes if they are not phonically regular words.

Selecting Words to Teach: Three Tiers of Vocabulary

Tier	Description	Examples
Tier 1: Do Not Teach	Basic words—words that children are familiar with	*table, crayon, coat, jump, goat, room*
Tier 2: Teach	High-frequency words that are more difficult than basic words	*logical, basically, intertwine, absurd, relevant, significance*
Tier 3: Teach	Domain-specific vocabulary (content-area words with content-area definitions)	*peninsula, photosynthesis, isosceles, the Great Depression* (of the 1930s)

Grammatical Function

Grammatical function is the role played by a word or phrase in a sentence or clause. Essentially, this is language about language (called meta-language), and it helps people to communicate more effectively when discussing grammar. Grammatical function becomes important in reading because it "rules" the syntax or structure of language. To discuss grammatical function, parts of speech—the building blocks of a language—should be understood. Parts of speech explain the use and/or role of particular words. The eight parts of speech in the English language as traditionally defined are as follows:

- **Noun:** A person, place or thing. (*oven, boy, love*)
- **Verb:** An action or state of being word (*run, is*)
- **Adjective:** Describes or modifies a noun (the *blue* dress)
- **Adverb:** Describes a verb, adjective, or another adverb (laughing *loudly*)
- **Pronoun:** Used in place of a noun (The girl misplaced *her* doll.)
- **Preposition:** Shows position (*under* the table)
- **Conjunction:** Joins other words (black *and* white, milk *or* water)
- **Interjection:** Expresses strong feeling (*Oh!, Yikes!*)

As shown by the definitions above, each part of speech has grammatical functions in our language. For example, two of the more commonly known grammatical functions of a noun are as the subject of a sentence or as a direct object. One well-known function of a verb is as a predicate. The grammatical function of a word or phrase posits the word or phrase in the structure of our language, or the cueing system of syntax, and aids in identifying unknown words.

When children enter school, they usually have the structure of the language internalized. They have learned where parts of sentences go without the labeling. When reading, students can use syntax to help them determine an unknown word. Let's try this little exercise:

Use the following words to fill in the four blanks in the sentence below: *boy, from, pick,* and *tall.*

The _____ man lifted up the little _____ so he could _____ an apple _____ the tree.
    1   2   3   4

The answer you surely arrive at is the following:

The __tall__ man lifted up the little __boy__ so he could __pick__ an apple __from__ the tree.
    1   2   3   4

You are probably thinking, well, that was easy. But not so for young students who may miscue with a noun where a verb should be, perhaps reading: "The duck went into the pond." as "The duck water into the pond." In this miscue, the child sees the word *pond* and the "w" of *went* and simply substitutes a "w" word that is related to water—a word that does not make grammatical or syntactic sense.

Looking closely at the above cloze sentence, you can analyze the syntax a bit. The word that fills in blank #1 had to be descriptive (*tall*) (an adjective because it modifies a noun). The word that fills in blank #2 must be a noun (*boy*) because an adjective (*little*) comes before it as a modifier. Blank #3 has to be a verb (*pick*) because there is a pronoun (*he*) that is the subject of the action. Finally, blank #4 begins a prepositional phrase, so the word *from* fits there. Filling in the blanks as in the classic game Mad Libs can be challenging, especially for young students and English Language Learners (ELLs).

The following terms are often used in elementary school, as they refer to some of the simpler grammatical functions.

Subject: Person, place, or thing (can also be an idea) that acts upon the verb. Example: *The <u>bunny</u> hopped around the yard.*

Predicate: Verb phrase that contains any object, modifier, or complement. Example: *The bunny <u>hopped around the yard</u>.*

Direct object: That which the subject acts upon; answers the question *who* or *what*. Example: *The bunny hopped around the <u>yard</u>.* (What did the bunny hop around? It hopped around the yard.)

Prepositional phrase: Made up of a preposition and a noun phrase. Example: *The bunny hopped <u>around the yard</u>.*

Vocabulary About Vocabulary: Words Worth Knowing and Understanding

Meta-language is defined as language about language. Words such as *nouns, verbs,* and *adjectives* are considered meta-language because they label types of words. In reading, there are a number of words that label specific types of words, such as the following:

acronym: An abbreviation that is pronounced and used as a word. Examples: *ASAP* (as soon as possible), *laser* (light amplification by stimulated emission of radiation), and *sonar* (sound navigation and ranging).

affix: A letter or group of letters added to a root word to change its meaning. Prefixes and suffixes are affixes. Prefix examples: *re-* ("to do again"), *un-* ("opposite of"), and *pre-* ("before"). Suffix examples: *-less* ("without"), *-er* ("one who does"), and *-acy* ("state or quality").

anagram: A word or phrase that can be made by rearranging the letters of another word; all letters in the word must be used. Examples: *era/are, ocean/canoe,* and *south/shout.*

antonyms: Words that mean the opposite of one another. Examples: *hot/cold, guilty/innocent,* and *exciting/dull.*

base word: A base word is a word that stands alone, but affixes can be added. Examples: *test→retest, pretest, testing, tester.*

compound words: Two words that are joined together to form one word. Examples: *upstairs, hairdresser,* and *shoelace*. *Note:* Not all compound words must be written as one word. Examples: *high school* and *ice cream.*

contraction: One word that abbreviates a two-word combination, using an apostrophe to substitute for the omitted letter or letters. Examples: *can't, don't, wouldn't,* and *could've.*

etymology: The study of the history of words or phrases. Examples: *pizza* (Italian, meaning "pie" or "tart"), *bagel* (most likely from the Yiddish word *beygl,* which is likely from the German dialect word *beugel,* meaning "ring" or "bracelet"), and *T-bone* (taken from the shape of the steak bone).

euphemism: An expression or word that is substituted for something that is considered too harsh or vulgar. Examples: *in the family way* for *pregnant; darn* for *damn; let go* for *fired.*

homographs: Words that are spelled the same, but have multiple meanings and may not be pronounced the same. Examples: *fair, bow, desert,* and *minute.*

homophones (or homonyms): Words that sound the same, but are spelled differently and have different meanings. Examples: *bare, bear; pail, pale;* and *surf, serf.*

idiom: A phrase that has a different meaning than what is expected. Examples: *go jump in the lake, at the drop of a hat,* and *the ball is in your court.*

palindrome: A word that is spelled the same forward and backward. Examples: *mom, madam,* and *racecar.*

prefix: A morpheme that is connected to the beginning of a word. Examples: *re-* ("to do again"), *un-* ("opposite of"), and *pre-* ("before").

suffix: A morpheme that is connected to the ending of a word. Examples: *-less* ("without"), *-er* ("one who does"), and *-acy* ("state or quality").

synonyms: Words that mean the same thing or nearly the same thing. Examples: *nice/polite, cold/chilly,* and *sleepy/drowsy.*

Wide Reading for Vocabulary Growth

It cannot be stressed enough that wide reading supports and impacts vocabulary growth, and that knowledge of vocabulary increases comprehension. The more students read inside and outside the classroom, the more vocabulary they will learn. Not only will students learn more words through wide reading, but they will also learn the meaning of words at a more in-depth level. Wide reading allows for the following:

- Multiple exposures to new and known vocabulary
- Use of new and known words in different contexts
- Practice in using context to identify unknown words
- Exposure to derivatives of known and unknown words
- Multiple exposures to word roots and bases used with known and unknown affixes
- Connections from known information to new information, increasing the understanding of words and word usage

Assessing and Monitoring Vocabulary: An Overview

It is important to recognize that knowledge of vocabulary transcends word recognition. Students who have learned to read in a school district that uses a strong, systematic phonics approach can often correctly pronounce words even though they may not know meaning. Vocabulary assessment includes not only pronunciation, but also word meaning and word usage, which are assessed through observation and analysis of student work. Vocabulary is informally assessed through tracking of students' word usage in oral and written language. Teachers will often have students provide a definition using their own words in order to ensure that the students have a good command of the meaning. In addition, teachers can assess a student's word knowledge by asking for an association if the student cannot state a definition. For example, if a child cannot give a definition of the word *important,* the teacher can ask the child to state something that is important to him. Association indicates that students have an idea of how the vocabulary word is applied. Vocabulary is also assessed through teacher-created tests, vocabulary games, and word banks.

Chapter 11
Assessment and Differentiation for Optimal Growth

Assessments, both formal and informal, are an important part of the process of teaching reading. They are used to identify starting points for instruction and to monitor student progress, and they can guide teachers in how best to help students meet or exceed grade-level reading expectations. Since teachers are held accountable for students' academic growth, this continual or periodic monitoring is essential.

Formal Reading Assessments

Standardized tests are formal assessments. They include standardized measures that are based on research regarding expectations for specific age or grade groups and on corresponding statistics that allow for results comparison. The data are standardized, and scores appear as percentiles, stanines, standard scores, or grade-level equivalents.

Standardized tests are created in two formats: norm-referenced and criterion-referenced.

- **Norm-referenced test:** This format compares students with others and produces a percentile score that "ranks" each student at a percentile against other students. If a student receives a score in the 75th percentile, this means that the child has scored higher than 75% of the students who took the test, and lower than 25%. The norm is at the 50th percentile; therefore, receiving a score in the 75th percentile places the student above the norm.
- **Criterion-referenced test:** In this format, the test is structured to measure against certain criteria. The child is not compared with other test-takers, but instead is evaluated based on the content being measured on the test. A criterion-referenced reading test can test word-attack knowledge, vocabulary, homophones, contractions, comprehension, and so forth.

Some standardized tests are a hybrid—a mix of norm-referenced and criterion-referenced assessments. Such tests are arranged in sets of "batteries" or content matter, where each of the content areas has been "ranked" in percentiles.

Scoring

Standard deviation is sometimes referred to as the "mean of the mean." Think about a bell curve. The closer a score is to the middle of the bell curve, the closer the score is to the norm. If a bell curve is high and narrow, then the individual scores are not too spread out from the norm. If the bell curve is low and flat, then there is a huge spread in the scores. Standard deviation is determined through calculation. One standard deviation from the norm comprises 34% of the test-takers in the group. So when going one standard deviation from each side of the mean, that would be the scores of 68% of the test-takers. A high standard deviation indicates a larger spread in scores. A stanine is a 9-point scale used for normalized test scores: 1 to 3 is considered below average, 4 to 6 average, and 7 to 9 above average. Therefore, a student whose scores land in the 4 to 6 stanine is considered to have scored in the average range, 5 being the average.

Determining Test Validity and Reliability

A test is valid if it measures what it says it will measure. For example, if an assessment says it is measuring inferential comprehension, but it asks only literal questions, the assessment is not valid. (Literal questions ask for what was said explicitly in the text, not what was inferred.)

A test is deemed reliable if it would produce the same results with a different set of people in a different setting. If you can give the California Achievement Test to third graders in California, Kentucky, Florida, and Massachusetts and each state's results produce approximately the same curve, then the test is considered reliable.

Check Your Understanding

Read each of the following statements and determine whether it describes validity, reliability, a criterion-referenced test, or a norm-referenced test. Explain your answer.

1. A student is in the 47th percentile for this standardized test.

2. This norm-referenced test was given in New York, Missouri, and Oregon, in both rural and urban areas in each of the three states. The student scores in all of these areas were comparable.

3. There is some concern about this test because it asks for alphabetical order in a question that says it is measuring inference.

4. From the testing results, the teacher can see that Brendon needs to work on his word identification skills, vocabulary, and inferential comprehension.

Answers

1. Norm-referenced test: The test has been measured on the normal curve, and this student has 46 percent of the students who took it below him and 53 percent above him.

2. Reliability: The test is normed and has been given in various locations in order to assure its reliability, yielding comparable scores in all locations.

3. Validity: The issue at hand is whether alphabetical order measures inferential comprehension. In order to be valid, a test must measure what it says it will measure. As illustrated by this statement, the test is not valid.

4. Criterion-referenced: The test results have pinpointed content in which Brendon has a weakness.

Monitoring Students' Reading and Writing Progress

Monitoring a student's reading and writing progress is an ongoing process. Three concepts are described in the chart below: progress monitoring, how assessment guides instruction, and formative assessment. To aid in your understanding of these concepts, a concrete example is provided, using a scenario with a child named Sarah.

Concept	Description and Purpose	Scenario
Progress monitoring	Progress monitoring is used to ensure that "no child is left behind." Scores from assessments are recorded, student weaknesses are identified, instruction is given, and, finally, a follow-up assessment will show whether progress has been made. This is a constant cycle in both reading and writing instruction to ensure that all students learn. The teacher must keep excellent records regarding a child's progress, and continually use formative assessment to ensure the child improves.	Sarah has been assessed using a running record, and the teacher has found her to be weak in identifying multisyllabic words.
Assessment guide instruction	The idea behind this concept is that a child is assessed in some form and the results of the assessment inform his goals for learning. Instruction is then aligned to these goals.	A goal for Sarah would be instruction that improves her ability to identify multisyllabic words. Sarah would be taught chunking skills and morphemic analysis (looking for smaller words or word parts that are known to the reader), and perhaps using context cues more frequently to aid in word identification.

Concept	Description and Purpose	Scenario
Formative assessment	Formative assessment consists of a variety of assessments, often used in daily instruction, that inform teachers of students' needs. A student's progress assessment entails daily monitoring on multiple fronts. When a teacher sees that a child is struggling in an area, she uses this formative assessment information to set goals for improvement in the weak areas. In addition, if a teacher sees that a child is "breezing through" the concept and skills being studied, the teacher knows it is time to give that child more challenging tasks.	After Sarah has practiced using her new strategies to identify multisyllabic words, her teacher listens to her read. Sarah is given a text in which she can apply and demonstrate these new skills. If Sarah does well in this formative assessment, it will be time to create new goals for her. If she does poorly, the teacher will need to try a different instructional approach. (This is all within the cycle of progress monitoring.)

Reading Levels

As discussed in Chapter 9, "Reading Fluency and Assessing Accuracy," the three reading levels are defined as follows:

- **Independent:** When a child can read 95% or more of the words in a text correctly and shows excellent understanding of the text, this is the child's independent level; the material is considered too easy for the child to be challenged.
- **Instructional:** When a child reads 90%–94% of the words in a text correctly and shows good understanding of the material, this is the child's instructional level—what is called the "just right" reading level for the child's optimal learning.
- **Frustration:** When a child reads 89% or fewer of the words in a text correctly and shows minimal understanding of the text, this indicates that the material is too difficult for the child.

Vygotsky and the Zone of Proximal Development

Reading levels are important because student assessments at these levels help determine the optimum level for instruction. Lev Vygotsky, a learning theorist with a sociocultural approach to cognitive development, posited that cognitive development depends on a zone of proximal development (ZPD). To simplify, the ZPD is a range in which a person can learn. If something is too difficult (frustration level), true learning cannot occur. If something is too easy (independent level), a person can't "learn" what he already knows. Therefore, the ZPD is at the instructional level, where someone can be taught by a more learned individual. This is because at that level, there is sufficient material to learn—but not so much as to be frustrating. As a person learns the new material, the ZPD shifts forward, and the learning cycle continues at the adjusted instructional level.

Informal Reading Assessments

Informal assessments are conducted almost daily in the classroom and are driven by content and performance; unlike formal assessments, they are not standardized. Although the procedures are usually somewhat standardized, scoring in informal assessments is often subjective. If a teacher is concerned about a student's understanding of contractions, for example, an informal assessment could be made. The teacher could choose to use small-group instruction to improve each student's performance, assembling lower-scoring students in a skills group. In the case of a rubric (defined below), weaknesses and strengths would be identified in particular areas and goals would then be generated from that assessment.

Types of Informal Assessments

The following list is not exhaustive, but it provides an overview of the various informal assessments currently in use in classrooms.

Early literacy assessments:

- **Letter identification:** Very young students should be assessed to see whether they can identify letters by name and letter-sound identification.

- **Concepts of print:** The teacher will ask a student if he can show her the concepts of print, such as a book's title, a sentence, end marks, and so forth. (For a more complete list of the concepts of print, see Chapter 3.)

- **Phonemic awareness:** In this assessment, students are told a word orally and asked to blend, separate, segment, or substitute sounds.

- **Retellings:** Retelling entails a child explaining to the listener what a story or informational text is about. In a story retelling, a teacher might use a rubric to score the child's retelling (oral or written), and watch for inclusion of the following: characters, setting, a problem, attempts to solve, a solution, inferences, and voice or mood, depending on her expectations and the student's grade level. Retellings are usually scored with a checklist or rubric.

- **Running records:** A student reads a passage orally, and the teacher codes the miscues (errors) made. Miscues include omitting a word, pronouncing a word incorrectly, appealing for help, and substituting a word. If a student corrects an error, this is designated as self-correction, and is not counted as a miscue. Teachers analyze running records in order to ascertain word identification needs and reading levels of students. (For more on running records, see Chapter 9.)

Assessments used at all levels:

- **Portfolios:** A portfolio is an orderly and systematic collection of a student's work. The work is selected carefully so as to demonstrate student progress, or lack of progress. For example, the working portfolio may show a scored writing sample from weeks 1 and 5 in order to explain the goals that were set in week 1 and the progress made by week 5. Any of the assessments discussed in this "at all levels" section may be part of a working portfolio. (A showcase portfolio, on the other hand, is work that the student and teacher select as the student's best examples.)

- **Rubric:** A rubric is used to score work, and represents what is expected from a student at that grade level in the content or skill being assessed. It is usually structured like a grid, with the work delineated by the expected criteria, such as voice, content, or word choice in writing. Then, a thorough explanation of these expectations is written in boxes that are arranged as a continuum of developing to proficient. Scoring for each criterion may range from unacceptable to acceptable to target, and is represented in gradients that run the gamut from "best" to "needs to do better." A student might be scored at the target level in voice, for example, but do poorly in content. The separate scores for various criteria allow for formative-assessment data and goal setting for students.

- **Spelling inventories:** A widely used spelling "test" was popularized in the book *Words Their Way*, written by Donald R. Bear, Marcia Invernizzi, Shane Templeton, and Francine Johnston. The results highlight the spelling patterns where individual students are weak. Teachers can then group the students by skills needed, using formative assessment for progress monitoring.

- **Informal reading inventories (IRIs):** Although considered informal assessments, many IRIs have been normed by grade levels and include standardized directions for administration. An IRI usually consists of grade-level word lists designed to assess word recognition levels, grade-level passages to assess reading comprehension; these, along with word recognition, will enable the teacher to determine a student's grade level for reading. The passages can be read orally and miscues can be recorded, or the IRI can constitute a silent comprehension check. IRIs are one commonly used measure to decide what level book a child needs for "just right" reading.

- **Cloze procedure:** This is an assessment in which every fifth or sixth word is left blank. The student reads the text, and, using context and semantic cues, tries to fill in the blank with the correct word or a synonym. The cloze procedure may also be used to assess the student's reading level and his use of syntax (structure of language) and semantics (meaning) when selecting words to place in the blanks. Once the student fills in the blank, the replacement word is scored as correct only if it is identical to what had been omitted. If the text is at the child's instructional level, then 40%–59% of the words will be correct. A result of 60% and above places the student at the independent reading level; below 40% constitutes frustration level.

Assessing the Affective Domain

The Affective Domain refers to dealing with feelings and emotions, which do affect learning. This may include attitude toward reading, whether a child values literacy, and whether reading gives the child any satisfaction. Ideally, all children would love reading, understand its importance, and be very satisfied to read! Knowing this information about students can aid teachers in setting goals and choosing instructional activities.

- **Attitudinal survey:** This is an informal gathering of information regarding students' attitudes about various subjects, such as speaking, reading, and writing. A survey might ask questions such as "Do you like to read at home?" This question pinpoints whether the student likes recreational reading, whereas "Do you enjoy reading at school?" focuses on academic reading. (An online search for "elementary speaking, reading, and writing attitude surveys" will reveal dozens of examples.)

- **Interest inventories:** This is a series of questions that teachers ask students in order to learn more about them, and to gauge their interests for reading and writing.

Using Diagnostic Reading Data to Differentiate Instruction

Differentiation occurs in a classroom when a teacher matches a student with the materials and instruction that will help him improve. This process may be used with a struggling reader who needs slower-paced instruction, or a gifted student who has already mastered the material being taught and needs to be challenged, as they deserve the opportunity to learn. To differentiate instruction, data need to be collected and analyzed at predetermined intervals. This information is then used to differentiate instruction in the classroom. Progress monitoring is continuous, as a teacher must always be ready to "take a student to the next step." That is, when a student shows progress, he must be given more complex work so that he continues to learn. Or, if progress is not apparent, then the instruction needs to be modified so that the student can learn. Regular progress monitoring ensures that students are learning at their optimal level and pace.

What Will Data Tell You?

Data Source	What Can Be Determined
Norm-referenced test	Where each child performs compared with others in his age group and grade. Depending on the type of test, student needs can also be determined.
Criterion-referenced test	The student's strengths and weaknesses regarding the content the test is assessing (letter-sound correspondence, mechanics, comprehension, and so forth); the test is scored specifically to pinpoint these strengths and weaknesses. A child may score at the "ceiling" level; that is, he performed above the limits of the assessment.
Informal assessment	Myriad information, depending on the assessment, as noted previously in the list of informal assessments. If a rubric in fluency is used, for example, a child's data may say the child is weak in reading rate, but strong in expression.
Group/class data	If each child in the class had the same assessment, class data exist, but the data must be organized as such. Class data are used to group students for specific needs. The scores are analyzed for each class in order to set up instructional groups, such as leveled reading groups, writing strategy groups, or word enrichment groups. For example, with word-attack skills, if seven students in a class struggle on a criterion-referenced assessment with medial vowels, then these seven students would be placed in a group that concentrates on skills and strategies to help identify medial vowel sounds.

Ways to Differentiate

The main reason teachers gather data is to place each child where he can best learn what he needs—whether in a group, a class, or an individual setting. This is done through differentiation.

Tiers of Differentiation

"Tiers" essentially means "levels." In differentiation, an activity is "cloned" to an easier or more complex level so that all students can learn at their optimal level of instruction. Considered the "mother" of tiered differentiation, Carol Tomlinson has written extensively about differentiated instruction. She posits that differentiation occurs in three basic ways: through content, process, and product. Although teachers are careful to differentiate students' activities, the desired outcome or objective of the lesson does not change.

- **Content:** Differentiation through content means that the materials or information is differentiated in tiers to meet the learners' needs.

  Example: The desired outcome is for students to learn about ants and ant colonies. Students are given leveled books with at least three levels: one for the struggling readers; another for the on-grade readers; and finally, a more complex text for the students who need a challenge. The information required to achieve the desired outcome is included in the easiest text; the other two levels also contain that information, as well as more detailed or complex information.

- **Process:** Differentiation through process means that the instruction is tiered to meet the needs of the learner.

  Example: The desired outcome is student improvement in inference skills. During group time, the teacher is more explicit with the struggling group as she explains and models how, together, they can infer what the author is saying and find support in the text. With the on-grade-level group, the teacher models her inferences and support and then has students practice with her. Finally, the students work together to discuss additional inferences and support they glean from the text. For the advanced group, the teacher explains that she wants the students to read and state at least three inferences from the text and the supporting evidence. The teacher models with a few examples to ensure all students understand.

- **Product:** Differentiation through product means that the end result is tiered.

  Example: The desired outcome is to have students write directions. A teacher will have the struggling readers write directions for a three-step art project, the on-grade group write directions for a five-step project, and the group that needs a challenge write directions for a seven-step project. The key is that all students will be writing directions with different levels of complexity.

Curriculum Compacting

In curriculum compacting, a child "compacts out," which means that an assessment has shown that the child already knows the material being studied. Once that is clear, the teacher gives the child a project, or allows him to choose an individual project (or group project, if there is more than one child compacting out) that will foster new or extended learning related to the topic or goals.

Interest

Interest triggers motivation. If children are highly motivated to learn something, they will work harder and "go beyond" in their learning. Often, because of their interest, they have more background knowledge on a topic, which places them at a higher level of learning at the outset.

Learning Centers

Learning centers may be chosen by interest or assigned by need. They may be supplied with materials to differentiate learning, and the time needed at each center can be set differently for each child. For example, a word work center could have manipulatives for struggling students to make the "ent" word family (such as *bent, cent, dent, lent, rent, sent, tent, went*). The middle-level students could have a cloze (fill in the blank) activity in which they put one of the "ent" words into a sentence like "The campers put up their _____." The highest-level group could be told to write their own sentences using the "ent" word family.

Multiple Intelligences

The theory of multiple intelligences, proposed by developmental psychologist Howard Gardner, states that people are smart in many different ways and that there is not just one type of intelligence. When differentiating students by their various intelligences, teachers may allow students to choose an activity that capitalizes on their strength. Gardner has identified the following eight different intelligence types:

1. **naturalistic:** Smart with items in nature; seeing patterns in the natural.
2. **bodily-kinesthetic:** Learns through hands-on experiences; tactile.
3. **musical-rhythmic:** Learns musical instruments easily; learns through music and rhythm.
4. **intrapersonal:** Strong with inner thoughts; understands self.
5. **interpersonal:** Friendly; understands the needs and feeling of others.
6. **logical-mathematical:** Smart with math, reasoning, and logical thinking.
7. **verbal-linguistic:** Strong with the use of language to present ideas for various purposes.
8. **visual-spatial:** Creates and learns from visual images; thinks spatially and three-dimensionally.

There are numerous school-age assessments online to determine which intelligences are a child's strengths. Such assessments are usually in a survey format with questions that children answer. For example, a question might say, "Would you prefer to be drawing a picture or writing a song?" (visual or musical). Some assessments are checklist style and have the intelligence written with a list of "I like to do" under each. The intelligence with the most boxes checked off would be the strongest.

Differentiating through the intelligences is a fun and creative way of teaching and is relatively easy to incorporate into literacy instruction. Using the story *Little Red Riding Hood,* reader responses can be assigned using the different intelligences, without differentiating the outcome. In this example the outcome would be to have students retell the story in a sequential order. Some response choices could be:

- Draw five to six pictures that tell the story. (visual-spatial)
- Tell the story orally to the teacher. (verbal-linguistic)
- Number scenes from the story in the correct order. (mathematical-logical)
- Write a retelling of the story and give your opinion. (intrapersonal)
- Write a song that tells the story. (musical-rhythmic)

Although these choice are different, they would be assessed by the same criteria. How well did the student include the events in the story and were they in the correct sequence?

Scaffolding

The term *scaffolding* is derived from the word *scaffold,* a raised wooden platform used for work on out-of-reach areas. In the classroom, teachers provide scaffolding for students by asking guided questions, giving partial answers, or dividing a lesson into smaller parts. The idea is that as students grow proficient at a skill, teachers can take the "scaffold" away. Scaffolding is a major aspect of Vygotsky's zone of proximal development (see Chapter 8, "Reading Comprehension Across Genres and Text Types"), whereby teachers scaffold learners so that they can work on slightly challenging material.

Reading or Writing Workshop

When students are reading or writing more independently of the teacher, the class may be taught "workshop" style. Books and writing topics are often self-selected; students are then supported with flexible group mini-lessons on content the teacher deems necessary from analyzing different works. Although reading and writing workshops are driven by student interest, the teacher remains very much the classroom leader as she facilitates learning, monitors progress, and informally assesses students to offer mini-lessons in their areas of need.

Literature Discussion Groups

There are two principal ways to discuss literature in the classroom: literature circles and reciprocal teaching. Both are described below.

- **Literature circles:** Traditionally, students are given roles such as discussion director, vocabulary finder, clarifier, visualizer or artist, questioner, and so forth. Students are trained in their roles so that groups will be productive. For example, the "vocabulary finder" could be told to find one or two of the following: a new word, an unusual use of a word, or an interesting word and be prepared to share and discuss with the group. Literatures circles have evolved over time and now focus on a "dinner style conversation" about the text instead of roles. In this case, the teacher may have students use sticky notes to annotate while reading and share their thoughts with the group.

- **Reciprocal teaching:** In this grouping, students have four major strategies that guide their discussion: summarizing, clarifying, question generating, and predicting. The premise of reciprocal teaching is that it uses multiple strategies simultaneously, not just one strategy at a time. Summarizing can be oral, written, or a completed graphic organizer that will be shared with the group. Clarifying has students marking confusing passages or unfamiliar vocabulary to be discussed. Question generating has students making up questions as they read the text. The goal is to get students to think of questions that will allow all students to get to a deeper level of understanding. Finally, predicting has students thinking ahead as they read the text. These strategies are first modeled and then practiced before groups are allowed to operate without teacher guidance. These strategies are used differently at various grade levels; for example, in second grade, the students may be told to partner-read two pages and summarize orally what they just read. In older grades, a student may lead the group discussion.

Flexible Grouping and Guided Reading

Flexible grouping and guided reading are similar ways to differentiate, as guided reading groups should be flexible. These methods are described in detail below.

Flexible Grouping

Flexible grouping allows the teacher to differentiate instruction to maximize student learning; the flexibility refers to the composition of student groups as well as the content being taught. Students are brought together in small groups to receive instruction matched to their needs based on assessments. Progress monitoring is the key to flexible grouping. Such grouping is premised on the teacher's freedom to switch students from one group to another, depending on the level and needs of each student. Students do not remain in the same group all year; some advance faster than others, and a student will be moved from a group where he has mastered the content being taught. As students advance, they shift to more advanced learning groups or move to a newly created group. With effective teaching, all students should continually be advancing.

Flexible grouping may be used for, but is not limited to, the following:

- reading groups (discussed more in the "Guided Reading" section that follows)
- writing groups, focusing on instruction in a particular trait in writing
- word identification skills
- reading skills and strategies
- vocabulary instruction
- English Language Learners (ELLs; teachers must recognize that these students may be at different levels from one another, depending on their knowledge of the English language and of the content being taught)

Guided Reading

Guided reading is reading instruction designed to provide differentiated learning. This method enables the teacher to work with small groups of students on the same reading level and often with the same needs. Components of guided reading include the following:

- Students are grouped by assessment level; four to six students is considered an optimal group size.

- Assessment is continual; it may include daily observations, running records, and IRIs.

- Groups meet for about 20 minutes to read, with teacher scaffolding; discuss the reading; and participate in daily skill or strategy focus activities.

- Three to four guided reading groups are recommended per class.

- Small group size allows the teacher closer attention to each student's reading, and to design instruction to their needs. Groups are flexible and students are switched between groups when needed to ensure they are reading at their instructional reading level.

- When a reading group meets with the teacher, the other groups are kept well occupied with an academically focused task such as learning centers, literature discussion groups, independent reading, or reader response work.

Chapter 12

Test-Taking Strategies

Chapter 1 prepared you for studying for the Praxis (5204). Chapters 2–11 contained the material to be studied. The main focus of this chapter is to prepare you to actually take the test. To start, review the 3-day countdown for some last-minute test-preparation tips. Then, take this book's two practice tests, following the recommendations detailed toward the end of this chapter in order to simulate a real testing experience. Simulating test conditions can help make you more comfortable in anticipation of the actual test. The last section of this chapter gives you some tips for test day.

Countdown to the Praxis (5204)

The following timeline is recommended as you prepare for your test.

Three Days Before the Test

Go to the Praxis website (www.ets.org/praxis) and look for helpful tidbits and suggestions. There may be updates essential to your test-taking experience. Watch any videos, read any updates, and check your "My Praxis" account.

The Praxis (5204) includes three constructed-response questions. Take some time to focus on this question type. Think about how you might begin any of your essay responses for these questions. While you obviously don't know the questions in advance, there are some generic essay beginnings that can get you started, such as:

- After reviewing the material on …
- The teacher's notes suggest …
- When looking at the information provided, …
- In the case of this particular student, it appears …
- According to reading research and theory, …
- When analyzing the available assessment(s), …

Think about possible transitional phrases to begin your concluding essay paragraph. Again, each transitional phrase must be appropriate for the particular question, but some generic endings include:

- In conclusion, the evidence offered in this …
- The final point that is important to state …
- To summarize, …
- Finally, in support of what was said, …

You have 2 hours to complete the Praxis (5204). Decide how much time you will need to write the three short essay responses. Think about how much time you will need to answer 90 selected-response questions. Think carefully about what will work for you. If you are undecided, try the following approach:

1. Answer the constructed-response questions first. They are the most laborious, requiring significant thought. Give yourself no more than 45 minutes total; this allows 15 minutes for each short essay response. This is not a lot of time, but you are already prepared with your beginning and ending phrases. **Remember:** The constructed-response questions account for approximately 25% of your score. Be sure to save enough time to answer the 90 selected-response questions, which account for 75% of your score.

2. After 45 minutes, switch to the selected-response questions. You now have 75 minutes left, and you are hoping to devote the final 10 to 15 of those minutes to go back and check your constructed responses and any questions you are uncertain about. When you start the selected-response questions, look at the time and calculate what time it will be in 30 minutes. You should be at least halfway through the selected-response questions at that point. For example, if you start the selected-response questions at 10:00 a.m., you should be on at least question 45 by 10:30 a.m. And, with all the studying you've done, you will most likely be further along—which is good, as this will allow more time to review your constructed responses and perhaps some of the selected-response questions you find confusing.

3. Try this timing breakdown on one of the two practice tests in this book, and then tweak the timing as needed to make a timing plan for test day.

Two Days Before the Test

If unexpected complications have kept you from studying for the Praxis (5204), you do have a problem. But don't panic. There's still time to react. If you need to "pull an all-nighter," do so two nights before the test. Do not stay up all night the night before the test.

If, however, you have adhered to your study plan, just review, at this point. Review, study, and make sure you have everything clear in your head. When reviewing the reading content, focus on what you consider your weaker areas. Go over your notes. Make yourself confident.

Finally, if you overeat like this author does when she's anxious, put all (okay, most) of your junk food in a basket, and ask your neighbor to hold it for 48 hours. Seriously, you don't need a stomachache when taking the test!

The Night Before the Test

- Recheck the Praxis website for any updates.
- Verify your test center location (do so through your "My Praxis" account).
- Even if you plan to use a GPS for driving to the test site, if you have never been there, look it up on a map to ensure that you have a visual of where you are going.
- Print your admission ticket and have it ready to bring with you.
- Assemble your identification documents.
- Do not bring personal items; they are not allowed. No one at the site will take responsibility for any personal items.
- Put your ID and admissions ticket (and map, if needed) in a place where you will remember to take them (in the car if necessary!).

You should pay proper attention to your physical health as you prepare for the test. Make sure you have decent meals the night before and the morning of the test. It is essential to enter that testing room feeling physically and mentally alert.

Calculate what time you need to go to bed in order to get 8 hours of sleep, and adhere to that bedtime.

The Morning of the Test

- Eat. This may be the one time that a doughnut might help.
- Dress comfortably. Layers may be useful, in case the testing center is too hot or cold for you.
- Watch your liquid intake so you are not uncomfortable.
- Get to the testing center early. Expect a line at the entrance.

How to Take the Practice Tests to Simulate Real Testing

Pretend that the practice tests in this book are real tests, and prepare as if you were going to a test center to take the actual Praxis (5204). Use the study approach that you have decided is best for you. If there is any topic that is still unclear, do an online search to clarify and alleviate your concerns. You should go into the test knowing and understanding this material.

When taking the practice tests, try to mimic test-day conditions:

- Sit at a table or desk with a computer or laptop to answer the constructed-response questions.
- Have two or three No. 2 pencils ready for filling in the selected-response bubbles on the provided answer sheets.
- Set a timer for 2 hours.
- Pace yourself. Use the plan you made previously (in the "Three Days Before the Test" section). *Remember:* 90 selected-response questions and three constructed-response questions. So, if you plan to spend 45 minutes on the constructed-response questions and 60 minutes on the selected-response questions, that leaves you 15 minutes to review.
- Decide which question type you are going to tackle first. Many students prefer to do the writing first—the approach suggested above if you are undecided—because that seems to require the greater amount of energy. Decide what time limit you will observe.
- Start the selected portion of the test, stop at the previously decided time, and go to the second part.
- If you have time left at the end, use it to review what you have written. Check over conventions, spelling, and sentence structure.
- Stop when the timer goes off. Do not exceed the 2-hour testing time when taking the practice tests.

After you have taken both practice tests, you will have a better idea of how long each portion of the real test will take you, so you can plan your test-taking time accordingly. Furthermore, after scoring the practice tests, you will know if there are any areas where you need to focus your final review prior to the actual test.

Constructed-Response Tips

Remember the points on the Praxis (5204) scoring rubric for scoring the writing. Make sure that you have answered all parts of each question. Your response should be clear, with supporting details, and show strong knowledge of the reading content.

In your essay writing, use reading terminology carefully and in the appropriate context. If you use a reading term, either define it or support it in your response, as in the following example:

> You are asked to analyze a running record. The running record shows that a child reads the following words with short vowel sounds: *beat, tail, boat, bait,* and *pail.* With analysis, you can see that the child needs to learn that vowel digraphs say the long sound of the first vowel. In your essay response, you may write the following: Since all of the words with vowel digraphs ("ea" in *beat,* "ai" in *tail,* "oa" in *boat,* "ai" in *bait,* and "ai" in *pail*) had errors, the child's weakness is in vowel digraphs. A vowel digraph is when two consecutive vowels make one sound.

Test Day

At the test center, you will have 30 minutes to complete a tutorial before you start the timed test.

When the test begins:
- Check the time. You have 2 hours (120 minutes) for this test.
- Go to the section you plan to start with.

- Remember your timing plan. When should you be done with the constructed-response questions? The selected-response questions? Divide that time mentally in order to pace yourself.
- When the first section (whether constructed response or selected response) is done, begin the other section immediately, remembering to pace yourself so as to adhere to your timing plan.
- Keep calm and test on.

After the test:

Don't start second-guessing yourself and beating yourself up. It is what it is. Congratulate yourself for your great preparation! Now, go to your neighbor's house and get that junk food. You deserve it!

Chapter 13

Practice Test 1

Answer Sheet

Remove this sheet and use it to mark your answers to the selected-response questions.

Selected-Response Questions

1 Ⓐ Ⓑ Ⓒ Ⓓ		46 Ⓐ Ⓑ Ⓒ Ⓓ
2 Ⓐ Ⓑ Ⓒ Ⓓ		47 Ⓐ Ⓑ Ⓒ Ⓓ
3 Ⓐ Ⓑ Ⓒ Ⓓ		48 Ⓐ Ⓑ Ⓒ Ⓓ
4 Ⓐ Ⓑ Ⓒ Ⓓ		49 Ⓐ Ⓑ Ⓒ Ⓓ
5 Ⓐ Ⓑ Ⓒ Ⓓ		50 Ⓐ Ⓑ Ⓒ Ⓓ
6 Ⓐ Ⓑ Ⓒ Ⓓ		51 Ⓐ Ⓑ Ⓒ Ⓓ
7 Ⓐ Ⓑ Ⓒ Ⓓ		52 Ⓐ Ⓑ Ⓒ Ⓓ
8 Ⓐ Ⓑ Ⓒ Ⓓ		53 Ⓐ Ⓑ Ⓒ Ⓓ
9 Ⓐ Ⓑ Ⓒ Ⓓ		54 Ⓐ Ⓑ Ⓒ Ⓓ
10 Ⓐ Ⓑ Ⓒ Ⓓ		55 Ⓐ Ⓑ Ⓒ Ⓓ
11 Ⓐ Ⓑ Ⓒ Ⓓ		56 Ⓐ Ⓑ Ⓒ Ⓓ
12 Ⓐ Ⓑ Ⓒ Ⓓ		57 Ⓐ Ⓑ Ⓒ Ⓓ
13 Ⓐ Ⓑ Ⓒ Ⓓ		58 Ⓐ Ⓑ Ⓒ Ⓓ
14 Ⓐ Ⓑ Ⓒ Ⓓ		59 Ⓐ Ⓑ Ⓒ Ⓓ
15 Ⓐ Ⓑ Ⓒ Ⓓ		60 Ⓐ Ⓑ Ⓒ Ⓓ
16 Ⓐ Ⓑ Ⓒ Ⓓ		61 Ⓐ Ⓑ Ⓒ Ⓓ
17 Ⓐ Ⓑ Ⓒ Ⓓ		62 Ⓐ Ⓑ Ⓒ Ⓓ
18 Ⓐ Ⓑ Ⓒ Ⓓ		63 Ⓐ Ⓑ Ⓒ Ⓓ
19 Ⓐ Ⓑ Ⓒ Ⓓ		64 Ⓐ Ⓑ Ⓒ Ⓓ
20 Ⓐ Ⓑ Ⓒ Ⓓ		65 Ⓐ Ⓑ Ⓒ Ⓓ
21 Ⓐ Ⓑ Ⓒ Ⓓ		66 Ⓐ Ⓑ Ⓒ Ⓓ
22 Ⓐ Ⓑ Ⓒ Ⓓ		67 Ⓐ Ⓑ Ⓒ Ⓓ
23 Ⓐ Ⓑ Ⓒ Ⓓ		68 Ⓐ Ⓑ Ⓒ Ⓓ
24 Ⓐ Ⓑ Ⓒ Ⓓ		69 Ⓐ Ⓑ Ⓒ Ⓓ
25 Ⓐ Ⓑ Ⓒ Ⓓ		70 Ⓐ Ⓑ Ⓒ Ⓓ
26 Ⓐ Ⓑ Ⓒ Ⓓ		71 Ⓐ Ⓑ Ⓒ Ⓓ
27 Ⓐ Ⓑ Ⓒ Ⓓ		72 Ⓐ Ⓑ Ⓒ Ⓓ
28 Ⓐ Ⓑ Ⓒ Ⓓ		73 Ⓐ Ⓑ Ⓒ Ⓓ
29 Ⓐ Ⓑ Ⓒ Ⓓ		74 Ⓐ Ⓑ Ⓒ Ⓓ
30 Ⓐ Ⓑ Ⓒ Ⓓ		75 Ⓐ Ⓑ Ⓒ Ⓓ
31 Ⓐ Ⓑ Ⓒ Ⓓ		76 Ⓐ Ⓑ Ⓒ Ⓓ
32 Ⓐ Ⓑ Ⓒ Ⓓ		77 Ⓐ Ⓑ Ⓒ Ⓓ
33 Ⓐ Ⓑ Ⓒ Ⓓ		78 Ⓐ Ⓑ Ⓒ Ⓓ
34 Ⓐ Ⓑ Ⓒ Ⓓ		79 Ⓐ Ⓑ Ⓒ Ⓓ
35 Ⓐ Ⓑ Ⓒ Ⓓ		80 Ⓐ Ⓑ Ⓒ Ⓓ
36 Ⓐ Ⓑ Ⓒ Ⓓ		81 Ⓐ Ⓑ Ⓒ Ⓓ
37 Ⓐ Ⓑ Ⓒ Ⓓ		82 Ⓐ Ⓑ Ⓒ Ⓓ
38 Ⓐ Ⓑ Ⓒ Ⓓ		83 Ⓐ Ⓑ Ⓒ Ⓓ
39 Ⓐ Ⓑ Ⓒ Ⓓ		84 Ⓐ Ⓑ Ⓒ Ⓓ
40 Ⓐ Ⓑ Ⓒ Ⓓ		85 Ⓐ Ⓑ Ⓒ Ⓓ
41 Ⓐ Ⓑ Ⓒ Ⓓ		86 Ⓐ Ⓑ Ⓒ Ⓓ
42 Ⓐ Ⓑ Ⓒ Ⓓ		87 Ⓐ Ⓑ Ⓒ Ⓓ
43 Ⓐ Ⓑ Ⓒ Ⓓ		88 Ⓐ Ⓑ Ⓒ Ⓓ
44 Ⓐ Ⓑ Ⓒ Ⓓ		89 Ⓐ Ⓑ Ⓒ Ⓓ
45 Ⓐ Ⓑ Ⓒ Ⓓ		90 Ⓐ Ⓑ Ⓒ Ⓓ

Time: 2 hours

Selected-Response Questions

90 questions

1. Mrs. Carson has labels at various places in her first-grade classroom. For example, she has labels naming the light switch, whiteboard, clock, and calendar. What does this labeling convey about Mrs. Carson's knowledge about learning?

   A. She doesn't know that direct instruction works better than other methods for teaching vocabulary.
   B. She likes to motivate students by using posters.
   C. She understands the importance of environmental print.
   D. She is trying to teach her students the importance of labeling.

2. Using the language experience approach, Ms. Lawton begins her lesson by having students plant a seed in a pot. Next, using large chart paper, she asks students to help her write directions on how to plant a seed. Which statement below best describes the reason Ms. Lawton used this instructional technique?

   A. This approach allows students to use and apply vocabulary from speaking, listening, reading, and writing as they discuss and record their experiences.
   B. Using the chart paper with the students' words is an extremely effective technique to teach letter-sound correspondence.
   C. Ms. Lawton is modeling good listening skills for students to learn good listening habits.
   D. The classroom is in an urban area, and planting the seeds enables students to watch the plants' growth.

3. Mrs. Welch is reading a novel to her students, stopping to discuss the author's use of metaphors. Mrs. Welch writes the metaphor on the board and has the class discuss the image that it evokes. Which of the following best describes Mrs. Welch's goal?

   A. She is using a text to increase oral vocabulary.
   B. She is determining which metaphors make sense.
   C. She is using a mentor text to show students the author's craft.
   D. She is using genre study to show students the criteria.

4. Which of the following is an effective instruction technique for helping young children to develop concepts of print?

   A. Using decodable text when reading with students
   B. Showing students where a sentence begins and ends
   C. Asking literal questions to aid students in recall
   D. Clapping out syllables while reading

5. Mr. Benson wants to create a positive learning environment for the English Language Learners (ELLs) in his classroom. Which of the following is the best way for Mr. Benson to accomplish this?

   A. Send home a newsletter with reading tips for parents.
   B. Have the ELLs read on the computer and click on words to hear pronunciation.
   C. Use multicultural books for read-alouds.
   D. Give students books in their own language.

GO ON TO THE NEXT PAGE

6. Of the following words, which is the best to use in teaching structural analysis?

    A. *desert*

    B. *fair*

    C. *vacation*

    D. *unclearly*

7. Mrs. Little is assessing her kindergartners for phonemic awareness. Which statement below best describes one way she may do this?

    A. Show the words *bat, cat,* and *fat* and ask what letters these words end with.

    B. Show a bag with a letter "B" on it and have students fill the bag with pictures of words that begin with "B."

    C. Say the word *cat* and have the students segment the sounds.

    D. Give the students cards or pieces of paper with the letters "a," "b," "c," and "d" and have them put the letters in alphabetical order.

8. Which of the following groups of terms are often used synonymously to indicate letter-sound correspondence?

    A. Alphabetic principle, breaking the code, phonics

    B. Phonemic awareness, phonics, alphabetic principle

    C. Decoding, encoding, alphabetic principle

    D. Breaking the code, decoding, phonemic awareness

9. A first-grade teacher is assessing a child's oral reading by coding the errors and then analyzing to pinpoint reading goals for the student. Which of the following terms characterizes this informal assessment?

    A. Spelling inventory

    B. Oral language analysis

    C. Running record

    D. Context intervention

10. A fifth-grade teacher has noticed that a number of students do not comprehend some of their reading. He decides to work on developing their metacognitive skills. Which of the following best describes one technique the teacher can use?

    A. Have the students start asking themselves, "Does this make sense?"

    B. Break the reading down into smaller pieces of text and discuss.

    C. Check the students' oral reading to ensure that they are reading words correctly.

    D. Have the students read two pages, stop, and discuss the reading with a partner.

11. A first-grade teacher has determined that a number of her students are lacking in oral language. Their vocabulary is basic, such as the sentence "I fell on the black stuff and hurt my knee." Her past students would have stated, "I fell on the blacktop (or asphalt) and hurt my knee." Which of the following best explains why this may be a concern?

    A. Students who don't have a command of vocabulary are not as smart as students who do.

    B. The more oral language a student knows, the more this positively impacts reading comprehension.

    C. These students are not able to comprehend what the teacher is saying.

    D. The vocabulary building activities are taking time allotted for other parts of the curriculum.

12. Of the sentences below, which one would be considered the most likely to confuse an English Language Learner (ELL)?

  A. *In winter, bears hibernate and then wake up in the spring.*
  B. *Don't be upset; the kids are just pulling your leg.*
  C. *It couldn't have happened that soon.*
  D. *Water covers most of the Earth's surface.*

13. Students in a fifth-grade history class are reading a chapter on the causes of the Revolutionary War. Which of the following strategies is most likely to help the students remember and comprehend the various causes of the war?

  A. Having students write comments on sticky notes for later study
  B. Having students underline the most important details in each paragraph
  C. Aiding students in filling out a graphic organizer connecting important events
  D. Warning students that they need to remember details for a quiz

14. Use the terminology below to answer the question that follows:

  real-life events

  primary documents

  interviews

  outside author

The terminology listed above would most likely be used in teaching which of the following genres?

  A. Narrative
  B. Persuasive
  C. Autobiography
  D. Biography

15. Which of the following best describes how parents can help their child develop phonemic awareness?

  A. Show and read environmental print.
  B. Teach children the ABC song.
  C. Read rhyming stories and poems.
  D. Teach children letters and their corresponding sounds.

16. Mrs. Clark is administering a running record to one of her first-grade students. The principal reason she is doing this is

  A. to assess word identification skills and determine reading level.
  B. to find the cause of the student's lack of comprehension.
  C. to see if the student understands the text.
  D. to assess letter discrimination.

17. Mr. Harper reads aloud to his class daily. He chooses interesting books that are one to two years above his students' reading level. Which of the following best describes the main purpose for his reading selections?

  A. He needs to go above grade level to find interesting books.
  B. He has determined that the discussions about the higher-level books lead to deeper conversation.
  C. He wants his students to become familiar with oral vocabulary above their grade level.
  D. He wants to leave the on-level books for the students to read independently.

GO ON TO THE NEXT PAGE

18. Mr. Samuels' class is reading a historical fiction text. After each chapter, Mr. Samuels has his students write in their literacy journals about a particular aspect of the chapter, and asks them to include what they are thinking and feeling. Which of the following best explains the reason Mr. Samuels would assign these journal responses?

    A. He is interested in seeing whether the students' opinions are similar to his own.
    B. He wants students to think more about the events in the chapter to gain deeper understanding.
    C. He wants the students to stay engaged as he works with a group of students on skills work.
    D. He wants to assess students' ability to tell the events in chronological order.

19. Although he is able to identify words, a student reads very slowly and with numerous pauses. In which of the following aspects of reading does this student need help?

    A. Letter-sound correspondence
    B. Comprehension
    C. Self-monitoring
    D. Fluency

20. After reading a book that explains the layers of the rainforest, students are instructed to draw a diagram of the layers and label and explain the importance of each layer. Which of the following reasons best describes why the teacher would have the students create this diagram?

    A. To build the students' vocabulary
    B. To apply the reading-writing connection
    C. To provide opportunities for the students to write
    D. To help the students discover what they think

21. A teacher reads the following sentence: "After Mark came in from outdoors, there was mud on the floor." She then asks students to tell her what they think happened. Which of the following terms best describes what the teacher is asking her students to do?

    A. Predict
    B. Make connections
    C. Summarize
    D. Infer

22. A standardized test is evaluated for validity. Which term below best describes what this means?

    A. The test contains terms and concepts the students know.
    B. The test measures the skills and content that it states that it measures.
    C. The test will produce the same results in various populations.
    D. The test has been edited for any mechanical or grammatical errors.

23. A third-grade class is reading an informational text about Australia. A piece of the text states the following:

    Long ago, many Aboriginal peoples lived by hunting and gathering. Today, most of the Aboriginals live in towns.

Which of the following selections best describes the text structure of this sentence?

    A. Cause and effect
    B. Enumeration
    C. Compare and contrast
    D. Problem and solution

Use the following scenario to answer questions 24–26.

Mrs. Mackenzie, a fifth-grade teacher, has her students read the following passage. First, she activates prior knowledge on friendship by having the students fill out a semantic web. She then tells them that while reading, they should think about Sarah's attitude and behavior.

> Sarah was totally upset. Jasmine was to meet her exactly at 6:00 p.m. to go to the movies. Jasmine was always late. Maybe she would stop being friends with Jasmine. She was that mad and didn't want to miss the beginning of the movie she had begged her mom to see. Then, Jasmine's mom drove up and Jasmine jumped quickly out of the car. Sarah noticed a really big dent on the front of the car. Jasmine yelled, "Sorry I'm late. We had a fender-bender on the way here." Sarah smiled; she was just glad that Jasmine was not hurt. She was stupid to have been mad.

24. Of the questions below, which would make an effective inferential question regarding this text?

    A. How would you feel if your friend was late to go to the movies? Explain.

    B. Why was Jasmine late?

    C. How did Sarah feel at the beginning and end of the passage?

    D. Describe Sarah and Jasmine's friendship.

25. Why did Mrs. Mackenzie have students fill out a semantic web on friendship?

    A. To have the students state vocabulary words that might be in the text

    B. Comparing and contrasting the meaning of friendship relates to this text and aids in comprehension.

    C. Activating prior knowledge helps students make sense of the text by enabling them to connect what they already know to new information.

    D. To encourage students to treat their friends and classmates kindly

26. Why might the term *fender-bender* be confusing to English Language Learners (ELLs)?

    A. It is a euphemism.

    B. It is a contraction.

    C. It is a multisyllabic word.

    D. It is an idiom.

27. Miss Baker is working with her young students on vowel digraphs. She explains the phonics generalization that when two vowels are together the first vowel says its name. She shows and discusses this generalization by using the words *pail, steal, lied, boat,* and *bay*. She then shows a video that that has a song about this rule: "When two vowels go walking, the first one does the talking." The class practices the following words together: *hail, stay, feed, beat, pie,* and *toad*. After this practice, Miss Baker tells the students that she is giving them words that follow the rule, and asks them to work with partners to sort and say the following words: *beam, paid, coat, field, steed, hay, sail, head,* and *spray*.

Which of the following best critiques Miss Baker's lesson?

    A. She did an adequate job on the whole lesson to prepare her students for reading vowel digraphs.

    B. Her performance was excellent. She went over the phonics generalization and prepared well for the students' independent application.

    C. She has confused some of her content.

    D. She spent too much time on her teaching and not enough time in the students' application of the new content.

GO ON TO THE NEXT PAGE

28. A kindergarten teacher holds a pointer as she shares a big book with her students. She moves the pointer across the page as she reads. Which of the following best describes what the teacher is doing?

    A. Showing the names of letters
    B. Showing the directionality of reading
    C. Helping students to identify the words
    D. Pointing out print features

29. Which of the following is considered an effective teaching technique for English Language Learners (ELLs)?

    A. Ask questions that can be answered with a very short response.
    B. Speak in one-syllable words.
    C. Introduce students to grade-level words daily.
    D. Don't hold the students accountable for difficult work.

30. Which of the following terms best describes word pairs that have similar meaning?

    A. Synonyms
    B. Antonyms
    C. Homonyms
    D. Acronyms

31. Mrs. Silva has been focusing on getting her students to use Standard American English. She models it when speaking, reading, and writing. She sees improvement in the classroom discussions, but not on the playground. Which of the following selections best describes how Mrs. Silva should react to this?

    A. She should hold a discussion on the need to use Standard American English whenever speaking.
    B. She should correct the nonstandard use and have the students in question repeat their words using Standard American English.
    C. She should rely more on the reading and writing connection to help students make the transition to Standard American English more easily.
    D. She should not judge students' speech on the playground, but should continue to model Standard American English in the classroom.

32. A first-grade teacher is using the cloze sentence procedure in her classroom. She writes the following three sentences on the board with missing words:

    1. Samantha rode the _____ to school.
    2. Justin was so excited; he jumped _____ and down.
    3. Alex's pencil broke, and he had to _____ it.

She then reads the sentences with the students and asks them to fill in the blank in each sentence. Which of the following reflects the best reason the teacher is doing this exercise?

    A. To make sure the students are paying attention to the lesson
    B. To show the students sentence formation and the structure of the language
    C. To explicitly teach how context can be used to decode unknown words
    D. To make game-like learning to motivate the students

33. Miss Barker's fourth-grade-level group was about to read an informational article on the Mayan ruins in Mexico. Prior to reading, Miss Barker "walked" her group through the article by reading the headings and subheadings and discussing what each section of the article might contain. Which of the following best describes why Miss Barker is using this technique with her students?

  A. To give the students the information in case they don't read the text
  B. To allow the students to read the text with more speed
  C. To give the students a mental map of the information, allowing them to focus on key ideas in the text
  D. To make sure the students have explicit instruction on vocabulary prior to reading the text

34. A first grader writes the following two sentences.

  i lst mi bik yestrdae mom fond it n mi nabors yd

Which of the statements below best describes the first phonics instruction goal that the teacher should set for this student?

  A. Consonant blends and then understanding that "ay" makes the sound of long /a/ at the end of a word
  B. The initial and ending consonant phonemes
  C. That "er" spells the /er/ sound
  D. That all words contain vowels

35. Which of the following groups of signal words indicates a cause-and-effect text structure?

  A. *In order to, as a result, so that, therefore*
  B. *Also, then, furthermore, besides*
  C. *However, but, yet, despite*
  D. *To solve, it was recommended, now, this is a concern*

36. Which of the following words contains three phonemes?

  A. *oak*
  B. *duck*
  C. *possible*
  D. *plug*

37. Mr. Rich has his timer next to him as Tommy reads orally an instructional level passage that has been predetermined to have 312 words. Mr. Rich is using a rubric that scores how well Tommy uses expression as he reads. Which of the following best describes what Mr. Rich is assessing?

  A. Word accuracy
  B. Comprehension
  C. Inference skills
  D. Fluency

GO ON TO THE NEXT PAGE

Use the following scenario to answer questions 38–39.

At the beginning of the month, a third grader was given a spelling inventory. Five weeks later, a post-test was given to monitor progress. The chart below monitors the student's progress.

Spelling Word	Pre-Test	Post-Test
lifting	lifing	lifting
trapping	taping	traping
biking	bikeing	biking
dollar	doler	dolerr
fright	fite	frite
quack	kwak	kwack

38. In which of the given rules or areas has the student most improved?

    A. When a word has the consonant-vowel-consonant (CVC) pattern, double the last consonant and add an ending.

    B. When adding an ending to a consonant-vowel-consonant-silent "e" (CVCe) word, drop the "e" and add the ending.

    C. The long sound of /i/ can be spelled with "igh."

    D. The sounds of double consonants

39. Which word in this spelling inventory shows improvement with using a consonant digraph?

    A. *quack*

    B. *fright*

    C. *lifting*

    D. *trapping*

40. After looking over the reading material for one of her reading groups, Mrs. Temple realized that some of the vocabulary was very challenging for this group. She decided to explicitly teach four of the most difficult words prior to having the students read. Which of the following statements best explains why Mrs. Temple would pre-teach vocabulary?

    A. She is concerned that the difficult words will slow down the students' reading rate.

    B. She understands that the challenging vocabulary will probably frustrate the group.

    C. She understands that vocabulary is essential to comprehension.

    D. She wants the students to understand basic relationships among words.

41. Which of the following would best assess phonemic awareness in a student?

    A. Give the student a piece of paper with the letters "b," "t," and "d" written on it and ask him to pick out the letter "b."

    B. Say the word *duck* and ask the student to separate the sounds he hears in the word.

    C. Give the student a picture with a bed, a bird, and a table, and ask him to select the word that begins with the letter "t."

    D. Say the word *tip* and ask the student to write the letters for the sounds he hears.

42. In a kindergarten classroom, the teacher has assembled the students to contribute to the "morning message." She asks students to share news with the class, and then she writes this information on the morning message chart. Which of the following best explains why this technique is being used in this classroom?

    A. To build a community in the classroom

    B. To increase students' listening skills

    C. To increase students' awareness that text is speech written down

    D. To have students learn new words as the teacher writes

43. Julio can sound out the words in his instructional level text, but his method is slow and laborious. Although he is reading on grade level, his teacher is concerned. Which of the following best describes why a concern is valid?

   A. The slow reading could indicate that Julio is not at the right reading level.

   B. Julio needs some targeted phonics lessons to ensure that he knows essential sounds.

   C. The text is too easy for him.

   D. Fluency is a bridge to comprehending a text, and Julio may not understand what he is reading because he is distracted by decoding the text.

44. Jayden reads rapidly and with accuracy. However, his teacher has noticed through conversation that Jayden has limited comprehension about the text he has read. Which of the following would be best to address this issue?

   A. Metacognitive strategies

   B. Fluency techniques

   C. Structural analysis

   D. Look-back strategies

45. While monitoring Ava's progress in reading, her first-grade teacher has noticed that Ava does not read words accurately or with any expression. Which of the following would most effectively enable the teacher to help Ava progress?

   A. Structural analysis and affix definitions

   B. The introduction of various genres for reading and motivation

   C. Decoding strategies and sight word recognition

   D. Metacognitive comprehension strategies

46. Which of the following words contains an open syllable?

   A. *baker*

   B. *mantel*

   C. *carton*

   D. *mention*

47. Mr. Stanley has given his students an interest inventory with the following questions:

   1. What is your favorite sport?

   2. What is your favorite animal?

   3. Is there a hobby you have or would like to have? Describe it.

   4. What would you like to learn?

Which of the following selections best describes how Mr. Stanley could use the gathered information in his reading instruction?

   A. To choose appropriate-level text

   B. To be attentive to the students' cultural backgrounds

   C. To create writing activities to support reading

   D. To motivate reading, taking into account student interests when he chooses books

GO ON TO THE NEXT PAGE

48. A teacher is explicitly teaching his class syllabication rules, such as when two consonants are together and a vowel comes before and after the pair of consonants, the word is divided between the two consonants. For example: *but/ton* and *lit/ter*. Which of the following best explains why the teacher feels this is important enough to be taught?

    A.   Breaking words into syllables makes it easier for students to read phoneme by phoneme.

    B.   Understanding syllabication aids students in comprehension of the text.

    C.   Knowing how to break words into syllables can help readers identify and pronounce a word through use of accented and unaccented syllables.

    D.   Using word parts gives students a deeper meaning of concepts in the text.

49. A principal is concerned that his students are not reading up to national level. He decides to assess them in reading to find out. Which of the following types of standardized tests should he use?

    A.   Norm-referenced

    B.   Percentile-referenced

    C.   Criterion-referenced

    D.   Percentage-referenced

50. The grammatical function of a word—what a word does as a unit of language—often depends on the placement of the word in a sentence. For example, a word may be a subject in one sentence and a direct object in another. Which sentence below best shows *father* as the subject of the sentence?

    A.   The ice cream cone belonged to the father.

    B.   The son ate his father's ice cream cone.

    C.   The father ate his son's ice cream cone.

    D.   The father's ice cream cone was given to the son.

51. Which of the following best describes the syllabication rule for digraphs and diphthongs?

    A.   Digraphs and diphthongs are always separated.

    B.   Digraphs are not separated; diphthongs are.

    C.   Digraphs and diphthongs are never separated.

    D.   Digraphs are separated; diphthongs are not.

52. A new kindergarten student, Joshua, arrived midyear. The teacher is concerned because Joshua has been in class for more than 3 weeks, but he never voluntarily contributes to classroom conversations, and when called upon, he gives short static answers. The teacher has started taking anecdotal notes regarding Joshua's speech in order to monitor his progress. Which of the following would be most effective for the teacher to do at this point?

    A.   Since Joshua is new, give him more time with the class to see if he is just shy.

    B.   Provide more opportunities for Joshua to speak, and encourage him to expand on what he is saying.

    C.   Assume that Joshua's static speech is developmental and will improve by the year's end.

    D.   Model good speech patterns for Joshua to emulate.

53. Mrs. Julio has created a bulletin board with labeled areas: poetry, mystery, nonfiction, fable, myth, legend, and tall tale. After she read a book of poems to the class, she wrote the name of the book on an index card and placed the card under "poetry" on the board, and explained the structure of the poems. She is planning on doing this with all the book types on the board. Which of the following best explains why she is doing this?

    A.   She wants to hold herself accountable for doing read-alouds to her class.

    B.   She wants to make sure that the students are getting a variety of topics as she reads to them.

    C.   She wants to motivate her students as they watch the bulletin board fill up.

    D.   She understands that knowing a variety of text genres and how they are structured aids in comprehension.

54. An analysis of the errors on a running record shows that a student had missed numerous multisyllabic words, some of which he should have been familiar with. Which of the following instructional techniques would be best to use with this student?

    A. Teach the student to use metacognitive strategies to glean what is being said.

    B. Have the student create a personal dictionary with the multisyllabic words.

    C. Teach the student structural analysis to separate words into smaller, familiar parts.

    D. Have the student slow down and read each phoneme, then blend the word.

55. A second-grade teacher is working with the following pairs of words: *fare-fair, high-hi, ate-eight, blue-blew,* and *dear-deer.* Students are having difficulty differentiating the meanings of these words. Which of the following approaches would be best for the teacher to employ?

    A. Discuss the meaning of homonyms, sometimes called homophones, and have students draw a picture conveying the meaning of each word in the pair.

    B. Discuss the meaning of antonyms and have students draw a picture conveying the meaning of each word in the pair.

    C. Discuss the meaning of homographs and have students draw a picture conveying the meaning of each word in the pair.

    D. Discuss the meaning of synonyms and have students draw a picture conveying the meaning of each word in the pair.

56. Mrs. Smith is reading a book to her students. She makes sure to stop and show the pictures and explain any unusual vocabulary. Every few pages, she pauses to discuss concepts in the book with the students. What is the teacher's main reason for doing this?

    A. She is using the learning experience approach in order to broaden vocabulary.

    B. She is modeling book handling skills.

    C. She is fostering active engagement in reading, making sure the students understand the vocabulary and concepts.

    D. She is taking these steps to select difficult vocabulary that should be explicitly taught.

57. Which student below is in most need of reading intervention?

    A. A kindergarten student who is not yet phonemically aware

    B. A third-grade student who is struggling with structural analysis

    C. A fourth-grade student who reads accurately but doesn't comprehend difficult concepts

    D. A second-grade student who is working on short vowel sounds

Use the following second-grade-level Informal Reading Inventory (IRI) section to answer questions 58–59.

Word List	The Passage
ball	Mark was playing ball with his little sister, Kara. The ball went into the street. Kara ran after the ball. Mark yelled, "Stop!" He saw a car was coming. Kara stopped. Mark hugged her, and after the car went by he got the ball.
little	
street	
sister	
after	

58. Katrina, a second grader, read the word list orally, pronouncing all words accurately. However, when she read the passage, she missed the words *was* and *went* and pronounced the word *yelled* as *yield.* Which of the following gives the best synopsis of Katrina's reading skills?

    A. Katrina is getting all phonetically regular words correct.

    B. Katrina is reading too fast and therefore misses words she should know.

    C. Katrina appears to be strong in phonics but does not seem to use context to help her in word identification.

    D. Katrina's results indicate a problem with "r"-controlled vowels.

GO ON TO THE NEXT PAGE

59. Andy, a first grader, missed the words *street* and *sister* in the word list, yet he read the passage orally with complete accuracy. Which of the following statements gives the best synopsis of Andy's reading skills?

    A. Andy appears to use context cues to help him in word identification.

    B. Andy is experiencing problems reading multisyllabic words.

    C. Andy is strong in phonics, as evidenced by his getting most words in the word list correct.

    D. Andy's comprehension is affected by his lack of decoding skills.

60. The comprehension questions given in the Informal Reading Inventory after the passage is read are identified as literal, inferential, or evaluative. This allows the teacher to check for weaknesses in particular areas. Which of the following comprehension questions would be identified as an inferential question?

    A. Whom is Mark playing with?

    B. How would you describe Mark as a good big brother?

    C. Is Mark a good ball player?

    D. Where did the ball go?

61. Which of the following describes the grammatical function of a predicate?

    A. It contains a preposition and a descriptive word.

    B. It contains an adverb.

    C. It contains a verb and states something about the subject.

    D. It is an indirect object.

62. Mrs. Alves is starting to teach her class an instructional unit on writing summaries. She begins by discussing the difference between important and interesting. She explains that only important ideas are included in a summary. She then puts a passage on the interactive whiteboard and circles important information. As she circles, she explains to the students why the information is important to the text. What technique is Mrs. Alves using in this scenario?

    A. She is using systematic, explicit instruction.

    B. She is engaging the students in the text.

    C. She is using systematic, implicit instruction.

    D. She is monitoring the students' reading comprehension.

63. The fourth-grade teachers at North Elementary School have decided to group students according to their reading instruction areas of need. As one indicator of need, teachers use scores from the students' last standardized reading test. Which of the following standardized test results will the teachers use?

    A. Norm-referenced

    B. Percentile-referenced

    C. Validity-referenced

    D. Criterion-referenced

64. A teacher has noticed that one of her second-grade students is very quiet and soft-spoken. The student actively participates in class activities, such as morning circle, and performs adequately, with follow-through. But when he speaks, he uses short, simple sentences; his writing mirrors his speech. Which of the following best describes the possible root of the student's lagging in these areas?

    A. The student lacks phonemic awareness.

    B. The student's expressive language is below the teacher's expectations at his developmental level.

    C. The student's receptive language is below the teacher's expectations at his developmental level.

    D. The student's telegraphic speech needs to be further developed.

Use the following information to answer questions 65–67.

Mr. Michaels, a fourth-grade teacher, is teaching a unit on Lewis and Clark's expedition and its influence on westward expansion. He begins the unit with a semantic web on explorers. He then builds background on what the Northwest Territory was like in the early 1800s, shares a map outlining Lewis and Clark's journey, and pinpoints the various rivers the expedition followed. After explicitly teaching some of the more difficult vocabulary, Mr. Michaels has the students read with a partner. They are directed to stop at three specific places in the text and explain to each other what they have just read. He also tells them to think about how Lewis and Clark's work may have encouraged settlers to move farther west.

65. Which of the following best describes the purpose of using a semantic web in this lesson?

   A.   The semantic web will be placed on a bulletin board so that students can refer back to it.
   B.   Using a semantic web to activate prior knowledge aids students in comprehension, as it allows them to connect new information to known information.
   C.   The semantic web helps explain concepts about the expedition.
   D.   It is effective practice to use a semantic web to summarize important information in the reading.

66. Classroom time is limited and must be used wisely. Which of the following best explains why Mr. Michaels is having students stop and talk instead of just assigning independent silent reading?

   A.   The activity helps those students who cannot read the text independently.
   B.   The teacher understands that the time used for dialogue about text topics helps the lesson go faster.
   C.   The teacher understands that interacting with the text is an effective practice, enabling students to gain broader and deeper understanding of what they have read.
   D.   The teacher wants to walk around and hear the students' dialogue so that he can correct any misconceptions they may have.

67. The students are going to read a lot of information about Lewis and Clark's expedition and discoveries. Why does Mr. Michaels first teach the students about the American West in the 1800s and Lewis and Clark's mapping of rivers and territory?

   A.   Mr. Michaels realizes that this unit contains some complicated concepts, and students will need scaffolding in order to fully comprehend the text they will be reading.
   B.   Mr. Michaels is having the students actively participate in learning background knowledge.
   C.   Mr. Michaels wants to ensure that his students know this information because some of the students are very low-level readers and cannot sufficiently understand the text.
   D.   Mr. Michaels wants to ensure that his students will be able to infer the conceptual relationships in the text.

68. In adherence with the third-grade curriculum and standards, the teacher wants to have her students work on recognizing differences. Which of the following text structures would be the best for her to use in a lesson on this skill?

   A.   Compare and contrast
   B.   Description
   C.   Chronological
   D.   Persuasive

GO ON TO THE NEXT PAGE

69. A teacher has her first position teaching inner city students. The students speak in their cultural dialect, which doesn't always mimic Standard American English. Which of the following best describes how the teacher should react to this speech pattern?

    A. Model Standard American English and correct students when they speak in their cultural dialect.

    B. Explicitly teach oral language conventions by having students pronounce words after the teacher says them.

    C. Model the rules of Standard American English but remain respectful of the cultural dialect.

    D. Model the rules of Standard American English and encourage students to use it, then engage students by having them tape record themselves speaking, and listen to see if they have said words correctly.

70. The kindergarten teacher has gathered her group on the rug and is reading a *Jack and the Beanstalk* big book to the class. She has told the students to watch the pointer carefully as she reads; she explains that she will point to each word and then read it. What is the teacher's main purpose in conducting this activity?

    A. To show children the different parts of the book so as to review the story's plot

    B. To explicitly teach beginning phonemes

    C. To reinforce one-to-one word correspondence in reading

    D. To explicitly teach book handling skills

71. The school system has just begun using a new standardized reading test for fourth-grade students. The curriculum specialist had mentioned specifically that this test has a high reliability rating. Which of the following best describes what that means?

    A. A test is deemed reliable if the test questions have been checked for accuracy.

    B. A test is deemed reliable if it has been used for over a 3-year period.

    C. A test is deemed reliable if it would produce the same results with a different set of people in a different setting.

    D. A test is deemed reliable if it measures what it is supposed to measure.

72. After giving his class a spelling inventory and analyzing students' writing samples, a teacher has determined that the students have different needs in order to be successful in encoding. Which of the following selections best describes what instructional technique this teacher should employ to ensure optimal growth for all of his students?

    A. The teacher should decide which skills are needed by most students and just teach those particular skills.

    B. Students should be placed in flexible groups with other students who need the same skills.

    C. The teacher should continue to model excellent spelling and writing skills.

    D. The teacher should place students in peer conferencing groups, enabling them to support each other in their encoding.

73. A teacher writes the following on the whiteboard: "My boots are brown with a black zipper. The zipper is hard to pull up." She then reads the sentence and purposely stops at *zipper,* saying, "I don't know that word. It begins with a 'z' so must begin with the /z/ sound. I'll have to read on to see if I can get an idea of what the word means from the next sentence." She then reads "The /z/ is hard to pull up," after which she adds, "Oh, I think I know it; it must be *zipper* because it's on a boot and hard to pull up. Let me check the word to see. I'll try to chunk the word." She then covers the "per" part of the word and says, "Yes, look, here's the word *zip,* so it is *zipper.*" The teacher then reads the two sentences correctly and says, "Yes, that makes sense." Which of the following best describes what the teacher is doing?

    A. She is teaching her students the word *zipper*.

    B. She is modeling the chunking strategy for word identification.

    C. She is showing students that what they are reading needs to make sense.

    D. She is modeling that multiple strategies may be used for word identification.

Use the following to answer questions 74–75.

A fifth-grade class is reading an article on bullying titled "Five Ways to Avoid Bullying." The text begins with a list of behaviors that a bully may exhibit, and tips on how to identify bullying behavior. The text then discusses how to avoid bullying by stating the five strategies described in the title and explaining each one. Finally, it includes a paragraph summarizing the importance of avoiding bullying. The teacher hands the students the text and asks them to read it. After they do so, the teacher has the students re-read it and fill in a graphic organizer, and then they discuss the article as a class. Although the students do well with the graphic organizer, the teacher thinks they still do not really understood how to identify a bully.

74. Which of the following best describes how the teacher might have better prepared students to understand the behaviors of a bully?

    A.   Teach the students the behaviors of bullying before reading.
    B.   Discuss with the students how this article may have been written by someone who had been bullied.
    C.   Activate prior knowledge on bullying behaviors.
    D.   Tell students to read for information on how to avoid bullies.

75. What is the main type of text structure the author likely used in this article?

    A.   Problem-solution
    B.   Enumeration
    C.   Cause-and-effect
    D.   Descriptive

76. A teacher reviewing scores on a standardized test notices that one student has scored in the 97th percentile in reading comprehension. Which of the selections below best explains what this score tells her?

    A.   The student is weak in comprehension, as he received a score of 97 and there were 202 questions on the exam.
    B.   The student is extremely strong in reading comprehension because he got 97 out of 100 questions correct.
    C.   The student is average in reading comprehension, as the normal curve shows that the majority of students score in this range.
    D.   The student is extremely strong in reading comprehension because he scored higher than 97% of the students who took this exam.

77. A teacher is working with his intermediate-grade students on the following roots and their meanings: *tri* (three), *port* (carry), *later* (side), and *infra* (below). Which of the following best describes why the teacher would work with these unusual word parts?

    A.   The teacher understands that teaching students to pronounce chunked pieces of a word will aid them in the pronunciation of the whole word.
    B.   The teacher understands that knowing root words allows students to understand multiple words when they use structural analysis techniques to approach unknown words.
    C.   The teacher understands that knowing these roots will aid students in dividing syllables and placing accents for word pronunciation.
    D.   The teacher understands the important influence Latin has had on the English language, and she wants her students to learn Latin.

78. Mrs. Thomas is preparing to read a fable to her class. Which of the following best describes a fable?

    A.   A story that may be based on fact
    B.   A story involving occurrences or creatures that do not exist
    C.   A story involving some sort of wrongdoing
    D.   An imaginary short story that has a moral

GO ON TO THE NEXT PAGE

79. The teacher is previewing a text to check for vocabulary that should be pre-taught. She reads the following paragraph:

    > Mark was being introspective as he hastened to the bus. If he were late for work, he would be terminated. That would be a catastrophe, as he needed the money. Actually, he hated his job, so maybe getting fired wouldn't be so bad after all.

    The teacher then decides to teach one of the words. Which of the following vocabulary words should she select for pre-teaching?

    A. *introspective*
    B. *hastened*
    C. *terminated*
    D. *catastrophe*

80. Which of the following reading modes will best increase student fluency?

    A. Silent reading
    B. Popcorn reading
    C. Choral reading
    D. Partner reading

81. Which of the following groups of words demonstrates that different letters and letter combinations can represent the same phoneme?

    A. *know, gnu, now*
    B. *through, though, thus*
    C. *table, cable, fable*
    D. *can't, didn't, shouldn't*

82. As Mrs. Sullivan works with her group of kindergarten students, she holds up the letter "P." She says, "Boys and girls, look carefully at this letter. It is the letter 'P.' Can you say the letter 'P'?" She draws the letter "P" on the board in both uppercase and lowercase, and once again says, "This is the letter 'P,'" asking the students to repeat the letter. She then holds up the letters "H," "J," and "P" and asks students to pick out the letter "P." Which of the following best describes the purpose of this lesson?

    A. It is explicit instruction of letter-sound correspondence.
    B. It is implicit instruction of letter-sound correspondence.
    C. It is explicit instruction of letter recognition.
    D. It is implicit instruction of letter recognition.

83. Which of the following describes components of close reading?

    A. Activating prior knowledge and building background
    B. Analyzing short pieces of text for deeper meaning
    C. Pre-teaching vocabulary and examination of word meanings
    D. Activating prior knowledge and re-reading

84. Students are reading a coming-of-age novel in Mrs. Stark's sixth-grade class. She is having them respond to the reading by writing about the changes the main character undergoes. Which of the following best describes the main purpose of this reader response?

    A. To use writing as a vehicle to support the students' reading comprehension
    B. To get students to analyze the plot of the story
    C. To enable students to understand how their lives may parallel the main character's life
    D. To keep the students engaged as she works with another group

85. A teacher is preparing to read a picture book to a student. Before she begins reading, she asks the student to point to a letter, a word, the first sentence on the page, and the last sentence on the page. Which of the following best describes what the teacher is assessing?

   A.   The structure of a sentence
   B.   Directionality
   C.   Letter identification
   D.   Print awareness

86. Which of the following would NOT be recommended for the teacher of a relatively new English Language Learner (ELL)?

   A.   Speak slowly so that students can hear your pronunciation.
   B.   Ask questions that force the ELL student to use a lot of oral language in his responses.
   C.   Offer the student multiple exposures to the same word.
   D.   Use rebuses to supplement written directions.

87. A fourth-grade teacher is trying to improve the fluency of some of the students in her classroom. She has the group of students reading a story in which each of them has been assigned a character. The students are to read the dialogue as if they were the character. Which of the following best describes the technique being used?

   A.   Readers' Theater
   B.   Retelling
   C.   Writing their own story
   D.   Puppet show using dialogue from the book

88. Mr. Everett assembles his class on the rug and previews a text. He is careful to point out the graphics and diagrams in the book and discusses what they show or explain. Which of the following best describes Mr. Everett's reason for doing this?

   A.   He has noticed that his students are ignoring these parts of the text and wants to highlight their importance.
   B.   He wants his students to read the text with greater speed and not get bogged down with the information on the graphics and diagrams.
   C.   He understands that graphics and diagrams support the information in the text and that analyzing these can enhance comprehension.
   D.   He is using the graphics and diagrams to show students how to find important vocabulary.

89. Which of the following correctly lists the four components of fluency?

   A.   Appropriate rate, automaticity, and pragmatics
   B.   Accuracy, appropriate rate, automaticity, and prosody
   C.   Accuracy, appropriate rate, automaticity, and pragmatics
   D.   Syntax, appropriate rate, automaticity, and semantics

90. A classroom teacher is selecting new multicultural literature for her classroom. As she looks at the possibilities, she focuses on the roles of each book's characters and its illustrator's portrayal of the culture depicted in the book. Which of the following best describes why the teacher is looking so analytically at these books?

   A.   The teacher wants to make sure that the books are engaging and contain enriching vocabulary.
   B.   The teacher wants to make sure that the stories and phrases in the books are written in Standard American English.
   C.   The teacher is determined to make sure that the literature authentically portrays its subject's culture.
   D.   The teacher wants to determine whether the pictures match what the text is saying so that her students can use these pictures to aid their word identification.

GO ON TO THE NEXT PAGE

Constructed-Response Questions

3 questions

Note: The Praxis Study Companion Teaching Reading (5204) provides one essay example and gives a suggested time of 10 minutes to answer the question. As recommended in Chapter 12, 10–15 minutes would be the best timing for each of the constructed-response questions.

Constructed-Response Question #1

Luke read the following passage to his teacher as she coded his oral reading. The plain print in the box below shows what was written in the text. The bold type above the plain print shows what Luke read orally. Look carefully at the following reading record and answer the questions that follow.

---

                    wait

Jake was <u>waiting</u> for his friends. They were going to the new park to play. Jake was

exkite   **clim**

<u>excited</u> because the new park has all these bars that he and his friends could <u>climb</u>.

                        pret

Last time they went, they made up a game and <u>pretended</u> the ground was a swamp. If

     took   **took**

anyone <u>touched</u> the swamp, they got bitten by a fish. No one wanted to <u>touch</u> the ground.

     go

They were <u>going</u> to go play again!

Coding: Substitution (error) has what student said above underlined word.

Analyze the above miscues. Using evidence from the teacher's coding, state one strength that Luke has as a reader and one weakness. State a learning goal for Luke and how you might instruct him to attain that goal.

Constructed-Response Question #2

Scenario:

The fourth-grade teachers have decided to include a bit of research in a unit on authors' study. They have selected the authors. They have determined that students will work in collaborative groups. The goal is to include the following: collaborative learning, authors' biographies, book reviews, and technology.

Task:

- Briefly describe the instructional organization and materials that would allow the teachers to meet these goals. Include how the materials should be selected.
- Briefly describe how technology would be incorporated into this unit of study, and how this supports the students' reading growth.

Constructed-Response Question #3

Briefly explain the three cueing systems and the role they play in reading development.

Answer Key

1. C	19. D	37. D	55. A	73. D
2. A	20. B	38. B	56. C	74. C
3. C	21. D	39. A	57. D	75. B
4. B	22. B	40. C	58. C	76. D
5. C	23. C	41. B	59. A	77. B
6. D	24. D	42. C	60. B	78. D
7. C	25. C	43. D	61. C	79. A
8. A	26. D	44. A	62. A	80. C
9. C	27. C	45. C	63. D	81. A
10. A	28. B	46. A	64. B	82. C
11. B	29. A	47. D	65. B	83. B
12. B	30. A	48. C	66. C	84. A
13. C	31. D	49. A	67. A	85. D
14. D	32. C	50. C	68. A	86. B
15. C	33. C	51. C	69. C	87. A
16. A	34. D	52. B	70. C	88. C
17. C	35. A	53. D	71. C	89. B
18. B	36. B	54. C	72. B	90. C

Answer Explanations

Selected-Response Answers

1. **C.** She understands the importance of environmental print, choice C. Choice A is incorrect because we don't know Mrs. Carson's stance on direct instruction of vocabulary. Choice B is incorrect because this scenario discusses labeling classroom items, not posters. She is not trying to teach the importance of labeling, choice D.

2. **A.** This approach allows students to use and apply vocabulary from speaking, listening, reading, and writing as they discuss and record their experiences, choice A. Choice B is incorrect; the focus of this lesson is not teaching phonics, and we know that explicit phonics instruction is most effective. While Ms. Lawton may be modeling good listening skills, choice C, this is not the best reason for this instructional technique, as the teacher should model good listening skills in every lesson. Choice D is incorrect; watching the seeds grow is not the focus of this instruction.

3. **C.** Mrs. Welch is using a mentor text to show students the author's craft, choice C. By using the book, Mrs. Welch is fostering the reading and writing connection and using a mentor text with metaphors as a model. Choice A, using a text to increase oral vocabulary, is incorrect; there is no indication of the level of vocabulary in the novel. Choice B, determining which metaphors make sense, is incorrect; the students are discussing the images that the metaphors evoke, not whether the metaphors make sense. Choice D, using a genre study to show students the criteria, is incorrect; just one book is being discussed, not multiple books from one genre.

4. **B.** The ability to identify where a sentence begins and ends, choice B, is part of the concepts of print. Choices A, C, and D are not considered concepts of print.

5. **C.** Using multicultural books for read-alouds will help create a positive learning environment for ELLs, choice C. The key words in this question are "positive learning environment," and it is essential to help

English Language Learners to see themselves in books. Choice A, sending a newsletter home with reading tips, will not necessarily affect the classroom environment. Choice B, reading on the computer and clicking on words to hear pronunciation, could help the ELLs, but it doesn't affect the learning environment. Choice D, giving students books in their own language, is not helpful, as this could isolate the ELL students from their peers.

6. **D.** Of the words listed, *unclearly,* choice D, would be best to use in teaching structural analysis. Structural analysis entails the ability to analyze parts of words to determine meaning. *Unclearly* has a prefix that means "not" and a suffix that means "in a way of." From this, the meaning can be determined as literally "not in the way of being clear." Choices A, B, and C do not contain smaller structures with meaning.

7. **C.** One way Mrs. Little can assess her kindergartners' phonemic awareness is to say the word *cat* and have the students segment the sounds, choice C. Phonemic awareness involves only sounds, not letters. Choices A, B, and D all involve letters.

8. **A.** The terms *alphabetic principle, breaking the code,* and *phonics* are often used synonymously to indicate letter-sound correspondence, choice A. Choice B is incorrect, as it includes *phonemic awareness,* which covers only sounds. Choice C is incorrect, as it includes *decoding* and *encoding,* which do refer to letter-sound correspondence, but are processes, not synonymous terminology; decoding is reading the sounds, and encoding is writing the sounds. Choice D also includes *decoding* and *phonemic awareness,* making it incorrect.

9. **C.** The informal assessment described here is a running record, choice C. A running record is a type of miscue analysis. The teacher analyzes the child's reading behaviors in order to determine what the child is doing correctly and incorrectly. Choices A, B, and D do not include a child reading orally to a teacher.

10. **A.** The teacher can have the students ask themselves, "Does this make sense?" (choice A). This technique fosters students' ability to self-monitor their own comprehension. Metacognition is "thinking about thinking," meaning that students need to think about what they understand. Choices B, C, and D may all help with comprehension in some way, but they are not metacognitive techniques.

11. **B.** The more oral language a student knows, the more this positively impacts reading comprehension, choice B. If children have a large oral vocabulary, they are more likely, when reading, to encounter words they already know, giving them a deeper understanding. Choice A is incorrect, as lack of exposure to vocabulary building experiences is often the culprit. Choice C, students' inability to comprehend what the teacher is saying, is not evidenced in the scenario. Choice D is incorrect, as vocabulary building activities can and should be incorporated in all areas of the curriculum.

12. **B.** Choice B, *Don't be upset; the kids are just pulling your leg,* contains an idiom, a saying that does not have a literal meaning, but rather a definition of its own. In this case, *pulling your leg* means teasing, not the physical pulling of a leg. Idioms can be confusing to ELLs. Choice C is incorrect, as there are no confusing words. Choices A and D are incorrect, as the terms are straightforward, although they do contain some content vocabulary (*hibernate* and *Earth's surface*).

13. **C.** Aiding students in filling out a graphic organizer connecting important events, choice C, is most likely to help students remember and comprehend the various causes of the Revolutionary War. This choice allows discussion and support as students identify these causes. Choice A, writing comments on sticky notes for later study, may help students recall the information, but it doesn't aid with understanding the causes. Choice B, underlining details, does not allow for processing the information learned. Choice D, warning students they need to remember details for a quiz, again does not support understanding, only literal facts.

14. **D.** This terminology would most likely be used when teaching about the biography genre, choice D. Choice A, narrative, would not use interviews or an outside author. Choice B, persuasive, would likely use emotive terms and testimonials, not the terminology listed. Choice C would not allow for an outside author, as an autobiography is written by the person whose life is being recorded.

15. **C.** Reading rhyming stories and poems, choice C, can help children develop phonemic awareness; it allows children to hear words that sound alike, and to begin distinguishing words that sound alike from words that do not rhyme. Choice A, showing and reading environmental print, would include reading sight words or symbols, but phonemic awareness entails only sounds, not letters. Choice B, teaching children the ABC

song, does not include sounds of letters, and phonemic awareness is the ability to hear, isolate, and manipulate individual speech sounds. Choice D, teaching children letters and the corresponding letter sounds, involves phonics, not phonemic awareness.

16. **A.** Mrs. Clark is administering a running record to assess word identification skills and determine reading level, choice A. Choices B and C are incorrect, as a running record is not used to assess reading comprehension. Choice D, to assess letter discrimination, is incorrect, as reading text does not necessarily measure letter discrimination skills.

17. **C.** He wants his students to become familiar with oral vocabulary above their grade level, choice C. Listening is a receptive component of gaining vocabulary, and hearing higher-level vocabulary will help prepare students to understand these words when reading. Choice A is incorrect; there are interesting books at all levels. Choice B is incorrect, as there is no evidence to support that the discussions about the higher-level books lead to deeper conversation. Choice D is incorrect, as there are numerous books on different levels.

18. **B.** Mr. Samuels assigns journal responses because he wants students to think more about the events in the chapter for deeper understanding, choice B. Choices A, wanting to know if the students' opinions agree with his own, and C, keeping the students engaged as he works with a group of students on skills work, might be true, but neither is the best answer. Choice D, wanting to assess students' ability to tell events in order, can be eliminated, as Mr. Samuels is asking the students to explain what they are thinking and feeling about a particular issue, not to recall events in order.

19. **D.** This student needs help in fluency, choice D. Fluency includes reading rate, automaticity, accuracy, and prosody (expression). The student is reading slowly and with pauses, which indicates he needs help with fluency. There is no basis for choice A, letter-sound correspondence, as the student is able to identify words. Choice B is incorrect, as there is nothing stated about comprehension. Choice C is incorrect, as the pauses in the child's reading may indicate that he is self-monitoring.

20. **B.** Making a diagram of the layers of the rainforest and labeling and explaining the importance of each layer applies the reading and writing connection, choice B. Research has shown that when students write about what they have learned, they think about the material, deepening their understanding. Choice A is incorrect; although the students may be learning new words, building vocabulary is not the best reason to create a diagram and explain the importance of each layer. Choices C, providing an opportunity for students to write, and D, helping students discover what they think, are possible additional benefits, but these are not the focus of the assignment.

21. **D.** The teacher is asking her students to infer, choice D. When readers derive clues from a text and think about what they know, they are using inferential comprehension skills to determine what the author is saying. Predicting, choice A, also utilizes inferential comprehension—but to determine what will happen next, not what just happened. Choice B, making connections, was not something the teacher required, although students may have thought about a time when they brought mud into their home. Students were not asked to summarize, choice C.

22. **B.** A valid standardized test measures the skills and content it states that it measures, choice B. Choice A, contains terms and concepts students know, would not make the test valid, but it would most likely characterize a criterion-referenced test. Choice C, producing the same results in various populations, is a measure of reliability, not validity. Choice D, edited for any mechanical and grammatical errors, should be done for any test—standardized or informal.

23. **C.** This text selection has a compare and contrast text structure, choice C. Choice A, cause and effect, is not covered in this text. Choice B, enumeration, is a list within a text, and is not shown here. Finally, the text does not state a problem and solution, choice D.

24. **D.** Choice D (Describe Sarah and Jasmine's friendship) is an effective inferential question about this text. This question is inferential because it encourages the students to think outside the scope of the passage. There is enough information in the text—Sarah being upset, frustrated that Jasmine was always late, glad that Jasmine was okay—to infer and describe their friendship. Choice A (How would you feel if your friend was late to go to the movies? Explain.) is incorrect, as it is a beyond-the-text question and can be answered

without reading the passage. Choices B (Why was Jasmine late?) and C (How did Sarah feel at the beginning and end of the passage?) are literal questions. Choice B's answer is right there: Jasmine was in a fender-bender. Choice C, how Sarah felt in the beginning and end, is also right in the text, although it is a "think and search" question, as the full answer is found in two places: She was upset; she was glad.

25. **C.** Mrs. Mackenzie had students fill out a semantic web on friendship because activating prior knowledge helps students make sense of the text by enabling them to connect what they know to new information, choice C. A semantic web allows students to record what they know about a topic, helping them make connections to new information. Choice A, stating vocabulary that is in the text, is incorrect, as this cannot be guaranteed. Choice B, comparing and contrasting, is incorrect, as Mrs. Mackenzie did not request it. Choice D, encouraging kindness in the classroom, sounds lovely, but was not the purpose of this semantic web.

26. **D.** It is an idiom. Choices A, B, and C may be confusing to ELLs, but the term *fender-bender* may be confusing because it is an idiom. An idiom is a term that means something else than what it states literally. *Fender-bender* means a minor collision between two vehicles; no one necessarily bends a fender.

27. **C.** She has confused some of her content, choice C. Miss Baker correctly states the phonics generalization that when two vowels are together the first one says its name. However, some vowel patterns are phonetically irregular, and she has included phonetically irregular words in the students' lesson, even though she told her students all of the words followed the rule. The words *field* and *head* do not follow the rule. *Field* has a long /e/ sound, and *head* has a short /e/ sound; the first vowels in these two words do not say their name and that would be confusing to the students at this time. Therefore, choices A and B are incorrect; she has not done an adequate job, nor was her performance excellent. Choice D is also incorrect; there is no way to tell how much time was spent on different parts of the lesson.

28. **B.** By moving the pointer across the page as she reads, the teacher is showing the directionality of reading, choice B. Choice A, showing the names of letters, is not being done in the scenario. Choice C, identifying words, is incorrect; although she is moving the pointer, she is not pausing at each word. Choice D, pointing out print features, is incorrect, as the discussion does not bring up pictures or graphs, or titles.

29. **A.** Asking questions that can be answered with a very short response is an effective teaching technique to use for ELLs, choice A. Initially, when working with ELLs, it is best to ask questions that can be answered with one or two words. This can be lengthened as the students gain confidence in the new language. Choice B, speaking in one-syllable words, is incorrect, as it would be nearly impossible to do so, and ELLs need to learn high-frequency words. Choice C is incorrect, as ELLs may not be at grade level and may need high-frequency words. Choice D is incorrect, as no student should be given work that is too difficult for him.

30. **A.** Synonyms, choice A, are words with similar meanings, such as *big, large,* and *huge*. Choice B, antonyms, are words with opposite meanings, like *big* and *little*. Choice C, homonyms, are words that are spelled differently and have different meanings but sound the same, like *beat* and *beet*. Choice D, acronyms, are words composed of initials from an abbreviation, such as *radar* (an acronym for *radio detection and ranging*).

31. **D.** She should not judge students' speech on the playground, but should continue to model Standard American English in the classroom, choice D. Students will learn the difference between their home language and school language and should not be judged during this transition to Standard American English. Choices A, holding a classroom discussion about using Standard American English whenever speaking, and B, correcting the nonstandard use and having students repeat their words using Standard American English, are not considered effective methods and could prevent students from volunteering to speak orally in the classroom in order to avoid possible embarrassment. Choice C, using the reading and writing connection, may be helpful, but it is not the most effective, as students need practice in their daily speech.

32. **C.** She is using cloze sentences to explicitly teach how context can be used to decode unknown words, choice C. The teacher uses the cloze procedure because all of the sentences contain enough context cues that an appropriate guess can be made to fill in the blank. This exercise explicitly teaches students that they don't need to know all the words in a sentence, but can use other words in the sentence to help them discern the unknown word. There is no evidence for choice A, making sure students are paying attention, in this

scenario. Choice B, showing students sentence formation and language structure, would not be the best reason, nor the most effective way, to teach decoding unknown words. Although guessing may constitute a game-like format, choice D, this is not the best reason to use the cloze procedure.

33. **C.** Miss Barker "walked" her group through the article prior to their reading to give the students a mental map of the information, allowing them to focus on key ideas in the text, choice C. Using headings and subheadings to preview a text has been shown to increase comprehension; it provides readers a mental map and activates prior knowledge on a topic, helping the reader make the connection from known information to new information. Choice A, giving the students the information in case they don't read the text, is incorrect, as students should be held accountable for text they have been assigned to read. There is no evidence that knowing the headings and subheadings will increase reading speed, choice B. Choice D, making sure students have explicit instruction on vocabulary, is incorrect; reading headings and subheadings does not constitute explicit vocabulary instruction, although the headings may contain some important vocabulary.

34. **D.** The first phonics instruction goal for this student should be understanding that all words contain vowels, choice D. Using inventive spelling, the child has written the words *lost, in,* and *yard* without any vowels. Choice A, consonant blends and then understanding that "ay" makes the sound of long /a/ at the end of a word, cannot be assessed, as the "nd" blend is used correctly in *fond,* and these sentences have no other blends (the "gh" in *neighbor* is silent, not a blend). Choice B, the initial and ending consonant phonemes, is incorrect, as the child shows knowledge of beginning and ending phonemes. Choice C, that "er" spells the /er/ sound, is incorrect, as this should not be the student's first goal, and "ar," "ir," "or," and "ur" can all make the /er/ sound.

35. **A.** *In order to, as a result, so that,* and *therefore* are signal words that indicate a cause-and-effect text structure, choice A. *Also, then, furthermore,* and *besides* (choice B) indicate a descriptive text structure. *However, but, yet,* and *despite* (choice C) indicate a compare/contrast text structure. *To solve, it was recommended, now,* and *this is a concern* (choice D) indicate a problem/solution text structure.

36. **B.** *Duck,* choice B, contains three phonemes. A phoneme is one sound, and in *duck* there are three sounds: /d/, /u/, and /k/. Choice A, *oak,* has two phonemes, /o/ and /k/. Choice C, *possible,* has three syllables but six phonemes: /p/, /o/, /s/, /i/, /b/, and /l/. Choice D, *plug,* has four phonemes: /p/, /l/, /u/, and /g/.

37. **D.** Mr. Rich is assessing fluency, choice D. Fluency assessments encompass reading speed, accuracy, and prosody (expression). In this scenario, Mr. Rich is doing an informal assessment of reading speed and prosody to see how many words per minute Tommy is reading. It is important to note that Mr. Rich has already determined the passage to be at Tommy's instructional level. The other answer choices are incorrect, as there is no indication that word accuracy (choice A), comprehension (choice B), or inference skills (choice C) are being assessed.

38. **B.** The student has most improved in adding an ending to a consonant-vowel-consonant-silent "e" (CVCe) word by dropping the "e" and adding the ending, choice B. In the post-test, *bikeing* was improved to *biking.* Choice A (when a word has the consonant-vowel-consonant (CVC) pattern, double the last consonant and add an ending) is incorrect, as *trapping* was still misspelled in the post-test. Choice C (the long sound of /i/ can be spelled with "igh") is also incorrect, as *fright* was still misspelled in the post-test. Although *fright* was still spelled incorrectly, the student improved on the phonetic spelling by changing *fite* into *frite,* but phonetic spelling is not among the answer choices. Choice D, the sounds of double consonants, is not evidenced in this spelling inventory, as *trapping* was spelled incorrectly both times, and *dollar* had the wrong consonant doubled.

39. **A.** *Quack,* choice A, shows improvement with using a consonant digraph. A digraph is two letters that make one sound. In the word *quack,* "ck" makes one sound. Choice B, *fright,* has a silent "gh," but "gh" is not a digraph in this word (note that "gh" is a digraph in some words, such as *tough,* where "gh" make the sound of /f/). Choices C (*lifting*) and D (*trapping*) both have consonant blends in which the letter sounds of "ft" and "tr" blend together.

40. **C.** Mrs. Temple opts to pre-teach vocabulary because she understands that it is essential to comprehension, choice C. In order to fully comprehend a text, students must understand the vocabulary within the text. If a challenging word's meaning cannot be discerned from context cues, the word needs to be explicitly taught.

Choice A, difficult words would slow down the students' reading rate, may be true, but it is not the best reason to pre-teach vocabulary. Choice B, challenging vocabulary will probably frustrate the group, is also incorrect; some concepts have challenging vocabulary and it needs to be taught explicitly. Choice D, understanding basic relationships among words, is unrelated to pre-teaching vocabulary; it refers to terms such as synonyms, antonyms, and derivatives—words that are related in some way.

41. **B.** Saying the word *duck* and asking the student to separate the sounds he hears in the word, choice B, is an example of phonemic awareness. Phonemic awareness involves only sounds, not letters. In this case, the student is being asked to segment sounds. Choice A, give the student the letters "b," "t," and "d" and ask him to pick out the letter "b," entails letter recognition; the child does not necessarily know the sounds. Choices C (give the student a picture of a bed, a bird, and a table, and ask him to select the word that begins with the letter "t") and D (say the word *tip* and ask the student to write the letters for the sounds he hears) both address phonics rather than phonemic skills, as they require the student to identify a sound with a letter.

42. **C.** This "morning message" technique is used to increase students' awareness that text is speech written down, choice C. Students at this young age must understand that there is a message and meaning in texts. Choice A, to build a community in the classroom, is important, but it is not the main reason to have morning messages. Choice B, to increase students' listening skills, is incorrect, as the teacher would then need to explain the behaviors of good listeners. Choice D, to have students learn new words as the teacher writes, may be beneficial for advanced students, but many kindergartners are just learning that print carries meaning, so this is not the best answer.

43. **D.** Fluency is a bridge to comprehending a text, and Julio may not understand what he is reading because he is distracted by decoding the text, choice D. If a student has to concentrate on decoding and is sounding out too many words, then his comprehension suffers. Choice A is incorrect because reading rate, although important in fluency, is not an assessment of reading level; in addition, the question states that this text is at Julio's instructional reading level. Choice B is incorrect because Julio is able to decode the words, so his current phonics instruction is working for him. Choice C is incorrect because the question states that this text is at Julio's instructional level, which means he can read it comfortably, although it does contain some new words.

44. **A.** Metacognitive strategies encourage readers to think about what they are thinking, and whether what they are reading makes sense. Jayden seems to be reading without thinking about what he is reading, so he would benefit from metacognitive strategies, choice A. Choices B, fluency techniques, and C, structural analysis, are not needed, as Jayden is a rapid and accurate reader. Choice D, look-back strategies, may be used to answer questions or aid with decoding, but they are not the best technique to use with this fluent reader.

45. **C.** Decoding strategies and sight word recognition, choice C, should be the teacher's focus to help Ava progress. As a developing reader, Ava must increase her alphabetic skills and sight words before working on more challenging areas. Once she has acquired some reading proficiency, the teacher can work on her prosody. Structural analysis and affix definitions, choice A, are for more advanced readers. Choice B, the introduction of various genres for reading and motivation, is incorrect because Ava must improve her alphabetic skills before she increases her reading volume. Choice D, metacognitive comprehension strategies, should be employed if needed, but only after Ava has acquired alphabetic skills and proficient sight word knowledge.

46. **A.** *Baker,* choice A, contains an open syllable: ba/ker. An open syllable is one that ends with a vowel (CV or V) that usually has a long vowel sound. Choices B, C, and D (*mantel, carton,* and *mention*) all contain closed syllables. A closed syllable ends with a consonant and usually has a short vowel sound.

47. **D.** Mr. Stanley could use the information to motivate reading, taking into account student interests when he chooses books, choice D. Research has shown that when students are interested in a topic, they are more involved in the reading. Using an interest inventory is an effective method for determining what students would like to learn or read about. Choice A is incorrect, as there is no evidence to support this, although choosing appropriate-level texts is important for reading success. Choice B, to be attentive to students' cultural backgrounds, is incorrect, although a question about students' cultural backgrounds would have

been a good addition to Mr. Stanley's interest inventory questions, as books on different cultures would be a sign of a culturally responsive classroom. Choice C, to create writing activities to support reading, is important, but is not evident in this scenario, although the survey does entail children reading and writing.

48. **C.** Knowing how to break words into syllables can help readers identify and pronounce a word through use of accented and unaccented syllables, choice C. This allows students to read words by chunking the parts of the words; in some cases, syllabication rules dictate which syllable is most likely to be accented or unaccented. Choice A, making it easier for students to read phoneme by phoneme, is incorrect because students should not read phoneme by phoneme, but rather, with automaticity, chunking parts of words if necessary. Choice B, aiding in comprehension, works only if they know what the word means. Choice D, to obtain a deeper meaning of concepts in the text, is incorrect; although word knowledge is crucial to comprehension, breaking words into syllables won't necessarily help with difficult conceptual knowledge.

49. **A.** The principal should use a norm-referenced test, choice A. Norm-referenced tests compare students with other populations, and produce percentile scores that "rank" students. Choice C, criterion-referenced, is incorrect; a criterion-referenced test measures specified criteria such as skills in letter recognition or inference. Choices B, percentile-referenced, and D, percentage-referenced, are not standardized test types.

50. **C.** In the following sentence, *father* is the subject: *The father ate his son's ice cream cone* (choice C). The subject of a sentence is a person, place, or thing (which may be an idea) that is doing or being something. In this sentence, the *father* ate. In choice A, *ice cream cone* is the subject and *father,* the object of a preposition. In choice B, *son* is the subject and *father's* is a possessive noun. In choice D, *ice cream cone* is the subject and *father's* is a possessive noun modifying the ice cream cone.

51. **C.** Digraphs and diphthongs are never separated, choice C. Digraphs are two letters that make one sound, such as the "oa" in *boat* and the "ph" in *graph,* so they should not be separated. Diphthongs are two vowels that make a glided sound, such as the "oi" in *boil* and the "ou" in *couch.* These glided sounds are also never separated into syllables. Therefore, choices A, B and D are incorrect.

52. **B.** At this time, the teacher should provide more opportunities for Joshua to speak and encourage him to expand on what he is saying, choice B. Joshua is still in a developmental stage with language, but he should be encouraged to "use his words" in order to improve his communication. Choice A, giving him more time because he may be shy, or C, assuming that his static speech is developmental and will improve by year's end, may result in Joshua's falling further behind in his oral language development. Choice D is not the best answer because a teacher should always model good speech patterns.

53. **D.** She understands that knowing a variety of text genres and how they are structured aids in comprehension, choice D. Understanding the structure of genres and various other text structures enhances comprehension. Choices A, B, and C are plausible answers, but the best answer (choice D) focuses on the students' acquisition of knowledge about genres.

54. **C.** The best instructional technique to use with this student would be to teach him structural analysis to separate words into smaller, familiar parts, choice C. Separating word parts (the root or base word and any affixes) aids the reader in determining word meanings. The meanings of affixes are taught to enable students to do this. So, if the prefix *un* means "not" and the suffix *able* means "to be able," then *unlikeable* means "unable to be liked." Choice A, using metacognitive strategies to glean the meaning of what is being said, may not help the student understand the multisyllabic word even if he can get the gist of what is being said. Choice B, creating a personal dictionary, can be beneficial, especially for struggling readers, but doing so will not help when that student tries to read an unknown new word. Choice D, reading phoneme by phoneme, is incorrect, as some phonemes may be silent, and sounding out a word does not necessarily aid in word meaning.

55. **A.** The best approach would be to discuss the meaning of homonyms, sometimes called homophones, and have students draw a picture conveying the meaning of each word, choice A. This question refers to words that signal relationships between words. Homonyms or homophones are words that sound the same, but are spelled differently and have different meanings (for example, *two, to,* and *too*). Antonyms, choice B, are words that mean the opposite (*up* and *down*). Homographs, choice C, are words that have the same spelling, but a different meaning (*fair*—a carnival; *fair*—treated the same). Synonyms, choice D, are words that have the same meaning (*kind, caring, generous*).

56. **C.** The teacher is fostering active engagement in reading, making sure the students understand the vocabulary and concepts, choice C. Exposing students to new words and giving them the opportunity to discuss the vocabulary and concepts deepens understanding. Choice A, to broaden vocabulary, is incorrect, as this learning approach uses hands-on experiences so that students connect spoken language to written text. Choice B, modeling book handling skills, is not the best answer; the teacher's focus is not on discussing how she is handling the book. Choice D, selecting difficult vocabulary for explicit instruction, is incorrect because if vocabulary is going to be explicitly taught, it should be done prior to the reading in order to scaffold understanding.

57. **D.** A second grader who is working on short vowel sounds is in most need of reading intervention, choice D. Short vowel sounds are the first vowel sounds taught in systematic phonics, so by second grade, students should be able to decode words like *cat, bet, fit, cob,* and *but.* Some kindergartners are at a developmental level in which they are still acquiring phonemic awareness, choice A, so a teacher should be aware, but not overly concerned at this point. A third grader struggling with structural analysis, choice B, is not a cause for concern, as this is often the beginning point for this type of word work. A fourth grader who reads accurately but is not comprehending difficult concepts, choice C, does need scaffolding on skills such as activating prior knowledge and building background, but is progressing adequately.

58. **C.** Katrina appears to be strong in phonics but does not seem to use context to help her in word identification, choice C. Katrina was able to decode the words in the list, but when she saw unknown words in the passage, she could not decode them. Had she used context as an aid, she would have been able to correctly decode the three missed words because of the meaning and/or syntax. Choice A is incorrect, as *yelled* is phonetically regular, with a short /e/ sound. Choice B is incorrect, as we have no way of knowing Katrina's reading speed. Choice D is incorrect, as she read *Mark, Kara, sister, car,* and *her* correctly. All of these words contain "r"-controlled vowels; the words she missed do not.

59. **A.** Andy appears to use context cues to help him in word identification, choice A. Andy missed the words *street* and *sister* in the word list; since the word list has no context, Andy must rely completely on sight recognition or decoding skills when reading the word list. However, he read *street* and *sister* correctly in the passage, indicating that he used context to help him decode the words. Choice B is incorrect, as only one of the two incorrect words is multisyllabic. Choice C is incorrect, as getting 60% correct in a word list is not a sign of strong phonics skills. Choice D is incorrect, as there is no basis to judge comprehension.

60. **B.** Choice B is an inferential question: How would you describe Mark as a good big brother? The reader would have to infer using evidence from the text to answer this question, such as the facts that he played with his little sister, he made sure that she was safe from the danger in the street, and he hugged her. Choice A (whom is Mark playing with?) is literal (he's playing with his little sister). Choice C (is Mark a good ball player?) is speculation, as there is no information in the text to answer this question. Choice D (where did the ball go?) is literal, as the answer is right in the text (the ball went into the street).

61. **C.** A predicate contains a verb and states something about the subject, choice C. Choice A is incorrect, as prepositions do not necessarily appear in the predicate of a sentence. Choice B is incorrect, as a predicate may not necessarily contain an adverb. Choice D is incorrect; an indirect object is a word or phrase that states to, or for whom, or for what, an action is performed, such as *me* in the sentence "My child gave *me* a drawing."

62. **A.** The teacher is using systematic, explicit instruction, choice A. She is showing students through steps how to define important details or information, and then explicitly modeling how to achieve this while reading a text. In good explicit instruction, the next lesson on this topic would be a guided practice where the students and teacher decide important information together. Choice B is incorrect because at this point in the instruction, students are watching, but not really engaged in the activity. Choice C is incorrect, as the instruction is not implicit, but explicit (direct). Choice D is incorrect; there is no indication that reading comprehension is being monitored.

63. **D.** The teachers will use the results from a criterion-referenced test, choice D. A criterion-referenced test measures specified criteria such as letter recognition, vocabulary, and comprehension skills, so the scores may serve as one indicator of a student's needs. Choice A is incorrect, as a norm-referenced test compares students with other populations and produces a percentile score that "ranks" the student. Choices B, percentile-referenced, and C, validity-referenced, are not types of standardized tests, although standardized tests, of course, should be valid and can produce percentile scores.

64. B. The student's expressive language is below the teacher's expectations at his developmental level, choice B. People process language through the receptive modes of listening and reading, and communicate via the expressive modes of speaking and writing. In this case, the student appears to be receiving and understanding the oral language, but his expressive modes of speaking and writing, shown through short simple sentences, are not showing adequate growth. Choice A is incorrect, as phonemic awareness is not being monitored in this case, and since the student's receptive abilities seem fine, he may have adequate phonemic awareness. Choice C is incorrect, as the teacher does not see any inadequacies in the student's receptive modes of language. Choice D is incorrect, as the student is using simple sentences, not telegraphic speech (telegraphic speech is shortened speech such as "me go now").

65. B. Mr. Michaels uses a semantic web in this lesson because activating prior knowledge aids students in comprehension, and the semantic web allows them to connect new information to known information, choice B. This allows students to make a mental map of the information and aids in connecting ideas presented in the text. Choice A, leaving the semantic web on a bulletin board as a reference may be helpful but not necessary, as much more information will be learned. Choice C is incorrect, as a semantic web is a brainstorming tool, not an explanatory tool. Choice D is incorrect, as the students haven't read the text yet, and it would more effective to use a concept map or a timeline than a semantic web to summarize Lewis and Clark's expedition's influence on westward expansion.

66. C. The teacher understands that interacting with the text is an effective practice, enabling students to gain broader and deeper understanding of what they have read, choice C. Discussing what was read with a partner helps students to learn new ideas, ask questions, and clarify information. Choice A is incorrect, as students who cannot read a text independently with the scaffolding Mr. Michaels has already provided should receive more aid; if they can't read it, they will have nothing to discuss with their partner. Choice B is incorrect, as the purpose of the interactive lesson is not to rush the process, but to provide opportunities to enhance comprehension. Choice D is incorrect; although the teacher should listen in on the dialogue in his classroom, this is not the best reason to have students discuss with a partner, as he won't be able to monitor all of the partner discussions.

67. A. Mr. Michaels realizes that this unit contains some complicated concepts, and students will need scaffolding in order to fully comprehend the text they will be reading, choice A. When concepts are difficult or entirely new to students, reading experts recommend that some background knowledge be taught. This knowledge should supplement the information students will learn from reading the text. Choice B is incorrect; there is no indication of active engagement by students in the building background portion of this lesson. Choice C is incorrect because background information should not encompass all the information taught in the text, and students who struggle should be scaffolded further. Choice D is incorrect, as he is using partner discussion to ensure that his students can comprehend conceptual relationships within the text.

68. A. Since the teacher wants her students to work on recognizing differences, she should use a text that follows the compare and contrast text structure, choice A. Choice B, description, is incorrect, as descriptive text would not necessarily contain differences. Choice C, chronological, is a text structure that gives information in a sequential order, but not necessarily differences. Choice D, persuasive, is a genre that focuses on one side of an issue or topic.

69. C. The teacher should react by modeling the rules of Standard American English and remaining respectful of the cultural dialect, choice C. It is best to show respect to students regarding their regional and dialectical speech variations. Choices A, B, and D all include corrections for the student. By listening to teachers' modeling of the correct rules of language, students will learn both Standard American English and situational use of dialectical English.

70. C. The teacher's purpose is to reinforce one-to-one word correspondence in reading, choice C. The teacher explicitly points to each word and reads it, demonstrating to the students that one spoken word equals one written word. Choice A is incorrect, as the teacher is not pointing out or explaining parts of a book or reviewing the plot. Choice B, teaching beginning phonemes, is incorrect, as there is no isolation of sounds. Choice D, teaching book handling skills, is incorrect, as the teacher is working with the text in the book, not addressing how to handle a book.

71. **C.** A test is deemed reliable if it would produce the same results with a different set of people in a different setting, choice C. Choice A is incorrect, although test questions should be checked for accuracy. Choice B is incorrect, although the pilot questions may have been tested for a period of time, as a test does need to be reliable over time. Choice D is incorrect, as a test is deemed valid, not reliable, if it measures what it is supposed to measure.

72. **B.** To achieve optimal learning growth for all of his students, the teacher should place them in flexible groups with other students who need the same skills, choice B. Flexible grouping allows for more differentiation. The teacher will explicitly teach the needed skills to the applicable group. Once students have mastered the skill, they can be reassigned to a new group that will be taught a different skill. Choice A, teaching just the most needed skills to the whole class, does not differentiate for students' individual needs. Choices C, modeling excellent spelling and writing skills, and D, placing students in peer conferencing groups, are both feasible activities in the classroom, but the most effective technique is choice B.

73. **D.** She is modeling that multiple strategies may be used for word identification, choice D. Choice A is incorrect, although the word the teacher happens to use is *zipper*. Choices B and C are incorrect, although each is ONE of the strategies the teacher is using.

74. **C.** To improve student understanding of this text, the teacher could activate prior knowledge on bullying behaviors, choice C. When prior knowledge is activated, it allows readers to take information that they know and connect it to new information. Choice A, to teach bullying behaviors before the students read, is incorrect, as students must learn to read for information and be held accountable for that information. If they are told in advance, some students may skip over that part of the text. Also, the discussion would assess their listening comprehension and not their reading comprehension. Choice B, discuss how the article may have been written by someone who has been bullied, is incorrect; there is no basis for this answer. Choice D, have students read for information on how to avoid bullies, is incorrect; this would be purpose setting for the reading, but the answer should also include reading to see how bullies behave.

75. **B.** The author of the article likely used enumeration, choice B. Both the behaviors of bullies and five ways to avoid bullies are provided as lists, and an enumeration text structure can be considered a list. Choice A, problem-solution, is incorrect, as the two sections are separate, and the article is not written to convey "if this happens, do that." Choice C, cause-and-effect, is incorrect, as there is no mention of the cause of bullying. Choice D, descriptive, is incorrect, as the descriptive text structure entails an author presenting a main topic and then expanding on it. Note that in the enumeration text structure, a list may contain short paragraphs that are descriptive, but these paragraphs do not constitute the main text structure.

76. **D.** The student is extremely strong in reading comprehension because he scored higher than 97% of the students who took this exam, choice D. Choices A and B are incorrect, as the score is represented in a percentile, which means that the test is norm-referenced; a percentile does not indicate the raw score. Choice C is incorrect, as the normal curve is around the 50th percentile (68% of the test-takers fall within a range of one standard deviation below and above the 50th percentile).

77. **B.** The teacher understands that knowing root words allows students to understand multiple words when they use structural analysis techniques to approach unknown words, choice B. If a student knows the meaning of a root and various affixes, the student can then use structural analysis to figure out an unknown word. Choice A, chunking for pronunciation, may be helpful, but it is not the best reason to learn these Latin roots. Choice C is incorrect because knowing these Latin roots may not help with dividing syllables and placing accents. Choice D, that Latin has influenced the English language, is true, but although learning Latin can be invaluable, it is not a goal in most intermediate classrooms. ·

78. **D.** A fable is an imaginary short story that has a moral, choice D. It also usually has two or three animals as main characters. Choice A, a story that may be based on fact, is a legend. Choice B, a story involving occurrences or creatures that do not exist, is a fantasy. Choice C, a story involving some sort of wrongdoing, refers to a mystery.

79. **A.** The teacher should pre-teach *introspective,* choice A. This word's definition cannot be determined from the context. You could replace this word with a number of different words, and the sentence would still make sense. Mark was *happy, worried, concerned, confused,* and so forth. But *introspective* means thoughtful, looking into oneself. Choices B, C, and D are incorrect. Their definitions can be gleaned from the context and therefore should not be explicitly taught. Students need to learn the strategy of using context to figure out meaning.

80. **C.** Choral reading, choice C, can be used to increase fluency. Choral reading requires students to read together in a group; the group practices reading by re-reading together. Choral reading is often used for "performances" such as reading a poem in front of the classroom, providing an incentive to practice and re-read. Re-reading builds fluency. Choices A, silent reading, and D, partner reading, may help build fluency, but these modes do not necessarily entail re-reading. Choice B, popcorn reading, is when a teacher arbitrarily calls on someone to read orally. It is not considered an effective instructional method.

81. **A.** The word group *know, gnu, now,* choice A, demonstrates that different letters and letter combinations can represent the same phoneme. In these combinations "kn," "gn," and "n" all make the /n/ sound. Choice B, (*through, though, thus*) is incorrect; these words simply show the same spelling for the /th/ sound combined with different vowel sounds. Choice C is incorrect, as *table, cable,* and *fable* are rhyming words. Choice D is incorrect, as *can't, didn't,* and *shouldn't* do not represent different letters making the same sound; they are contractions.

82. **C.** This lesson entails explicit instruction of letter recognition, choice C: directly teaching students the letter "P." The teacher does not address the sound of "P"; therefore, choices A and B are incorrect. Choice D is incorrect, as implicit instruction is not direct, but implied.

83. **B.** Analyzing short pieces of text for deeper meaning, choice B, is a component of close reading. In close reading, the teacher leads students through a short piece of text to analyze form, purpose, craft, language, meanings, ideas, concepts, and so forth. Choice A is incorrect, as close reading does not involve background building. Choice C is incorrect, as vocabulary and word meaning are discussed within the short passage; they are not pre-taught. Choice D is incorrect, as prior knowledge may not be activated in close reading, although the technique does include re-reading.

84. **A.** The main purpose of this reader response assignment is to use writing as a vehicle to support the students' reading comprehension, choice A. When crafting a written response, the reader must think about and analyze what happened in the text, leading to deeper comprehension. Choice B is incorrect, as the teacher has asked about changes in a character, not events in the plot. Choice C is not the best answer, although sixth graders may discover some parallels that would deepen their comprehension. Choice D, keeping students engaged as she works with another group, may be a side effect, but it is not the reason she initiated the reader response.

85. **D.** The teacher is assessing print awareness, choice D. Print awareness is the understanding of the nature and meaning of print—how print works, and that, like oral language, it carries meaning. Choice A, structure of a sentence, is incorrect, as that assessment would involve grammatical functions. Choice B, directionality, is incorrect; although directionality is an aspect of print awareness, the teacher is not asking any questions about the direction that people read. Choice C, letter identification, is incorrect; although the child points to a letter, he is not asked to identify it.

86. **B.** Asking questions that force the student to use a lot of oral language in his responses, choice B, is NOT recommended. Questions for relatively new ELLs should be able to be answered with just a few words. Choice A, speaking slowly, is highly recommended. Choice C, offering multiple exposures to the same word, is very important; all students need this, but especially ELLs. Choice D, use rebuses to supplement written directions, is a very helpful technique. Rebuses are small pictures that take the place of a written word. Using rebuses allows teachers to use words the ELLs know. Rebuses can also be used to add information so the ELL can still gain understanding of the text.

87. **A.** The students are preparing for Readers' Theater, choice A. Readers' Theater is used to build fluency, as the students re-read dialogue to prepare for sharing the story with the rest of the class. Choice B, a retelling, is incorrect, as the students are reading character parts, not retelling on their own. Choice C, writing their own story, is incorrect, as writing is not part of the scenario. The same can be said about choice D, a puppet show using the dialogue from the book; although the students are using dialogue, there is no mention of using puppets.

88. **C.** He understands that graphics and diagrams support the information in the text and that analyzing these can enhance comprehension, choice C. Choice A, that students are ignoring the graphics, would be a good reason, but not the best rationale for the close analysis Mr. Everett is modeling. Wanting students to read the text with greater speed, choice B, is incorrect, as teachers usually recommend that students slow down when reading informational text; concepts in informational text may be difficult, and students may be unfamiliar with the text structure. Choice D, using the graphics and diagrams to find important vocabulary, is incorrect, as the graphics may include vocabulary that is not important.

89. **B.** The four components of fluency are correctly listed in choice B: accuracy, appropriate rate, automaticity, and prosody. Choice A incorrectly includes pragmatics in place of prosody, and omits accuracy. Choice C also incorrectly includes pragmatics instead of prosody. Pragmatics is the way that expression can provide meaning to language, so it is a broader concept than prosody. Choice D omits accuracy and prosody and incorrectly includes syntax and semantics, two parts of the cueing system that also includes phonics.

90. **C.** The teacher is determined to make sure that the literature authentically portrays its subject's culture, choice C. It is important that the pictures are not stereotyping or exaggerated in any fashion, and that the cultural aspects portrayed in the books are authentic to the culture. Choice A, to make sure the books are engaging and contain enriching vocabulary, is likely true, but it is not the primary reason the teacher is looking so analytically at the texts. The teacher is not making sure the stories and phrases in the books are written in Standard American English, choice B. In fact, if a book was about the Spanish culture, to be truly authentic, it would include a few Spanish words or a dialect. Choice D, determining whether the pictures support the text to aid in word identification, is incorrect, as it is not the best reason, but rather a comprehension aid for beginning and struggling readers.

Constructed-Response Model Answers

Before you begin writing an answer, you should review what is expected to obtain a score of 3. To paraphrase expectations:

- Clearly and directly answer all parts of the question.
- Show that you know reading content and understand it. Be accurate in that content.
- Write a strong explanation—support what you say.

Constructed-Response Question #1

Model Answer 1

The teacher's coding on Luke's reading indicates a strength and a weakness in word identification skills. Luke's strength appears to be in reading sight words. Luke's weakness appears to be not reading through the word.

The teacher's coding shows that Luke had seven errors. These words—*waiting, excited, climb, pretended, touched, touch,* and *going*—are all Tier 1 words but not sight words, which Luke appeared to read with ease. Sight words are words that are frequently used in texts. When readers recognize sight words automatically it allows the reading to go much smoother. Luke was able to read words such as *was, were, the, that, and,* and *went* without any hesitation, showing his automaticity with sight words.

The teacher's coding shows that Luke does not read through the words when trying to decode an unknown word. Of the seven errors, six had incorrect endings. Four words did not have the ending sounds: He read *wait* for *waiting, exkite* for *excited, pret* for *pretended,* and *go* for *going.* Each of these words is multisyllabic, and Luke did not read the ending syllables.

At this time, one instructional goal for Luke would be to have him read through the word and pay attention to ending letters and to make sure what he is reading makes sense. He must be taught to chunk multisyllabic words and look for known parts of words to help with word identification. The teacher should model chunking multisyllabic words for Luke, and he should be monitored to make sure that he is using this new skill.

Model Answer 2

The running record of Luke's oral reading shows that he has one strength and one weakness in word identification skills. Luke's strength is reading initial phonemes. His weakness is not reading for meaning.

The coding on the running record shows that Luke got seven words wrong, yet every error indicates that he said the initial phoneme correctly. Luke read *wait* for *waiting, exkite* for *excited, clim* for *climb, pret* for *pretended, took* for *touched* and *touch*, and *go* for *going*. All of these errors show that he did begin the words with the correct initial phoneme, and that he is trying to sound out unknown words.

Luke's weakness, that he is not reading for meaning, is strongly evidenced by his errors and the fact that he did not make any self-corrections. Although his errors with *wait* for *waiting* and *go* for *going* may have made sense to him, the syntax was incorrect. The errors of *exkite* for *excited, clim* for *climb, pret* for *pretended,* and *took* for *touched* and *touch* made no sense in the sentences, which indicates Luke is not reading for meaning.

Luke needs to be mindful of what he is reading and begin to ask himself if something makes sense. He needs to use metacognitive strategies to make sure he is reading for meaning. He needs to be taught to stop and ask himself three questions: Did that make sense? Did it sound right? Did I understand it?

Constructed-Response Question #2

Model Answer 1

To aid in student motivation, author sign-up sheets will be used for students to be placed in groups reading books by the author of their choice. Prior to the sign-up sheets, teachers will conduct a book talk on two books by each author, so that students are able to make an informed choice. The authors will have been selected by the following criteria: They have written multiple books, many of which are highly recommended or have received awards, and the books are on a variety of topics and are at various reading levels. Collaborative groups, assigned by reading level, will be formed for the instructional organization of the authors' study unit. Once the groups have been formed, the teachers will model how to write a biography and its components: childhood, education, writing interests, and current status of the author. Each member of a group will be given a section of the biography to write about. One instructional level book review will be assigned to each group member.

Technology will be incorporated into the unit of study in two major ways. First, the biography research will be conducted online. As teachers model how to write a biography, they will also give recommendations on how to find credible sites for research. The authors' studies will be published on a grade-level blog that will be monitored by the teachers to ensure that publications are up to the expected standards. Each student will contribute at least one book review, and must include a link to something that connects to the topic of the book.

These activities support the students' reading growth in a variety of ways. Using the reading and writing connection has been shown to enhance and deepen comprehension. First, students will read about the author, and then they will read the book. As they write about each, they will need to organize and analyze information from their reading. In addition, having their work published on a blog gives the students an incentive to perform their best.

Model Answer 2

In order to involve the students from the beginning of the authors' study, the teachers will poll the students to learn their favorite authors. Choosing from the authors that the students suggested, the teachers will select highly recommended or award-winning authors. Students will each be allowed to select two authors and will be placed in a study group with one of their selected authors. Teachers plan to partner a higher reader with a lower reader for this particular unit of study. Students will be required to make a timeline with the biography. The higher reader will take the lead on writing the biography, while the lower reader will take the lead on creating the timeline. Teachers will model both to ensure student understanding of procedures and expectations.

Technology will be included in multiple ways. First, teachers will explain to students how to find credible and recommended websites to gather information on the author. Second, the timeline will be made on a program such as Timeliner and two links will be required: one to the author's birthplace and one to the town or state the author currently resides in, or where the author is buried. Each student will write a review of one of the author's books. The completed authors' studies will be shared with the class and uploaded to the class website for parental viewing.

Constructed-Response Question #3

Model Answer 1

The three main cueing systems are phonology, semantics, and syntax. These are important because each of the cueing systems can help readers identify unknown words. Phonology is the cueing system that encompasses phonics and phonics generalizations. Students can decode words by knowing the letter-sound correspondence. The semantics cueing system uses meaning to help students read unknown words. Students who cannot sound out a word can sometimes determine a word by using context cues in the sentences. When this happens, we say the student is using semantics for word identification. The third cueing system is syntax, which refers to the structure of the language.

These cueing systems play an important role in reading because they allow readers to learn new words. This is extremely important, as most vocabulary is learned through wide reading, which is primarily independent reading. When students are reading and they come across an unknown word, they can employ the cueing systems to identify the word. Over time and with more exposure to the word, its meaning broadens. This, in turn, deepens comprehension, as students recognize more words with automaticity.

Model Answer 2

The cueing systems are used by students to identify words they don't know. There are three main cueing systems: phonology, semantics, and syntax. Sometimes a forth cueing system, pragmatics, is included. The first cueing system, phonology, is used when students try to sound out words or look for familiar word parts to help them pronounce a word. For example, if a student did not know the word *cookout,* he could chunk the word into *cook* and *out* and figure out the word. Semantics entails meaning. Students need to be taught that they can sometimes guess what a word means by reading the rest of the sentence, surrounding text, or sometimes even the pictures. Consider the sentence, "The boy made a big splash when he jumped into the pool and everyone nearby got wet." If a reader didn't recognize the word *splash,* after reading the sentence and using context cues, he would most likely identify it. The third cueing system, syntax, refers to the structure of the language; it helps students determine what a word might be by encouraging them to think of the word's function. Consider the sentence, "The pretty bird flew into the tree." If the student didn't know the word *pretty,* the student's internalized language structure (syntax) would lead him to recognize that the word was describing the bird. With syntax, use of some phonics, and semantics, the student should be able to identify this unknown word as *pretty.* Finally, pragmatics, often referred to as the fourth cueing system, is the way that expression carries meaning. For example, a person can say "no" and be mean, questioning, or funny, depending on how the word *no* is expressed.

The cueing systems are crucial to both reading and oral language. Most vocabulary is learned through wide reading. Students are able to learn more words during the year than teachers can teach because of wide reading and the cueing systems. These systems also allow readers to learn new words in the receptive mode, reading, and eventually use these words in the expressive mode through speaking or writing. Once students begin to express new words, they are showing ownership of, and growth in, vocabulary.

Chapter 14

Practice Test 2

Answer Sheet

Remove this sheet and use it to mark your answers to the selected-response questions.

Selected-Response Questions

1 Ⓐ Ⓑ Ⓒ Ⓓ	46 Ⓐ Ⓑ Ⓒ Ⓓ
2 Ⓐ Ⓑ Ⓒ Ⓓ	47 Ⓐ Ⓑ Ⓒ Ⓓ
3 Ⓐ Ⓑ Ⓒ Ⓓ	48 Ⓐ Ⓑ Ⓒ Ⓓ
4 Ⓐ Ⓑ Ⓒ Ⓓ	49 Ⓐ Ⓑ Ⓒ Ⓓ
5 Ⓐ Ⓑ Ⓒ Ⓓ	50 Ⓐ Ⓑ Ⓒ Ⓓ
6 Ⓐ Ⓑ Ⓒ Ⓓ	51 Ⓐ Ⓑ Ⓒ Ⓓ
7 Ⓐ Ⓑ Ⓒ Ⓓ	52 Ⓐ Ⓑ Ⓒ Ⓓ
8 Ⓐ Ⓑ Ⓒ Ⓓ	53 Ⓐ Ⓑ Ⓒ Ⓓ
9 Ⓐ Ⓑ Ⓒ Ⓓ	54 Ⓐ Ⓑ Ⓒ Ⓓ
10 Ⓐ Ⓑ Ⓒ Ⓓ	55 Ⓐ Ⓑ Ⓒ Ⓓ
11 Ⓐ Ⓑ Ⓒ Ⓓ	56 Ⓐ Ⓑ Ⓒ Ⓓ
12 Ⓐ Ⓑ Ⓒ Ⓓ	57 Ⓐ Ⓑ Ⓒ Ⓓ
13 Ⓐ Ⓑ Ⓒ Ⓓ	58 Ⓐ Ⓑ Ⓒ Ⓓ
14 Ⓐ Ⓑ Ⓒ Ⓓ	59 Ⓐ Ⓑ Ⓒ Ⓓ
15 Ⓐ Ⓑ Ⓒ Ⓓ	60 Ⓐ Ⓑ Ⓒ Ⓓ
16 Ⓐ Ⓑ Ⓒ Ⓓ	61 Ⓐ Ⓑ Ⓒ Ⓓ
17 Ⓐ Ⓑ Ⓒ Ⓓ	62 Ⓐ Ⓑ Ⓒ Ⓓ
18 Ⓐ Ⓑ Ⓒ Ⓓ	63 Ⓐ Ⓑ Ⓒ Ⓓ
19 Ⓐ Ⓑ Ⓒ Ⓓ	64 Ⓐ Ⓑ Ⓒ Ⓓ
20 Ⓐ Ⓑ Ⓒ Ⓓ	65 Ⓐ Ⓑ Ⓒ Ⓓ
21 Ⓐ Ⓑ Ⓒ Ⓓ	66 Ⓐ Ⓑ Ⓒ Ⓓ
22 Ⓐ Ⓑ Ⓒ Ⓓ	67 Ⓐ Ⓑ Ⓒ Ⓓ
23 Ⓐ Ⓑ Ⓒ Ⓓ	68 Ⓐ Ⓑ Ⓒ Ⓓ
24 Ⓐ Ⓑ Ⓒ Ⓓ	69 Ⓐ Ⓑ Ⓒ Ⓓ
25 Ⓐ Ⓑ Ⓒ Ⓓ	70 Ⓐ Ⓑ Ⓒ Ⓓ
26 Ⓐ Ⓑ Ⓒ Ⓓ	71 Ⓐ Ⓑ Ⓒ Ⓓ
27 Ⓐ Ⓑ Ⓒ Ⓓ	72 Ⓐ Ⓑ Ⓒ Ⓓ
28 Ⓐ Ⓑ Ⓒ Ⓓ	73 Ⓐ Ⓑ Ⓒ Ⓓ
29 Ⓐ Ⓑ Ⓒ Ⓓ	74 Ⓐ Ⓑ Ⓒ Ⓓ
30 Ⓐ Ⓑ Ⓒ Ⓓ	75 Ⓐ Ⓑ Ⓒ Ⓓ
31 Ⓐ Ⓑ Ⓒ Ⓓ	76 Ⓐ Ⓑ Ⓒ Ⓓ
32 Ⓐ Ⓑ Ⓒ Ⓓ	77 Ⓐ Ⓑ Ⓒ Ⓓ
33 Ⓐ Ⓑ Ⓒ Ⓓ	78 Ⓐ Ⓑ Ⓒ Ⓓ
34 Ⓐ Ⓑ Ⓒ Ⓓ	79 Ⓐ Ⓑ Ⓒ Ⓓ
35 Ⓐ Ⓑ Ⓒ Ⓓ	80 Ⓐ Ⓑ Ⓒ Ⓓ
36 Ⓐ Ⓑ Ⓒ Ⓓ	81 Ⓐ Ⓑ Ⓒ Ⓓ
37 Ⓐ Ⓑ Ⓒ Ⓓ	82 Ⓐ Ⓑ Ⓒ Ⓓ
38 Ⓐ Ⓑ Ⓒ Ⓓ	83 Ⓐ Ⓑ Ⓒ Ⓓ
39 Ⓐ Ⓑ Ⓒ Ⓓ	84 Ⓐ Ⓑ Ⓒ Ⓓ
40 Ⓐ Ⓑ Ⓒ Ⓓ	85 Ⓐ Ⓑ Ⓒ Ⓓ
41 Ⓐ Ⓑ Ⓒ Ⓓ	86 Ⓐ Ⓑ Ⓒ Ⓓ
42 Ⓐ Ⓑ Ⓒ Ⓓ	87 Ⓐ Ⓑ Ⓒ Ⓓ
43 Ⓐ Ⓑ Ⓒ Ⓓ	88 Ⓐ Ⓑ Ⓒ Ⓓ
44 Ⓐ Ⓑ Ⓒ Ⓓ	89 Ⓐ Ⓑ Ⓒ Ⓓ
45 Ⓐ Ⓑ Ⓒ Ⓓ	90 Ⓐ Ⓑ Ⓒ Ⓓ

CUT HERE

Time: 2 hours

Selected-Response Questions

90 questions

1. Mrs. Williams is working with her kindergarten students to develop concepts of print. Which of the following activities would she utilize?

   A. Explaining that the illustrator is the artist who drew pictures for the book
   B. Using a pointer on a big book to model how to track words
   C. Choosing rhyming words within a text
   D. Using a graphic organizer to help summarize a story

2. Students in a fifth-grade science class are reading about the circulatory system. Which of the following strategies is most likely to help the students comprehend and remember the blood flow sequence and the parts of the heart?

   A. Having students talk to partners about what they are reading
   B. Having students outline the reading
   C. Having students fill in a diagram of the heart with sequencing arrows
   D. Making flash cards to study the circulatory sequencing

3. Mr. Cote, a second-grade teacher, spends time in the afternoon teaching his students about compound words. When the class walks in the next morning, they see neon green labels around the room. The labels, placed near the objects they identify, say the following: *light bulb, light switch, doorway, whiteboard, bookcase, cupboard, cardboard,* and *homework.* Which of the following best explains Mr. Cote's purpose for these labels?

   A. He wants his students to be surprised and welcomed by the brightly colored signs.
   B. He is intending to use these for a classroom game.
   C. He is using environmental print to reinforce the concept of compound words.
   D. He is interested to see if students recognize that these words label the objects within the classroom.

4. Use the terminology below to answer the question that follows:

   metaphors

   symbolism

   visual words

   sensory observation

   details

   The terminology listed above would most likely dominantly be used when teaching which of the following genres?

   A. Narrative
   B. Descriptive
   C. Expository
   D. Persuasive

GO ON TO THE NEXT PAGE

5. Which of the following best describes an at-home activity that parents can use to help their child develop phonemic awareness?

   A. Play a computer game that has the child match the letter to a picture that begins with the letter sound.
   B. Use magnetic alphabet letters and spell the child's name.
   C. Read stories and poems that contain rhyming words and alliteration.
   D. Place objects on a table and work with the child to take out the items that begin with the letter "B."

6. A first-grade class has just returned from a trip to a neighborhood pet store. The owner had shared some tips on the care of turtles and snakes. Now that the students are back in the classroom, the teacher has them tell her about the trip and what they have learned. As the students volunteer information, the teacher writes the students' words on large chart paper. Which of the following best describes the technique the teacher is using in this activity?

   A. Language experience approach
   B. Oral language development approach
   C. The writing process
   D. Guided writing

7. What is the primary reason for a teacher to administer a miscue analysis of a student's reading performance?

   A. To assess the student's comprehension grade level
   B. To measure the student's ability to recognize where a sentence begins and ends
   C. To identify the student's difficulties in oral reading and set instructional goals
   D. To evaluate the student's inferential comprehension and set instructional goals

8. Mrs. Carson is having her students complete a research project on the animal of their choice. Among her criteria are a requirement that each student include four citations—one hard-copy source and three online sources. Which of the following describes the most essential skill that Mrs. Carson should help her students develop before they start the online portion of the research project?

   A. The ability to cite a source found on the Internet
   B. How to use software to enhance a research project
   C. The ability to evaluate an online source for credibility
   D. Strategies to keep on task while searching the web

9. Which of the following would be considered an effective technique for working with English Language Learners (ELLs)?

   A. Provide long explanations so that the ELLs hear a large amount of English words.
   B. Stand or sit in close proximity when speaking to ELLs.
   C. Whenever you speak, write out the words so that ELLs can make the connection between the spoken and written words.
   D. Use visuals whenever possible to explain new vocabulary.

10. Which of the following terms best describes word pairs that are spelled differently and have different meanings but sound the same, such as *fare* and *fair*?

   A. Antonyms
   B. Homonyms
   C. Pseudonyms
   D. Acronyms

11. Which of the following groups of signal words indicates a compare and contrast text structure?

    A. *first, second, then, next*
    B. *besides, several, another, in addition*
    C. *however, but, yet, on the contrary*
    D. *for this reason, as a result, on account of*

12. Which of the following may be used to assess students' phonemic awareness?

    A. Say the word *bug* and have the students separate the sounds in the word.
    B. Hold up a pan with the letters "Pp" on it. Give each student an object such as a pencil, eraser, paper, and so forth. Tell them that if the object they hold begins with the letter "P," then they are to place it in the pan.
    C. Give students the letters "g," "i," and "p." Ask them to put the letters in the right order to spell *pig*.
    D. Ask students to say the beginning letter of the word *fan*.

13. A third-grade teacher has noticed that a few students, although reading at an appropriate rate and with accuracy, are not demonstrating full comprehension of text concepts. Which of the following techniques would be the most effective to employ with these students?

    A. Use computer reading programs.
    B. Activate prior knowledge before reading.
    C. Have students start a personal dictionary.
    D. Use word sorts.

14. When reading, a student demonstrates poor word accuracy. Which of the following strategies should the teacher implement to best help this student?

    A. Extensively teach grade-level vocabulary and structural usage.
    B. Use texts at the student's reading level while concentrating on decoding and sight word recognition.
    C. Supply diverse materials for the student to read and respond to.
    D. Employ computer games that foster inferential thinking and analysis.

15. Three terms are often used to refer to the alphabetic principle. Which of the following selections correctly states these terms?

    A. *decode, phonemic awareness, phonics*
    B. *breaking the code, phonics, phonemic awareness*
    C. *concepts of print, decoding, phonics*
    D. *breaking the code, letter-sound correspondence, phonics*

16. Which of the following words contains a closed syllable?

    A. *baby*
    B. *magma*
    C. *away*
    D. *agree*

17. In which of the following words is the second syllable the accented one?

    A. *declare*
    B. *bacon*
    C. *heater*
    D. *broken*

GO ON TO THE NEXT PAGE

18. A superintendent wants to prove that the students in his school district read as well as the rest of the nation. Which of the following test types should he select?

    A. Validity-referenced

    B. Norm-referenced

    C. Reliability-referenced

    D. Criterion-referenced

19. A grammatical function is the syntactic role that a word or phrase plays in a clause or sentence. For example, a word may be a subject in one sentence but a direct object in another. In which of the following sentences does the word *mitten* function as a direct object?

    A. *The missing item, a mitten, was found.*

    B. *The mitten was lost.*

    C. *The boy lost the mitten.*

    D. *The mitten belonged to the boy.*

20. Monitoring oral speech is an everyday task for Mr. Giles, a first-grade teacher. He has noticed that a number of students use limited oral vocabulary and show low comprehension skills. Which of the following strategies might Mr. Giles employ to best aid these students?

    A. Teach students good listening skills, such as keeping their eyes on the speaker.

    B. Use a talking stick or ball as a visual cue for determining whose turn it is to speak.

    C. Instruct students to take turns talking so that everyone gets a chance to speak.

    D. Read books with rich vocabulary, explain what is happening in the books, then have students turn and talk.

21. For the first time in her teaching career, Mrs. Carr has English Language Learners (ELLs) in her classroom. Which of the following describes the best way for her to create a positive learning environment for these students?

    A. Have the ELLs read books about the local area.

    B. When possible, use the ELLs' native languages in the classroom.

    C. Incorporate literature that includes cultures of all students into the students' reading.

    D. Send home books for the ELLs to re-read.

22. As the teacher monitors Bella's reading, she is concerned. Although reading the words correctly, Bella pauses to decode approximately every other word. Which of the following best describes what the teacher should consider doing for Bella?

    A. Give Bella some much-needed phonics instruction.

    B. Work with Bella to build her confidence in reading.

    C. Use techniques such as phrase sorts and repeated readings to build Bella's fluency.

    D. Teach Bella self-monitoring techniques to ensure word accuracy.

23. Which of the following best describes why a teacher should choose books above the students' grade level to read to her class?

    A. To expose students to a variety of genres

    B. To expose students to higher-level vocabulary

    C. To model rules of Standard American English

    D. To emphasize plot within a story

24. The teacher holds up a number of informational texts and tells the class that they will be completing a genre study. She then proceeds to point out the title page, the table of contents, chapters, headings and subheadings, and the glossary, depending on what the text offers. Which of the following selections best describes the teacher's main purpose in doing this?

   A. The teacher wants her students to know vocabulary defining different parts of a text.
   B. The teacher is providing an opportunity for students to read nonfiction text.
   C. The teacher understands that introducing the structures of nonfiction texts can enhance comprehension.
   D. The teacher is providing extensive practice with nonfiction text.

25. A fourth-grade teacher is reading a novel to her students. As she reads, she stops to discuss unfamiliar words. Every few pages, she stops reading and asks the students to "turn and talk" about what just happened in the story. What is the teacher's main reason for doing this?

   A. "Turn and talk" builds collaboration in the classroom.
   B. The teacher understands that actively engaging students in learning unknown words and concepts is effective instruction that deepens their comprehension.
   C. Modeling vocabulary for students learning new words is essential.
   D. Using the "turn and talk" technique keeps the students more attentive to what is being read.

26. Which of the following groups of words demonstrates that different letters and letter combinations can represent the same vowel sound?

   A. *couch, horse, tore*
   B. *field, biked, cried*
   C. *window, hold, broke*
   D. *sack, bake, beak*

27. Which of the following selections describes a student who is not progressing sufficiently?

   A. A second grader who is not yet able to identify all the letter sounds
   B. A third grader having difficulty pronouncing multisyllabic words
   C. A first grader who is still learning to figure out unknown words by using context
   D. A second grader who is struggling with understanding contractions

28. Tommy's teacher has been monitoring his reading behaviors. She has observed that he reads orally at a very slow pace and in a monotone voice. Which of the following best describes what the teacher might do to help Tommy improve his reading?

   A. Have Tommy read more challenging texts to become accustomed to more difficult words.
   B. Offer Tommy a selection of books for wide reading.
   C. Use Readers' Theater, and have Tommy assume the role of a character.
   D. Have Tommy complete more written responses, incorporating new reading vocabulary.

29. One of Ms. Ortiz's reading groups has just completed another chapter from *Sarah, Plain and Tall*. She has instructed this group to write in their reading journals about the events in the chapter. Which of the following best describes why she would do this?

   A. She wants the students to practice their writing skills so that she can assess their needs.
   B. She wants the students to keep track of the events in the book.
   C. She wants the students to record their thoughts on the chapter, giving them a means to think more about the story and their reaction to the events within it.
   D. She must meet with another reading group and needs to keep these students engaged in learning, and journal writing is considered an effective learning tool.

GO ON TO THE NEXT PAGE

30. A teacher is preparing to group her students according to their reading skills and provide differentiated reading instruction. For one measure, she looks at the scores students received on a standardized reading test. In order to group for skills, what kind of standardized test results should the teacher use?

    A. Criterion-referenced

    B. Phoneme-referenced

    C. Identification-referenced

    D. Norm-referenced

31. Mrs. Silva sits next to Sarah and has her read. As Sarah reads, Mrs. Silva codes Sarah's errors on her paper. Afterward, Mrs. Silva will analyze the oral reading to ascertain Sarah's oral reading behaviors. Which of the following best describes what Mrs. Silva is doing?

    A. Capturing Sarah's ability to recognize sentences

    B. Using reading to bond with students

    C. Assessing recognition of letters

    D. Taking a running record

32. Mr. Carlson read the following text with his students: "The big man walked slowly as he carried a bag." Mr. Carlson asked his students to look at the underlined words, *big* and *carried*. Starting with the word *big*, Mr. Carlson asked for more interesting words with the same approximate meaning as *big* to replace the word. The students suggested *huge, gigantic, large,* and *enormous*. Mr. Carlson then repeated this process for the word *carried*. Which term below best describes what word type Mr. Carlson was exploring with his students?

    A. Antonyms

    B. Synonyms

    C. Euphemisms

    D. Homonyms

33. Mr. Cohen is reading a book orally to his students. As he reads, he stops and asks questions about the text. For example, after he reads the sentence "Seeds can travel in many ways," he says to the students, "I am wondering in what ways seeds may travel. I'm thinking about dandelions and how the wind blows them around." As he continues to read, he stops when it seems appropriate and ponders more questions, sharing each with the class. Which of the following best describes the main purpose of this lesson?

    A. To allow students to participate in a read-aloud

    B. To help students learn information about seeds

    C. To use explicit instruction in order to develop comprehension skills

    D. To explicitly teach the concept of main idea

Use the following to answer questions 34–36.

A fifth-grade teacher is teaching a unit on the Louisiana Purchase. She begins the unit with a KWL, shown below. She then discusses the importance of this historic acquisition. She begins the text by reading the first page and orally discussing her thoughts and questions. She re-reads a few paragraphs, annotating her most important thoughts. She then has the students read the next three pages of the text. Next, she has the students re-read, but instructs them to annotate during their second read, using sticky notes to write questions, areas that need clarification, and general comments or thoughts. The teacher then goes through the text with the students to discuss areas in which they have questions or that need clarification. They will end the unit by trying to answer the questions in the "W" section of the KWL and filling in the "L" section. If the class cannot answer all the "W" section questions, the teacher will assign some exploratory online reading to find answers.

What I KNOW (K)	What I WANT to know (W)	What I LEARNED (L)
Louisiana is a state.	What is the Louisiana Purchase?	
NOLA is on the web.	Did we buy Louisiana?	
It's a long drive from here.	Who paid for Louisiana?	
Voodoo dolls come from Louisiana.	How much did it cost?	
	Who owned it before?	

34. Which of the following best describes what the fifth-grade teacher was able to assess about her students' knowledge of the Louisiana Purchase from their response to the "K" portion of the KWL?

   A. Doing the KWL has made the students excited to learn about the Louisiana Purchase.
   B. The KWL was useless in this lesson, as the students veered from the task and talked about the state of Louisiana.
   C. The students have essentially no knowledge of the Louisiana Purchase.
   D. The students are not interested in learning about the Louisiana Purchase.

35. What reading technique is mostly being used during this reading?

   A. Directed reading
   B. Scaffolded reading
   C. Close reading
   D. Silent reading

36. What is the teacher's main purpose for continuing the unit by researching the unanswered "W" questions?

   A. The teacher understands that wide reading increases a student's vocabulary and fluency.
   B. The teacher built this activity into the unit to provide herself more time to plan the next unit.
   C. The teacher understands that the students need their learning reinforced.
   D. The teacher wants the students to use technology in this unit.

37. Which of the following best describes an effective way to assess phonemic awareness?

   A. Give students five uppercase and five lowercase letters and have the students match them (for example, "B" and "b").
   B. Say the word *tap* and ask for the letter that begins *tap.*
   C. Say the word *duck* and ask students how many sounds they hear in the word.
   D. Give students the letters "s," "t," "o," "n," and "e" and see what words they can make.

GO ON TO THE NEXT PAGE

38. Mr. Baker was in the process of timing a group of students who were taking a standardized exam on silent reading comprehension. After reading about the exam, he was not pleased with the reliability rating. Which of the following best describes Mr. Baker's concerns?

A. The reliability of a test means that the test questions have been checked for accuracy.

B. The reliability of a test is determined by the percentage of students scoring in the 50th percentile.

C. The reliability of a test means that the test would have the same results over time in different settings.

D. The reliability of a test means that the test measures what is it supposed to measure.

39. Which of the following best follows the syllabication rule for words that end in the consonant-le pattern such as *subtle* and *bundle*?

A. The consonant-le syllable is usually unaccented.

B. The consonant-le pattern does not make its own syllable.

C. The consonant-le pattern is always preceded by two consonants.

D. The consonant-le syllable is usually accented.

40. Which of the following techniques best describes the application of the reading and writing connection?

A. Word sorts

B. Reader response journal

C. Language experience approach

D. Choral reading

41. A teacher has given her students an Informal Reading Inventory (IRI) and a running record. She has determined that her students span four distinct reading levels. Which of the following best describes what her instruction should reflect?

A. The teacher should partner lower readers with higher readers for reading instruction.

B. Students should be placed in flexible guided reading groups that allow them to read from an instructional level book the majority of the time.

C. Students should be able to select books that they want to read, and the level shouldn't matter, as the motivational factor will be so strong.

D. The teacher should consider combining students at the two lower reading levels into one group and those at the two higher reading levels into a second group, and have these two new groups read an instructional level book.

42. Research suggests that which of the following should be taught first as students transition from emergent readers to beginning readers through the use of systematic phonics?

A. Vowel-consonant-silent "e" rule (VCe)

B. Consonant blends

C. Sight words

D. Short vowel sounds

43. Which of the following techniques reinforces letter recognition?

A. Put three letters on index cards in a pile and have students select the card with the letter that makes the /b/ sound.

B. Hide index cards with the letter "S" around the room and have the students do a letter "S" hunt.

C. Using picture clues, ask students to say the beginning sound of *hat, ham,* and *hurt*.

D. Using the class sandbox, have students write their name in the sand.

44. Which of the following best describes why teachers should instruct students about the purpose of headings and subheadings?

    A.   Headings and subheadings allow more white space on the page, providing the reader with extra room to decode.

    B.   Instruction about headings and subheadings minimizes confusion when students see what looks like numerous titles in a text.

    C.   Headings and subheadings inform readers about the topic to be covered in their corresponding sections, aiding in comprehension.

    D.   Headings and subheadings cite all the main ideas and details in the text.

Use the following passage to answer questions 45–46.

A sixth-grade class is reading a text about the Boston Tea Party. The text conveys what transpired between the colonies and England, and why some of the colonists were upset. It then explains how the colonists rebelled, and the historical events that followed as a result of the Boston Tea Party. Before assigning the reading, the teacher builds background on the historical points and the era, making sure students understand that in the 18th century, colonists could not just telephone Great Britain to communicate their displeasure. After the students read the text and summarize its main points, the teacher has the students re-read. After the second reading, the teacher gives the students a graphic organizer for summarizing the events detailed in the text.

45. Why does the teacher discuss historical points and the era, including the lack of telephones, prior to having students read the text?

    A.   The teacher is a history buff and wants her students to love history too.

    B.   The teacher understands that students are completely unfamiliar with life during the time period, and that some historical perspective will enhance their comprehension.

    C.   The teacher is working with vocabulary strategies to enhance comprehension.

    D.   The teacher wants to assess what students already know about the Boston Tea Party.

46. What type of graphic organizer would the teacher most likely have given the students?

    A.   Compare and contrast

    B.   Cause and effect

    C.   Timeline

    D.   Descriptive

47. The school district superintendent has decided to implement a new standardized test in grades 3 and 6. She states that this new test has been proven to have higher validity than the test the district has been using. Which of the following best describes why this is important?

    A.   A valid test measures the skills and the content that it is supposed to measure.

    B.   A valid test is normed; therefore, the scores will be comparable to those of other school systems.

    C.   All the questions in this test would have been confirmed to be at grade level.

    D.   Test validity ensures that all the scores are converted into grade equivalencies.

48. A third-grade class is working on a literacy unit about legends. The teacher uses legends in her read-aloud and with instructional reading groups. The class discusses the components of each legend the teacher uses in preparation for writing their own legends. Which of the following accurately describes a legend?

    A.   It includes occurrences or creatures that do not exist.

    B.   It must contain humor.

    C.   It does not have to be fact-based.

    D.   It must be based on facts.

GO ON TO THE NEXT PAGE

49. Listening to one of her first graders read an instructional level text, Mrs. Caron uses her tablet to time the reading, coding the errors as she hears them. Which of the following best describes what Mrs. Caron is assessing?

    A. Comprehension
    B. Fluency
    C. Letter-sound correspondence
    D. Word accuracy

50. Which of the following best describes the vowel patterns in the following words: *women, head, some, have, busy,* and *field*?

    A. Some of the vowel patterns are regular; some are not.
    B. The ending consonants following the vowel pattern change the vowel sound.
    C. They are all phonetically regular vowel patterns.
    D. They are all phonetically irregular vowel patterns.

51. A teacher is explicitly teaching close reading techniques to his fifth-grade students. What kind of text should he be using?

    A. A challenging book that is above grade level so that students will have to use structural analysis and context cues to understand the text
    B. A short text passage that can be analyzed for form, craft, and structure
    C. An informational textbook with complicated concepts that can be arranged on a graphic organizer
    D. A mystery, as the clues will lead to deeper analysis of the author's craft

52. Mr. Mantle's advanced reading group has some very challenging words in their current text. As students partner read, he walks around and listens. When a reader stops because he doesn't know a word, Mr. Mantle has the student read the rest of the sentence, and then asks him to figure out the word. Sometimes, Mr. Mantle has the student re-read the complete sentence. Which of the following best describes why the teacher does this?

    A. To assess the students' reading levels
    B. To practice oral reading at a more challenging level
    C. To have students learn to use context to decode unknown words
    D. To encourage students to read with expression

53. An intermediate-grade teacher is working with his class on the Greek root *anti* (against or opposite). After discussing the meaning of the root, he creates the following diagram with his students.

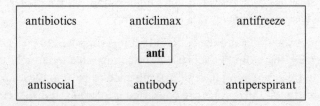

Which of the following best describes why the teacher does this activity?

    A. He understands that knowing the meaning of various roots can aid students in understanding the meanings of unknown words.
    B. He understands the importance of activating prior knowledge and is planning a literacy unit on Greek mythology.
    C. He is teaching the students a series of compound words, which he plans to introduce in alphabetical order.
    D. He understands that this exposure to these new words will aid students in their understanding of euphemisms.

54. Which of the following types of text would be most confusing for English Language Learners (ELLs)?

    A. Riddles

    B. Narratives

    C. Poetry

    D. Mysteries

55. A teacher reviewed Jamie's standardized test results and was surprised to find that Jamie had scored in the 48th percentile in reading comprehension. Which selection below best finishes the following statement regarding what this score indicates to Jamie's teacher?

The teacher can conclude that this test result shows that

    A. Jamie got 48 of the test items correct.

    B. Jamie needs to learn inference skills.

    C. Jamie is in the middle range in reading comprehension.

    D. Jamie is lagging in reading comprehension because the average student is at the 50th percentile.

56. Which word below contains four phonemes?

    A. *tack*

    B. *seriously*

    C. *boat*

    D. *flag*

57. Which of the following best describes how students' knowledge of oral language impacts their comprehension when reading?

    A. Oral language has no impact on reading comprehension.

    B. It aids them in phonemic awareness and, therefore, in phonics.

    C. Oral language allows clearer communication so students can be more concise in their explanations.

    D. If a student uses high-level oral vocabulary, the student is more likely to comprehend at a deeper level.

58. A fifth-grade class is reading a text about pollution, the changes in society that have brought about large amounts of waste, and the impact of this waste on the environment. Which of the following graphic organizers would be most effective in summarizing the main points of this text?

    A. Venn diagram

    B. Concept map

    C. Cause-and-effect map

    D. Main idea web

59. A teacher hands her student a small reproducible picture book. She reads the sentence under the first picture and asks the student to circle one word. Then she reads the next sentence and asks the student to circle one letter. Finally, she reads the sentence after that, asking the student to draw a circle around an uppercase letter. Which of the following best describes what the teacher is assessing?

    A. Phonemic awareness

    B. Print awareness

    C. Text structure

    D. Directionality

GO ON TO THE NEXT PAGE

60. A fourth-grade teacher is concerned because his students are using nonstandard English when speaking and writing. Which of the following would be the most current and effective advice for this teacher?

    A. Model Standard American English, allowing students to conclude that school language usage may differ from home language.

    B. Explain to students why they should use Standard American English, and demand that they begin immediately.

    C. Assemble a series of worksheets that students can complete to help them begin to use Standard American English.

    D. Tell students that they must use Standard American English whenever they are talking or writing.

Use the following scenario to answer questions 61–62.

At the beginning of the school year, a second-grade student was given a spelling inventory so that his needs could be assessed and goals could be set for his instruction. After 6 weeks, a post-test was given to monitor progress. Analyze the results of the chart below and answer the next two questions.

Spelling Word	Pre-Test	Post-Test
mat	mat	mat
bake	bak	bake
pail	pal	pail
say	sa	say
dark	drk	dark
house	hows	hous
stop	sop	stop
might	mit	mite

61. Examining the results of the pre- and post-tests, which of the following best describes this student's improvement?

    A. Understanding of consonant digraphs

    B. Knowing the various spelling of the long /a/ sound

    C. Learning that "igh" makes the long /i/ sound

    D. Knowing the short /a/ sound

62. Which word shows improvement with using diphthongs?

    A. *dark*

    B. *house*

    C. *stop*

    D. *might*

63. The grammatical function of a prepositional phrase is to express a relationship between a noun or pronoun and another word in the sentence. Which sentence below contains a prepositional phrase?

    A. *Bobby is the son of George.*

    B. *Sarah's long hair is brown and beautiful.*

    C. *My teacher is really nice.*

    D. *The dog does not mind, ever.*

64. In a fourth-grade classroom, students frequently write in their response journals about events happening in the text they are reading. Which of the following best describes why a teacher would have students keep a reader response journal?

    A. It provides the teacher time to create effective lessons around skills within the book.

    B. It fosters the reading and writing connection, and deepens comprehension by allowing students to devise their own interpretations of the text.

    C. It gives the teacher a means to assess whether students are capable of reading the selected text.

    D. The reader response journal allows students freedom of expression; it gives them a voice.

65. Readers use their schemata and information from the text to arrive at a conclusion about the text's events. Which of the following terms best describes this action?

    A. Inferring

    B. Clarifying

    C. Visualizing

    D. Predicting

66. Mrs. Marcum's class just completed a science experiment, mixing material to make a solution. After the students finished, Mrs. Marcum had them write a description of the procedure and record their results. Which of the following best describes Mrs. Marcum's reason for having the students document the procedure and results?

    A. As the students write the information, she can walk around and assess their experiments.

    B. Using a compare-and-contrast text structure, the students can analyze as they write.

    C. By writing the information, the students are using the sequential text structure and reinforcing domain-specific vocabulary.

    D. Writing the experiment will enable the students to do this again at home, fostering greater community relations.

67. The note below was written by a second grader to his teacher. Look carefully at his writing:

    Dr Miss Black, I thnk yu nise and I happe yu mi tesher. I lv yu and I lic yu tesh me.

Which of the following best describes what this second grader knows about phonics?

    A. Long vowels "say their name."

    B. All words contain vowels.

    C. The letter "c" can say the /s/ and /k/ sounds.

    D. Vowel digraphs make one sound.

68. Read the passage below and answer the question that follows.

    It is very easy to boil an egg. Put water in a pan and then place the egg in the pan. Put the pan on the burner and let the egg cook for 10 minutes. Take the egg out of the pan and let it cool before eating.

Which of the following best describes the text structure used in the passage?

    A. Compare and contrast

    B. Description

    C. Cause and effect

    D. Chronological

GO ON TO THE NEXT PAGE

69. What does *prosody* mean in reading?

    A. The expression and intonation used in oral reading

    B. The speed of oral reading

    C. The structure of the language

    D. The inability to infer

70. Mrs. Meeker has identified a group of students who are having difficulty reading unfamiliar multisyllabic words. She needs to create an instructional plan. Which of the following would be the most effective approach for these students' instruction?

    A. Give students books at a challenging level to read during their independent reading time.

    B. Use word trees to form derivatives of base and root words by adding affixes.

    C. Explicitly teach all the unfamiliar multisyllabic words that will be found in a particular text prior to assigning the text to the students.

    D. Have students look the words up in the dictionary and use them in a sentence.

Use the following scenario to answer questions 71–73.

A second-grade teacher has her students read the passage below. She tells them that as they read, they should think about what will happen next.

Brian went upstairs into his room to find his new baseball cap. It was brand-new and his grandmother had just given it to him. He looked under the bed. He looked inside his closet. He was trying hard to find it. It was so sunny outside. He looked on top of his bookcase. He came downstairs without his cap.

71. When the teacher asks the students to think about what happens next, which of the following terms describes the comprehension strategy she will most likely have the children use?

    A. Summarizing

    B. Guessing

    C. Predicting

    D. Clarifying

72. Which of the following questions requires that the students use inferential comprehension?

    A. Did Brian find his new baseball cap? Explain.

    B. Do you think Brian's baseball cap is important to him? Explain.

    C. Can you tell me about your favorite cap or hat?

    D. Where do you think the new baseball cap is?

73. The teacher then underlines the following words in the text: *upstairs, baseball, grandmother, inside, outside, bookcase, downstairs,* and *without.* She asks the students what kind of words these are. What response is she looking for?

    A. Contractions

    B. Synonyms

    C. Compound words

    D. Digraphs

74. Mr. Bacon is preparing a reading lesson on the manufacturing of cloth and has been reading through the informational text. He comes to the sentence "The shuttle is used to carry yarn to weave in a loom." He then decides to pre-teach the word *shuttle.* Which of the following best explains why *shuttle* should be pre-taught?

   A. Mr. Bacon understands how to select appropriate words for instruction.

   B. *Shuttle* is a new word, and all new words should be taught to students.

   C. Mr. Bacon should not pre-teach *shuttle* because it is explained in the sentence.

   D. Mr. Bacon realizes that the suffix "tle" may be confusing to students.

75. Mrs. Bradley assembles her kindergarten class around the whiteboard. She has written the following sentence frames on the whiteboard:

   My favorite animal is _____ because _____.

   I like to play _____ because _____.

   I like friends who _____.

Mrs. Bradley asks for volunteers to help complete the sentences, and writes down what the students say. Which of the following describes the best reason to do this?

   A. To organize the students' thinking and responses

   B. To get the students to know a little bit about each other

   C. To promote awareness of the relationship of speech to print

   D. To teach letter-sound correspondence

76. The teacher is previewing the students' text to decide if any vocabulary needs to be pre-taught. She reads the following sentence: "The kind man paid the exasperated young man with rupees." She then underlines *exasperated* and *rupees,* but decides NOT to teach one of the words. Which of the following best describes the word she will teach and why.

   A. *Exasperated,* as it has many synonyms.

   B. *Exasperated,* because it cannot be defined from the context.

   C. *Rupees,* as it is a foreign word and students need to know it.

   D. *Rupees,* as student can glean from the context it is some kind of money.

Use the following sixth-grade level Informal Reading Inventory (IRI) section to answer questions 77–79.

Word List	The Passage
anxious	Jerome was anxious to get home. His mother would be furious if he were late, and he would be grounded again. He was embarrassed to tell his friends he had to leave, as the game they were playing was almost over. He was in a dilemma because he didn't know what to do.
embarrass	
dilemma	
furious	
grounded	

77. Eric, an advanced fourth grader, read the word list for the sixth-grade level passage and missed the words *anxious, dilemma,* and *furious.* Since Eric had done well on a fifth-grade passage, his teacher had him read the passage. He accurately read all of the words except *dilemma,* which he read with a long /i/ sound. Which of the following is the best synopsis of Eric's reading skills?

   A. Eric appears to have problems with structural analysis.

   B. Eric has some small problems with reading sight words.

   C. The results of Eric's IRI suggest that he is using context cues for word identification in passages.

   D. Eric is an advanced reader and should not have been made to read this sixth-grade level passage.

GO ON TO THE NEXT PAGE

78. Angie, a sixth grader, read the word list and missed only the word *anxious.* She was able to read the complete passage accurately, yet could not answer the comprehension questions adequately. Which of the following is the best synopsis of Angie's reading skills?

    A. Angie is strong in phonics and should be placed in a sixth-grade level reading group.
    B. Angie needs to review affixes such as "ous."
    C. Angie's slow reading affects her ability to focus on comprehension.
    D. Angie appears to need explicit instruction on comprehension strategies.

79. The creator of this inventory has written questions about the passage. He has identified these questions as literal, inferential, and vocabulary-based. Which of the following questions is inferential?

    A. What would you do if you were Jerome?
    B. Would you say that Jerome is a good boy? Explain.
    C. Why wouldn't Jerome tell his friends he had to leave?
    D. How will Jerome's friends act if he leaves?

80. A fourth-grade teacher shows her students five books on different topics. She has each student sign up for the book and topic he wants to read. Which selection best describes the teacher's purpose in doing this?

    A. She wants her students to read a variety of texts.
    B. She understands that when students are interested in a topic, they are motivated.
    C. She knows how to motivate students through book talks.
    D. She intends to involve her students in a genre study.

81. A number of students are having a problem with comprehending instructional grade-level text. The teacher has determined that these students need to develop metacognitive skills. Which of the following best describes what she could do to help them?

    A. Read a passage orally and ask the students to discuss what they have read.
    B. Read a passage orally and ask herself about what she has just read, then model her thinking about the passage to the students.
    C. Ask the students to answer inferential questions at the end of their reading.
    D. Divide the students into groups and have them discuss important points after reading.

82. Mrs. Carol was reading orally to her students and sharing her thinking as she tried to comprehend the text. When Mrs. Carol came to a descriptive paragraph, she told her students that she was forming a picture in her mind, and that they should too. When she came to a sentence that was slightly confusing, she re-read the sentence, telling her students that sometimes she re-reads if she doesn't understand. When she came to a word she didn't know, she modeled for students how she was able to figure out the word by using context. When she read a part that resembled her experience, she explained that similarity to the students. From this type of modeling, which of the following selections best describes what Mrs. Carol understands about comprehension?

    A. That it may take a long time to truly understand a text
    B. That reading orally helps with text comprehension
    C. That students should use multiple strategies to enhance their understanding
    D. That visualization is a helpful tool

83. Mr. Pontis has a large selection of highly recommended multicultural literature in his classroom. Which of the following best describes why Mr. Pontis would have these books in his classroom?

    A. To invite students to read a variety of materials
    B. To teach students to respect and value all cultures
    C. To challenge students to read more difficult texts
    D. To identify cultural stereotypes in the texts

84. Mrs. Cole wants her students to be able to write a paper that demonstrates the differences between the lives of Native Americans in the 1800s and today. Which type of text structure should be modeled to convey these differences?

    A. Description

    B. Persuasive

    C. Compare and contrast

    D. Cause and effect

85. Which of the following is the best way to support a relatively new English Language Learner (ELL)?

    A. Expose the student to as many Standard American English words as possible to spur rapid language growth.

    B. Limit visuals in texts so that the ELL won't become confused when reading the print.

    C. Read books with lively and entertaining vocabulary words.

    D. Choose one or two target words and use them multiple times when speaking.

86. A second-grade teacher has been monitoring Carly's oral language development and listening skills because Carly does not follow through on directions. Although Carly appears to work hard, she also has not been completing class assignments and projects sufficiently. The teacher has noticed that when she visually shows Carly the expected steps, Carly performs much better. Which of the following best describes what the teacher should be most concerned about with Carly?

    A. There may be some developmental delays in Carly's expressive language.

    B. Carly lacks exposure to a variety of experiences, and that has limited her listening vocabulary.

    C. Carly needs to be placed in activities that encourage significant use of oral language.

    D. There may be some developmental or physical issues with Carly's receptive language.

87. Mr. Comec is teaching structural analysis to his fifth-grade class. Which of the following groups of words would be best for him to use?

    A. *duck, black, kick, clock*

    B. *heat, heater, preheat, reheat*

    C. *fair, fare, beat, beet*

    D. *liquid, solid, vapor, gas*

88. Mr. Oliver's rural classroom students speak in their regional dialect. Some of their spoken words do not reflect all the phonemes that should be pronounced. For example, his students' everyday speech includes "dudden" for *doesn't* and "iden" for *isn't*. What would a colleague familiar with current research on nonstandard speech suggest that Mr. Oliver do?

    A. Model Standard American English by speaking each sentence correctly, then writing the sentence on the board and having students read it orally.

    B. Model the rules of Standard American English, but be respectful of the students' regional dialect.

    C. Pair each student with a partner and have them use the mispronounced words such as *doesn't* and *isn't* correctly in a sentence and then read the sentence orally to each other.

    D. Model Standard American English. When a student speaks in his regional dialect, repeat the sentence correctly for him, then have him repeat the Standard American English.

GO ON TO THE NEXT PAGE

89. Prior to reading her class a story, the kindergarten teacher points out and explains to them the purpose of the book's front cover, back cover, title page, and first page. After a few days of doing this, she picks up a book and asks the students to name what she is pointing to, then points to the front of the book, the back of the book, the title page, and the first page. What is the teacher's main purpose in doing this?

    A. To explicitly teach directionality of print
    B. To preview the story prior to reading
    C. To explicitly teach that books have parts
    D. To reinforce visually for the students that all stories have a beginning and an end

90. A teacher has noticed that a group of her students is having problems with fluency. Which of the following techniques would be considered helpful in building fluency?

    A. Popcorn reading
    B. Readers' Theater
    C. Partner reading
    D. Cooperative learning

Constructed-Response Questions

3 questions

Constructed-Response Question #1

Katie read the following passage to her teacher as the teacher coded Katie's oral reading. The plain print in the box below shows what was written in the text. The bold type above the plain print shows what Katie read orally. Look carefully at the following and answer the questions below.

---

             is   **The duckies**   **fol-fol SC**
                                     ^

Mommy Duck <u>was</u> looking for her babies. <u>They</u> had been <u>following</u> her like good

                                                                   didn't

little ducks. Mommy Duck called, "Little ducks, come. Little ducks, come." But they <u>did not</u>

                                    —

come. They knew it was nap time and <u>they</u> did not want a nap.

                              —   **stard**

Mommy Duck knew what to do. She took <u>out</u> some crackers and <u>started</u> to eat.

          hear   **run**

The baby ducks <u>heard</u> Mommy Duck eating and they <u>ran</u> to her. They said, "Please give us crackers."

Mommy Duck said, "You can have crackers after you nap!" Then she put the little ducks to bed.

Coding
Substitution (error) has what student said above underlined word.
Dash (—) means an omission.
^ means a word has been inserted.
SC is a self-correction.

Analyze the above miscues. Using evidence from the teacher's coding, state one strength that Katie has as a reader and one weakness. State a learning goal for Katie and how you might instruct her to attain that goal.

GO ON TO THE NEXT PAGE

Constructed-Response Question #2

Directions: Read the scenario and then respond to the task that follows. Be sure to answer all parts of the task.

Scenario

School has just opened, and a new first-grade teacher, Miss Canton, is thrilled to have her very own classroom with 22 students. She was so happy to be awarded the position, but unfortunately, she was hired 3 days before school started. The classroom looks colorful, inviting, and ready for the students. Miss Canton is excited and wants to ensure that she promotes optimal growth in reading for her students. The kindergarten teacher has told her that three of these students were still learning letter identification when school ended last spring. Others were at various levels in reading and one student was already reading at the second-grade level. Miss Canton has a number of books in the classroom, and the school has a book closet with leveled books. She decides to do shared reading the first week of first grade, but knows she has to progress quickly into differentiated instruction.

Task

- Briefly describe what Miss Canton should prepare for the second week. Describe the instructional materials and how differentiation will take place.
- Briefly describe how technology will be infused and progress will be monitored in the classroom.

Constructed-Response Question #3

English Language Learners (ELLs) may easily become confused when listening to and speaking the English language. Certain words or phrases may be more confusing than others.

Task

- State and explain three types of words or word forms that would be confusing to an ELL.
- Cite and explain some instructional techniques that may aid ELLs in learning these words.

Answer Key

1. B	19. C	37. C	55. C	73. C
2. C	20. D	38. C	56. D	74. A
3. C	21. C	39. A	57. D	75. C
4. B	22. C	40. B	58. C	76. B
5. C	23. B	41. B	59. B	77. C
6. A	24. C	42. D	60. A	78. D
7. C	25. B	43. B	61. B	79. B
8. C	26. C	44. C	62. B	80. B
9. D	27. A	45. B	63. A	81. B
10. B	28. C	46. B	64. B	82. C
11. C	29. C	47. A	65. A	83. B
12. A	30. A	48. D	66. C	84. C
13. B	31. D	49. B	67. A	85. D
14. B	32. B	50. D	68. D	86. D
15. D	33. C	51. B	69. A	87. B
16. B	34. C	52. C	70. B	88. B
17. A	35. C	53. A	71. C	89. C
18. B	36. A	54. A	72. B	90. B

Answer Explanations

Selected-Response Answers

1. **B.** Using a pointer on a big book to model how to track words, choice B, will help Mrs. Williams' kindergartners develop concepts of print. Tracking the directionality of reading is considered a concept of print. Choices A, C, and D are not considered concepts of print.

2. **C.** Having students fill in a diagram of the heart with sequencing arrows, choice C, can help the students comprehend and remember the blood flow sequence and the parts of the heart. This answer allows students to study the material, label the parts of the heart, and visualize the blood flow sequence, which aids in understanding. Choice A, having students talk to partners about what they are reading, is helpful, but not as effective as choice C. Choice B, having students outline the reading, is also not as effective, as the outline may not include the necessary information or show the blood flow sequence. Choice D, making flash cards to study the circulatory sequencing, may allow for recall of facts, but not thorough comprehension of the sequencing.

3. **C.** He is using environmental print to reinforce the concept of compound words, choice C. While using brightly colored paper for the labels may be welcoming for students, choice A, this is not Mr. Cote's purpose. Choice B, using the labels for a classroom game, may be Mr. Cote's intention, but it is not the best explanation. Choice D is incorrect, as children at this grade level understand what labels are for.

4. **B.** The terms *metaphors, symbolism, visual words, sensory observation,* and *details* would most likely dominantly be used when teaching the descriptive genre, choice B. These terms reference literary devices that are dominantly used in descriptive writing. Choice A, narrative, is of a personal nature. Choice C, expository, alludes to factual writing and would not usually include a lot of sensory material. Choice D, persuasive, would include literary devices helpful in convincing others or taking a particular stance.

5. **C.** To help their child develop phonemic awareness, parents may read him stories and poems that contain rhyming words and alliteration, choice C. This allows the child to hear words that end with like sounds and words that have the same beginning sounds. Choices A (playing a computer game that matches a letter to a picture with that beginning sound), B (using magnetic letters to spell the child's name), and D (asking the child to identify objects that begin with the letter "B") all address letters and the letter-sound correspondence. Phonemic awareness relates to sound only.

6. **A.** The teacher is using the language experience approach, choice A. This is when a class has an experience and then talks and writes about it, using all types of vocabulary: listening, speaking, writing, and reading. This approach also allows children to connect speech to written words. Choice B, oral language development approach, is not a real technique. Choices C, writing process, and D, guided writing, are incorrect as well. The students aren't writing; rather, the teacher is writing what the students say, and the scenario does not include any mention of process. If collaborative writing were an answer choice, that would be acceptable.

7. **C.** The primary reason for a teacher to administer a miscue analysis of a student's reading performance is to identify the student's difficulties in oral reading and set instructional goals, choice C. The purpose of a miscue analysis is to determine what word identification skills students use and need. A running record can also aid in determining whether a book a child is reading is at his instructional level. Choices A, to assess the student's comprehension grade level, and D, to evaluate the student's inferential comprehension and set instructional goals, are incorrect because both refer to comprehension, and a miscue analysis is not the best evaluator of comprehension. Choice B, recognizing where a sentence begins and ends, is a concept of print measure.

8. **C.** Mrs. Carson should first help her students develop the ability to evaluate an online source for credibility, choice C. Sites recommended as being the most credible have URLs ending with .gov or .edu. Choice A, how to cite an online source, is an important part of a research paper, but not as essential as ensuring that the source is credible in the first place. Choice B, knowing how to use software to enhance a research project, is far too broad, although it is certainly true that online sources are accessed via software. Choice D, strategies to keep on task while searching the web, is not necessary to complete the research project.

9. **D.** An effective technique for working with ELLs is to use visuals whenever possible to explain new vocabulary, choice D. Showing a picture of a camel will teach an ELL much more effectively than trying to explain what a camel is when the student is unfamiliar with many of the words you are saying. Choice A, giving long explanations, would be confusing for ELLs. Choice B, being in close proximity to ELLs when speaking to them, would be useful if an ELL had a hearing loss or attention deficit, but is not usually necessary. Choice C, writing out the words whenever speaking, is simply not practical, and in any case, doing so would introduce too many words to ELLs.

10. **B.** Homonyms, also called homophones, are words that are spelled differently and have different meanings, but sound the same, choice B. Antonyms, choice A, are words with opposite meanings, such as *up* and *down*. Pseudonyms, choice C, are fictitious names such as Lemony Snicket, used by the author of the *A Series of Unfortunate Events* books. Acronyms, choice D, are words made from abbreviations. *Scuba*, for example, is an acronym for *self-contained underwater breathing apparatus*.

11. **C.** *However, but, yet,* and *on the contrary* (choice C) are signal words that indicate a compare and contrast text structure. The group *first, second, then, next* (choice A) indicates a chronological or sequential text structure. The group *besides, several, another, in addition* (choice B) indicates an enumeration text structure. The group *for this reason, as a result, on account of* (choice D) indicates a cause and effect text structure.

12. **A.** Saying the word *bug* and having students separate the sounds in the word allows a teacher to assess the students' phonemic awareness, choice A. Sound segmentation is part of phonemic awareness. However, students who are phonemically aware do not need to know that letters exist. Choices B, C, and D are incorrect because they all involve phonics skills, as students must connect spoken sounds to written letters.

13. **B.** Activating prior knowledge before reading, choice B, would be the most effective technique for students who are not demonstrating full comprehension of text concepts. Activating prior knowledge provides the reader an idea of what the reading selection is about, fosters connections to new knowledge, and promotes overall understanding of the text. Choice A, use computer reading programs, is not the most effective technique at this time; social learning, clarification, and summarizing skills are used in enhancing

comprehension and are better taught directly in the classroom, rather than by computer. Choices C, have students start a personal dictionary, and D, use word sorts, are incorrect, as the teacher is looking for comprehension that is in-depth rather than at the word level.

14. **B.** The teacher should use texts at the student's reading level while concentrating on decoding and sight word recognition, choice B. The student must learn alphabetic skills and develop increased sight word recognition before progressing to more difficult tasks. Choice A, extensively teach grade-level vocabulary and structural usage, may be helpful, but is not the best choice; structural usage is often difficult, and the student's grade level is not specified in this scenario. Choice C, supply diverse materials for the student to read and respond to, and choice D, employ computer games that foster inferential thinking and analysis, are incorrect, as the current goal for the student would be to improve word identification skills.

15. **D.** *Breaking the code, letter-sound correspondence,* and *phonics* are often used to refer to the alphabetic principle, choice D. Choices A and B both include *phonemic awareness,* which addresses only sounds, not letter-sound correspondence, and therefore should be eliminated. Choice C is incorrect, as *concepts of print* is not related to the alphabetic principle; concepts of print include directionality, knowing what a word is, and so forth.

16. **B.** *Magma (mag/ma),* choice B, contains a closed syllable. A closed syllable ends with a consonant and usually has a short vowel sound, as in the first syllable, "mag." An open syllable is one that ends with a vowel (CV or V) that usually has a long vowel sound, as in *ba/by, a/way,* and *a/gree* (choices A, C, and D).

17. **A.** In *declare (de/clare),* choice A, the second syllable is the accented one. Choices B (*bacon*), C (*heater*), and D (*broken*) are incorrect. The first syllable of these words is open, which usually indicates a long vowel sound as *declare* has. However, the syllabication rule states that if there is one consonant between two vowels, the first syllable is usually accented, which is the case with *ba/con, heat/er* and *bro/ken.*

18. **B.** The superintendent should choose a norm-referenced test, choice B. Norm-referenced tests compare students with other populations and produce percentile scores that "rank" the students. Choice D, criterion-referenced, is incorrect, as this type of test measures specified criteria such as letter recognition and inferential comprehension. Choices A, validity-referenced, and C, reliability-referenced, are not legitimate types of standardized tests.

19. **C.** In the sentence in choice C (*The boy lost the mitten*), *mitten* is a direct object. A direct object indicates who or what receives the action of the verb. In choice A, *a mitten* is an appositive that clarifies the missing item. In choices B and D, *The mitten* is the subject of the sentence.

20. **D.** Reading books with rich vocabulary, explaining what is happening in the books, then having students turn and talk will aid those with limited oral vocabularies and low comprehension skills (choice D). This is the only answer choice that focuses on developing vocabulary and then using it in oral speaking. Choice A, teaching students good listening skills, is a good strategy for listeners, but doesn't engage students in speech or encourage them to use new vocabulary. Choices B, using a talking stick, and C, instructing students to take turns talking, both entail additional oral language use, but they don't focus on increasing oral language vocabulary or comprehension.

21. **C.** Incorporating literature that uses cultures of all students into students' reading, choice C, will help create a positive learning environment for ELLs. It is important for ELL students to see themselves in books, and it helps when others see them too. The key phrase in this question is "positive learning environment," which pertains to the classroom climate; the teacher needs to make that environment as welcoming as possible. Choice A, have ELLs read books about the local area, while a nice gesture, will not improve the learning environment; furthermore, the students may not yet be capable of reading these books on their own. Choice B, use the ELLs' native languages in the classroom, is incorrect, as school districts may have a large number of different languages among their ELL students, making this highly impractical. Finally, choice D, sending books home, is acceptable, especially to re-read, but this won't directly impact the classroom environment.

22. **C.** The teacher should use techniques such as phrase sorts and repeated readings to build Bella's fluency, choice C. Slow reading and decoding pauses indicate the reader's lack of fluency. As fluency is a bridge to comprehension, Bella would benefit enormously from fluency techniques; her frequent pauses for decoding may certainly interfere with her comprehension of the text. Choice A, giving Bella phonics instruction, is

incorrect, as Bella's issue is not related to phonics. Choice B, working with Bella's confidence in reading, may be necessary, but it's not the best answer; gaining fluency will indirectly increase her confidence, anyway. Choice D, teaching self-monitoring techniques to ensure word accuracy, is incorrect, as Bella is reading the words accurately.

23. **B.** A teacher should choose books above the students' grade level to read to her class to expose the students to higher-level vocabulary, choice B. Listening to higher-level vocabulary entails receptive language, and will help students learn new words prior to seeing them in a text; this aids in comprehension. There is no basis for choice A, exposing students to a variety of genres, because the type of books the teacher is reading is not indicated. Choice C is incorrect, as not all texts use Standard American English. Choice D, emphasizing plot within a story, is incorrect because the read-aloud may not necessarily be a story, but rather, informational text.

24. **C.** The teacher understands that introducing the structures of nonfiction texts can enhance comprehension, choice C. Choice A, defining different parts of a text, is important because it makes communicating about the material easier, but this is not the most effective way to teach informational text. Choice B, providing the students an opportunity to read nonfiction text, is also essential, but it is not the primary reason for the activity. And, choice D, providing extensive practice with nonfiction text, is incorrect, as one exposure to new information does not constitute extensive practice with the material.

25. **B.** The teacher understands that actively engaging students in learning unknown words and concepts is effective instruction that deepens their comprehension, choice B. Choice A, "turn and talk" builds collaboration in the classroom, is true, but since the teacher is working with unknown vocabulary, choice B is more effective. Modeling vocabulary for students learning new words, choice C, and using "turn and talk" to keep students attentive, choice D, are not primary reasons to have students discuss concepts, because the teacher's goal is to foster comprehension and comprehension skills.

26. **C.** The word group *window, hold, broke* demonstrates that different letters and letter combinations can represent the same vowel sound, choice C. The "ow," "o," and "oke" all make the long /o/ sound. Choice A is incorrect, as *horse* and *tore* have an "r"-controlled vowel, while the "ou" in *couch* is a diphthong. Choice B is incorrect, as *field, biked,* and *cried* do not have all the same sounds; the "ie" in *field* makes the long /e/ sound, while the other words have the long /i/ sound. Choice D is incorrect, as there are no similar vowel sounds in the words *sack, bake,* and *beak*.

27. **A.** A second grader who is not yet able to identify all the letter sounds, choice A, is not progressing sufficiently. In second grade, this is a warning signal for the teacher that this child may need further intervention. Choice B, a third grader having difficulty pronouncing multisyllabic words, may be slightly below expectations, but with concentrated instruction this student would most likely improve. Choice C, a first grader who does not yet understand the use of context to figure out new words, lacks an essential skill, but his progress can still be considered proficient at this point. Choice D, a second grader who is struggling with contractions, is also progressing sufficiently at this point, but needs additional instruction in this area.

28. **C.** Using Readers' Theater, in which Tommy assumes the role of a character (choice C), would help him improve his reading. Fluency encompasses accuracy, speed, and prosody (expression). Tommy is said to read slowly and in a monotone voice, so he would certainly benefit from fluency techniques. When using Readers' Theater, students practice their parts to perform. As they practice, they re-read and use expression, both components of fluency. Choice A, reading more challenging texts, is incorrect, as reading at a frustration level will not help Tommy improve. Choice B, offering wide reading, is a good practice, but it does not include fluency techniques to help with prosody. Choice D, completing more written responses using new vocabulary, also does not help with prosody.

29. **C.** She wants the students to record their thoughts about the chapter, giving them a means to think more about the story and their reaction to the events within it, choice C. Choice A is incorrect, as journal writing is not the most effective way to get students to do their best writing. Choice B may be partially correct, but it demonstrates only literal understanding. Ms. Ortiz may be meeting with another group (choice D), but the reading response was selected for an academic purpose, not just to keep the students busy.

30. **A.** To group for skills, the teacher would use criterion-referenced test results, choice A. A criterion-referenced test measures a specific skill, such as vocabulary knowledge, comprehension, word usage, and so

forth. Therefore, the scores from a criterion-referenced test may be used as an indicator to differentiate instruction on that skill. Choices B, phoneme-referenced, and C, identification-referenced, are not real test types. Choice D, norm-referenced, refers to a standardized test that compares students with other populations, and produces a percentile score that "ranks" the student.

31. **D.** Mrs. Silva is taking a running record, choice D. She is coding Sarah's reading behaviors to pinpoint what Sarah is doing correctly and incorrectly when reading. Based on this analysis, Mrs. Silva will set goals for Sarah's reading growth. Choices A (capturing Sarah's ability to recognize sentences), B (using reading to bond with students), and C (assessing recognition of letters) do not include coding reading behaviors.

32. **B.** Mr. Carlson is teaching his students about synonyms, choice B. Synonyms are words that mean the same (*big: huge, gigantic, large, enormous*). Antonyms, choice A, are words that mean the opposite (*kind-mean*). Euphemisms, choice C, are words or phrases that express something offensive or embarrassing in a gentler way (for example, a euphemism for *the woman is pregnant,* is *the woman is in the family way*). Homonyms, choice D, sometimes called homophones, are words that sound alike but are spelled differently and have different meanings: *bear-bare; flour-flower*.

33. **C.** The main purpose of this lesson is to use explicit instruction to develop comprehension skills, choice C. Mr. Cohen is modeling how to ask questions, and how to think about the questions in order to enhance comprehension. Choice A, to participate in a read-aloud, is incorrect, as this lesson includes more than a read-aloud. Choice B, to help students learn information about seeds, may be partially true, but Mr. Cohen is using the book as a vehicle to teach questioning as a comprehension strategy; therefore, learning about seeds is not the main purpose of the lesson. Choice D, to explicitly teach the concept of main idea, is incorrect, as Mr. Cohen is not discussing main ideas; he is using questions to help clarify and comprehend information.

34. **C.** The students have essentially no knowledge of the Louisiana Purchase, choice C. They are confusing it with the state of Louisiana, which was a very small portion of the Louisiana Territory. So, the teacher will need to correct this misconception. Choice A, doing the KWL has made the students excited to learn about the Louisiana Purchase, may be true, as students would be interested to learn the answers to their questions, but the teacher wasn't looking to assess student motivation. Choice B is incorrect; the KWL was not useless in this lesson, as it showed the teacher that her students have limited to no knowledge about the Louisiana Purchase. There is nothing in the provided information to indicate that the students are not interested in learning about the Louisiana Purchase, choice D.

35. **C.** Close reading is the primary technique in this lesson, choice C. The teacher is using close reading techniques as she discusses her thinking and then re-reads to annotate. She subsequently has the students apply these techniques. Choices A, directed reading, and B, scaffolded reading, are incorrect, as both are pre-teaching techniques. Choice D, silent reading, is incorrect, as it is not a reading technique, but a mode of reading.

36. **A.** The teacher understands that wide reading increases a student's vocabulary and fluency, choice A. The teacher is giving students a compelling reason to read new material; the more students read, the more they will most likely improve their reading skills and increase their vocabulary. Choice B, to provide herself more time to plan the next unit, should never be a primary reason for a lesson. Choice C, the teacher understands that the students need their learning reinforced, is incorrect, as that may or may not be happening; it depends on the material students select to read. Choice D, the teacher wants students to use technology in this unit, is incorrect; using technology should never be a primary reason for any reading lesson. Technology should be used in effective and purposeful ways as a means of achieving literacy outcomes.

37. **C.** An effective way to assess phonemic awareness is to say the word *duck* and ask students how many sounds they hear in the word, choice C. Choices A, B, and D all involve letters; phonemic awareness relates only to sounds. Children do not even need to know letters exist to have phonemic awareness.

38. **C.** The reliability of a test means that the test would have the same results over time in different settings, choice C. Choice A, the questions have been checked for accuracy, would most likely be true, but this is not a measure of reliability. Choice B is incorrect; percentiles are determined by norm-referenced testing and are not a measure of reliability. Choice D is incorrect, as validity, not reliability, means that the test measures what it is supposed to measure.

39. **A.** The consonant-le syllable is usually unaccented, choice A. The consonant-le part of the word constitutes its own syllable, so choice B is incorrect. Choice C, the consonant-le pattern is always preceded by two consonants, is incorrect, as shown by the words *table* and *beagle*. The consonant-le syllable is usually unaccented, not accented, so choice D is incorrect.

40. **B.** A reader response journal, choice B, best describes the application of the reading and writing connection. When students respond to reading by writing, they are forced to think more about the text in order to decide what to write. This ultimately leads to deeper understanding. Choice A is incorrect, as word sorts do not necessarily require writing, although they may encourage students to think about word meaning. Choice C is incorrect, as the language experience approach helps students make the connection from the spoken word to the written word, not the reading and writing connection. Choice D is incorrect, as choral reading entails children reading a text together at the same time; it does not involve writing.

41. **B.** Students should be placed in flexible guided reading groups that allow them to read from an instructional level book the majority of the time, choice B. Instructional level texts are considered the "just right" level—not frustrating, but challenging enough that students keep improving their reading skills. Choice A, pairing lower and higher readers for reading instruction, is not fair to the high-level readers. Choice C, letting students select books they want to read, may be motivating, but it does not differentiate by skill level and would not be the most effective for all students. Choice D, making one large lower-level reading group and one large higher-level group in the classroom, does not differentiate enough to meet the needs of all students. The scenario doesn't say what the grade levels are. If, for example, some students are reading at a first-grade level and they are placed in a second-grade-level group, then this is not true differentiation; either the first-grade-level students will be reading at frustration level or the second-grade-level students will be reading material that is too easy.

42. **D.** Of the choices given, short vowel sounds should be taught first, choice D. Knowing consonant sounds is important, but that is not a choice. Short vowel sounds should be taught before the VCe rule (choice A), consonant blends (choice B), and sight words (choice C). Beginning readers start by reading decodable books with words like *mat, cat, fat, bit, hit, sit,* and so forth. Knowing short vowel sounds helps the beginning reader with decoding these high-frequency words.

43. **B.** Hiding index cards with the letter "S" around the room and having students do a letter "S" hunt reinforces letter recognition, choice B. The students know that they are looking for the letter "S" and will pick up any "S" they see, reinforcing the letter recognition. Choice A involves the /b/ sound, which is not identifying a letter. Choice C, saying the beginning sound of *hat, ham,* and *hurt*, involves phonemic awareness; no letters are involved. In choice D, the students will be writing letters in the sand, but little children can write their name without being able to name the letters.

44. **C.** Headings and subheadings inform readers about the topic to be covered in their corresponding sections, aiding in comprehension, choice C. Knowing what the next section of the text is about allows students to activate their prior knowledge and make connections to new knowledge. Choices A and B are incorrect; ample white space (choice A) may not aid in decoding, and headings are not known to confuse readers (choice B). Choice D is incorrect because headings may convey the topic, but not necessarily all the main ideas and details in the text.

45. **B.** The teacher understands that students are completely unfamiliar with life during the time period, and that some historical perspective will enhance their comprehension, choice B. Choice A, the teacher is a history buff, may be true, but it is not the best academic reason to build background. Choice C, working with vocabulary strategies, is incorrect, as vocabulary isn't mentioned as a focus. Choice D, to assess what students already know about the Boston Tea Party, is incorrect, as there is no basis for this in the question; if the teacher wanted to assess prior knowledge, she would most likely use a semantic web or a KWL chart in the instruction.

46. **B.** The teacher would most likely have given the students a cause-and-effect graphic organizer to summarize the events mentioned in the text, choice B. A text summary indicates the main action and the result, which indicates cause and effect. Choice A is incorrect, as nothing is being compared. Choice C is incorrect, as the text does not focus on the timeline of the events, but rather, the colonists' reactions. Choice D, descriptive, is incorrect, as students were not asked about what they already know; however, this is a good strategy to enhance comprehension.

47. **A.** A valid test measures the skills and content that it is supposed to measure, choice A. Choice B, a valid test is normed, is inaccurate, as a test can be valid without being normed. Choice C is inaccurate, as standardized tests are not necessarily at grade level; they must span students' abilities. Choice D, converting scores into grade equivalencies, is done on some standardized tests, but this conversion does not define the validity of a test.

48. **D.** A legend must be based on facts, choice D. This genre has elements of historical truth, but also includes imaginary events or heroes whose deeds are exaggerated. Choice A, includes occurrences or creatures that do not exist, describes a fantasy. Choice B, must contain humor, describes a tall tale, which is exaggerated but has no historical basis. Choice C, does not have to be fact-based, describes a narrative (however, personal narratives are fact-based).

49. **B.** Mrs. Caron is assessing fluency, choice B. Fluency encompasses word accuracy, reading rate, and prosody. In this scenario, Mrs. Caron is tracking both reading rate and word accuracy, thereby performing an informal fluency assessment. Choices A, comprehension, and C, letter-sound correspondence, are incorrect, as there is no evidence either is being assessed, although any phonics inaccuracies would be evident in the coding. Choice D, word accuracy, is partially correct, but not the complete or best answer.

50. **D.** They are all phonetically irregular vowel patterns, choice D. The "o" in *women* takes the short /i/ sound, and the vowels in *head* and *field* do not follow the phonics generalization that states when two vowels are together, the first is heard (vowel digraphs). *Some* and *have* do not follow the phonics generalization of the vowel-consonant-silent "e" (VCe) generalization in which the "e" is silent and the first vowel has the long vowel sound. Finally, *busy,* according to the CVC pattern generalization, should have a short /u/ sound, but instead has a short /i/ sound. Therefore, choices A, B, and C are incorrect.

51. **B.** A short text passage that can be analyzed for form, craft, and structure should be used to teach close reading techniques, choice B. Close reading is an analysis of text for form, craft, and structure, as well as language, meanings, ideas, concepts, and so forth. Choice A is incorrect, as a close reading does not involve a whole book, although the short passage should be at a challenging level. Choices C and D are incorrect, as close reading may be performed on any genre; it is not specific to informational texts (choice C) or mysteries (choice D).

52. **C.** Mr. Mantle is conducting this activity to have students learn to use context to decode unknown words, choice C. Having students read to the end of the sentence or re-read a sentence when coming to an unknown word is a standard procedure using context and meaning to aid students in decoding. There is no basis to say that Mr. Mantle is assessing the students' reading levels (choice A). Choice B, practicing oral reading at a more challenging level, is not an effective practice. Choice D is incorrect, as there is no indication that he is checking for expression (prosody).

53. **A.** The teacher is doing this activity because he understands that knowing the meaning of various roots can aid students in understanding the meaning of unknown words, choice A. With this knowledge, students can use structural analysis to decipher the meanings of most words. Choice B is incorrect, as learning Greek roots is an ineffective way to activate prior knowledge on Greek mythology. Choice C is incorrect, as *anti* is a root and not considered part of a compound word, defined as two words that take on a new meaning when combined (*light bulb*). Choice D is incorrect, as a euphemism is a word or phrase that expresses something offensive or embarrassing in a gentler way (i.e., describing someone who is overweight as being *pleasantly plump*).

54. **A.** Riddles, choice A, often contain puns, multiple meanings, or idioms that may be very confusing for ELLs. For example, the riddle *What has one eye, but cannot see?* (Answer: a needle), contains a pun, as the eye of the needle has a different meaning from the sensory organ. Choice B is incorrect, as narratives are typically straightforward. Choice C is incorrect; although poetry may contain tricky images and metaphors, most poems are not deliberately intended to confuse, as riddles are. Choice D is incorrect, although ELLs may need more scaffolding as they try to decipher clues to solve the mystery.

55. C. At the 48th percentile, Jamie is in the middle range in reading comprehension, choice C. The 50th percentile mark is at the exact mean, or average, on the normal (bell) curve. As long as Jamie is within one standard deviation of the 50th percentile mark, he will be considered average in reading comprehension. Choice A is incorrect, as this test utilizes percentile scoring, not raw test scores. Choice B is incorrect, as there is no indication that this was a criterion-referenced test, which would be able to isolate inference skills. Choice D is incorrect, as Jamie is not lagging, but in the average range, in reading comprehension.

56. D. *Flag,* choice D, contains four phonemes. A phoneme is a single sound; in *flag,* there are four sounds: /f/, /l/, /a/, and /g/. Choice A, *tack,* has three phonemes: /t/, /a/, and /k/. Choice B, *seriously,* has four syllables, not four phonemes. Choice C, *boat,* has three phonemes: /b/, /o/, and /t/.

57. D. If a student uses high-level oral vocabulary, the student is more likely to comprehend at a deeper level, choice D, because he already understands the words being read. Oral language vocabulary transfers into reading, and aids in comprehension. Choice A is false, as oral language does impact reading. Choice B, aids students in phonemic awareness and phonics, relates to word identification, not meaning. Choice C, oral language allows clearer communication so students can be more concise in their explanations, is a true statement and an attractive choice, but it doesn't answer the question posed here.

58. C. A cause-and-effect map, choice C, would be most effective in summarizing the main points of the text. The changes in society that have brought about large amounts of waste would be considered the cause, and the impact of this waste on the environment would be the effect. Choice A, a Venn diagram, is used for comparison and contrast. Choice B, a concept map, is used to establish connections between ideas, and to categorize information. Choice D, a main idea web, is used to write the main idea of a text and supporting details, but it cannot show causal relationships and the effects.

59. B. The teacher is assessing print awareness, choice B. Print awareness refers to understanding the nature and meaning of print, including the fact that print carries meaning. Choice A, phonemic awareness, is incorrect, as phonemic awareness involves only sounds, not print. Choice C, text structure, is incorrect, as this refers to the text's organizational structure, such as compare and contrast or sequential ordering. Choice D, directionality, is incorrect, as that would entail a teacher or student demonstrating with a finger that print is read from left to right.

60. A. Model Standard American English, allowing students to conclude that school language usage may differ from home language, choice A. With proper modeling, students will begin to realize that language usage styles may differ in different situations. Choices B and D entail demanding that students use Standard American English, and may be intimidating or make students uncomfortable speaking orally in the classroom, which is counterproductive. Choice C, using worksheets, would not be motivating for these students; furthermore, it would not model oral Standard American English.

61. B. The student's improvement can best be described as knowing the various spellings of the long /a/ sound, choice B. This is shown by the student's improvement on the post-test in the following: the VCe rule (progressing from spelling *bak* to *bake*); the vowel digraph rule, in which the first vowel has a long vowel sound (progressing from *pal* to *pail*); and that "ay" says the long /a/ sound (progressing from *sa* to *say*). Choice A, understanding of consonant digraphs, is incorrect, as there are no spelling words in the list that contain a consonant digraph (two consonants that make one sound). Choice C, learning that "igh" makes the long /i/ sound, is incorrect, as there was no improvement with the word *might*. Choice D is incorrect, as the student demonstrated that he already knew the short /a/ sound on the pre-test, with *mat*.

62. B. *House,* choice B, is the only choice given that contains a diphthong, and although the word was still spelled incorrectly in the post-test (*hous*), the diphthong was written correctly. Choice A, *dark,* has an "r"-controlled vowel, "ar." Choice C, *stop,* contains a consonant blend, "st." Choice D, *might,* contains the silent "gh," which is not a diphthong.

63. A. Choice A (*Bobby is the son of George*) contains a prepositional phrase. A preposition is placed before a noun to show its relationship to another noun or pronoun. In this case, the preposition *of* is before the noun *George,* showing George's relationship to Bobby (in this case, an actual familial relationship). Some examples of prepositions include *around, above, near, in, underneath, alongside, on, at, of,* and *for.* The sentences in choices B, C, and D do not contain a preposition, although the words *long, really,* and *ever* are adjectives or adverbs modifying a noun.

64. B. A reader response journal fosters the reading and writing connection, and deepens comprehension by allowing students to devise their own interpretations of the text, choice B. These journals encourage students to think more, and differently, about the events in the book when writing their responses. Choice A, providing the teacher time to create effective lessons, is incorrect; teachers should work with students, not plan, during class time. Choice C, a means to assess whether students are capable of reading the selected text, may be somewhat true depending on the nature of the response, but is not the best choice. Choice D is incorrect. With a reader response journal, students are often given a prompt or must respond to an event, essentially limiting their freedom of expression.

65. A. Using schemata and information from the text to arrive at a conclusion about the text's events constitutes inferring, choice A. Inferential comprehension combines background knowledge with information from the text to understand what the author implies but does not explicitly state in the text. Choice B, clarifying, is used when a reader is confused by something in the text, and frequently entails re-reading to clarify. Choice C, visualizing, entails the reader making a picture or "movie" in his head to "see" what is happening in the text. Choice D, predicting, involves using inference skills to think about what will happen next.

66. C. By writing the information, the students are using the sequential text structure and reinforcing domain-specific vocabulary, choice C. The students would have followed sequential directions to perform the experiment, so when writing down the steps and the results, they should follow the same text structure and use proper vocabulary. Choice A, to let the teacher assess the experiments, is not a reasonable answer. Choice B, using a compare-and-contrast text structure, is incorrect; writing the procedure employs a sequential text structure. Choice D, being able to redo the experiment at home, may or may not be true, but it's not the best reason.

67. A. The second grader's note shows that he knows that long vowels "say their name," choice A. The child doesn't have the long vowel sounds spelled correctly, but the letters he uses in the words *yu, nise, happe, mi, tesher, lic,* and *tesh* indicate that he understands the sounds. Choice B, that all words contain vowels, is incorrect, as the child wrote *Dr* (*Dear*), *thnk* (*think*), and *lv* (*love*) without vowels. Choice C, the letter "c" can say the /s/ and /k/ sounds, is incorrect; this rule is not used in *nise* (*nice*). Choice D is incorrect, as *teacher* and *teach* have vowel digraphs, but the child didn't use them in his spelling (*tesher, tesh*). A vowel digraph refers to two vowels together, with the first vowel making the long sound and the second, silent.

68. D. The text structure used in the passage is chronological, choice D, which is used when text must be written in a particular sequence. Choice A, compare and contrast, is incorrect, as nothing is being compared or contrasted in the passage. Choice B, description, is incorrect as there is no elaboration or senses that provoke an image. Choice C, cause and effect, is incorrect as there nothing in the passage to indicate this text structure; it simply gives the steps for boiling an egg.

69. A. Prosody is the expression and intonation used in oral reading, choice A; it is a component of fluency. Choice B, the speed of oral reading, is also a component of fluency, but refers to reading rate. Choice C, the structure of the language, is incorrect, as this defines syntax, not prosody. Choice D, the inability to infer, is also incorrect.

70. B. Using word trees to form derivatives of base and root words by adding affixes, choice B, is an effective approach for instructing students who are having difficulty reading unfamiliar multisyllabic words. This word study approach allows students to learn the meaning of affixes, and gives them a conceptual understanding of how multisyllabic words are formed. Giving students books to read that are at a challenging level (choice A) may leave the students at frustration level when reading, and will not necessarily aid in word identification. Choice C, explicitly teaching the text's multisyllabic words, is incorrect. Although this approach sounds feasible, if there are numerous multisyllabic words, the approach won't work well. Choice D is incorrect, as the students are likely to spend as much time with the dictionary as they are reading—or instead may pretend to know all the words.

71. C. The students will be predicting, choice C. Predictions are inferences; readers use evidence from the text to infer what might happen next (Brian leaves without his cap or he keeps looking, and so forth). Choice A, summarizing, entails putting information together, not thinking about what will happen next. Choice B, guessing, is not really a comprehension strategy, although children do guess sometimes! Choice D, clarifying, is used when the reader is confused and must take some action to understand what is happening in the text.

72. B. Asking students, "Do you think Brian's new baseball cap is important to him? Explain." (choice B) will require them to use inferential comprehension. This question is inferential because it takes what the students already know (if something is important to you, you look for it; his grandmother gave it to him; he needs it because of the sun) and connects the new information (Brian searched various places in his room). Therefore, the students, depending on their own knowledge and information from the passage, may answer, "Yes, because he cared enough to go upstairs," or "Yes, because he looked in so many places." Or, they might say, "No, because he didn't come down with the cap." Choice A (Did Brian find his new baseball cap?) is a literal question; the answer is right there in the text. Choice C (Can you tell me about your favorite cap or hat?) does not require students to read the text, so it cannot be used to evaluate text comprehension. Choice D (Where do you think the new baseball cap is?) is speculative; students would be guessing in order to answer the question, as there is no evidence in the text for inference.

73. C. The teacher wants the students to recognize these words as compound words, choice C. Compound words are two words that when combined, form a new word (*homework, light bulb*). Contractions, choice A, are two words that are shortened and combined into a single word (*wasn't* for *was not*). Synonyms, choice B, are words with the same meaning (*happy, glad*). Digraphs, choice D, are two consecutive letters that make one sound ("ea" in *beat*, "gh" in *tough*). The "ai" in *upstairs* and *downstairs* is an "r"-controlled digraph, but digraphs are not in all the listed words.

74. A. Mr. Bacon opts to pre-teach the word *shuttle* because he understands how to select appropriate words for instruction, choice A. The word *shuttle* has multiple meanings, and students may confuse this unknown usage with a bus shuttle or space shuttle. Not all new words should be explicitly taught (choice B). Choice C is incorrect because, while the sentence hints at the meaning of *shuttle*, it is still not clearly defined. Choice D is inaccurate because the "tle" in *shuttle* is not a suffix, but part of the word.

75. C. The teacher wants students to be aware of the relationship of speech to print, choice C. When students see their words written down, they begin to realize that print has meaning. Choice A, to organize the students' thinking and responses, is incorrect, although the activity does provide a sentence organization for each frame. Choice B, to get students to know a little bit about each other, is a nice thought, but not the best reason; also, not all students will volunteer. Choice D, to teach letter-sound correspondence, is incorrect; the most effective method for teaching phonics is through direct, explicit instruction, such as explaining that "b" says /b/.

76. B. The teacher will pre-teach *exasperated* because it cannot be defined from the context, choice B. For example, the word could be switched to *excited, exhilarated, worried,* or a number of other words and still make sense in the text. Choice A is incorrect because the numerous synonyms for *exasperated* is irrelevant here. Choices C and D are incorrect, as *rupees* is not a frequently used word, and students can glean from the text that it entails some form of money.

77. C. The results of Eric's IRI suggest that he is using context cues for word identification in passages, choice C. To identify words on the isolated word list, a student would need to use either sight word recognition or phonics. Since Eric got some words on the word list incorrect, but was able to read them correctly in the passage, he appears to be using context cues. Choice A, that Eric has problems with structural analysis, is incorrect, as two of the words he missed, *anxious* and *dilemma,* cannot be separated into smaller words. Furthermore, he did get *furious* correct; this does have a common root with the word *fury.* Choice B is incorrect, as all sight words (*was, and,* and *were*) were read correctly. Choice D is incorrect because when administering an IRI, the teacher must assess the student up to frustration level to ensure that she has the student placed at the highest instructional level.

78. D. Angie appears to need explicit instruction on comprehension strategies, choice D. Angie was able to decode the words, so she could read them orally. However, Angie could not understand what she was reading, as the scenario indicates that she could not answer the comprehension questions accurately. Choice A is incorrect, as Angie should not be given a frustration level text (although her progress should be monitored because as her comprehension improves, she should certainly be advanced to higher-level texts). Choice B is incorrect, as Angie self-corrected the word *anxious* in the passage. Choice C is incorrect, as there is no way of knowing Angie's reading speed.

79. B. The question in choice B is inferential: "Would you say that Jerome is a good boy? Explain." Although there is evidence in the text for an answer, the answer is not explicitly stated. A student could answer that Jerome is a good boy because he was worried about getting home on time. Or, the student could answer that Jerome was not a good boy because he was thinking of disobeying his mother and he had been grounded before, so he had already misbehaved at some point. Choice A (what would you do if you were Jerome?) encourages a nice personal connection with the reader, but there is no information in the text to help the reader form a response. The same is true for choice D (how will Jerome's friends act if he leaves?). Choice C (why wouldn't Jerome tell his friends he had to leave?) is literal, as the answer is right there in the text (he was embarrassed).

80. B. She understands that when students are interested in a topic, they are motivated, choice B. Effective reading instruction includes choosing texts that are at an appropriate ability level, and that interest the students. Choice A is incorrect, as the students are selecting only one text. Choices C and D are incorrect, as neither book talks nor genre studies are mentioned in the scenario, although both are effective motivators.

81. B. The teacher could help these students by reading a passage orally and asking herself about what she has just read, then modeling her thinking about the passage to the students, choice B. When a teacher does this, she is modeling her own metacognition (thinking about thinking) and showing students that they need to not only read, but also think about what they are reading and ask themselves if it makes sense. Choices A and D, which both incorporate discussion, may be helpful, but they are not metacognitive strategies. Choice C, using inferential questions after reading, would assess whether students are using metacognitive strategies, but it would not help them learn these skills.

82. C. This type of modeling shows that Mrs. Carol understands that students should use multiple strategies to enhance their understanding, choice C. Choice A, that it may take a long time to truly understand a text, is incorrect, although readers should slow down their reading if they don't understand. Choice B, that reading orally helps with text comprehension, is incorrect, as silent reading is usually best for comprehension. Choice D, visualization, was only one of the tools that was modeled, so it is not the best choice.

83. B. Mr. Pontis likely has a large selection of highly recommended multicultural literature in his classroom in order to teach students to respect and value all cultures, choice B. Having high-quality multicultural literature in a classroom allows minorities to see themselves in literature and allows others to learn about different cultures, creating respect and understanding. Choice A, inviting students to read a variety of materials, would be only one aspect of the reason to select multicultural literature; it is not the best answer. Choice C, to read more difficult texts, may not be true at all; the difficulty level of the books is not indicated. Choice D, to identify cultural stereotypes in the texts, is incorrect, as highly recommended multicultural literature would have been vetted for this type of information in both the text and pictures.

84. C. Compare and contrast, choice C, is the best text structure for this assignment. The students are to show differences, which indicates comparison. Choice A, description, would elaborate on one topic, but not convey differences between the 1800s Native Americans and the Native Americans of today. Choice B, persuasive, would use convincing language and evidence; this does not entail the kind of difference Mrs. Cole wishes to convey. Choice D, cause and effect, would shows a causal relationship, which is not required when writing about differences between groups or issues.

85. D. Choosing one or two target words and using them multiple times when speaking is the best way to support a relatively new ELL, choice D. This enables the ELL to capture the word by hearing it in context numerous times. Choice A, exposing the ELL to as many Standard American English words as possible, would be totally confusing to most ELLs and would not help in their English language growth. Choice B, limiting visuals in texts, is incorrect, as visuals aid ELLs in their learning. Choice C, read books with lively and entertaining vocabulary words, is also incorrect; such books would be too difficult for a relatively new ELL to comprehend.

86. D. There may be some developmental or physical concerns with Carly's receptive language, choice D. People receive language through the receptive modes of listening and reading, whereas they communicate via the expressive modes, speaking and writing. In this scenario, Carly demonstrates more understanding with visuals than with oral directions, which may indicate some type of language processing concern. Choices A and C are incorrect, as there is no mention of problems with Carly's writing (expressive language) or speaking (oral language). Choice B is incorrect, as the scenario does not include background information regarding a lack of exposure to a variety of experiences, and Carly is performing well enough when shown visual directions.

87. B. *Heat, heater, preheat,* and *reheat* (choice B) can be analyzed by the meaning of the word *heat* and the affixes (*pre-* meaning before, *re-* meaning again, and *-er* meaning one who does). Choices A, C, and D do not include words that would be useful as a set to teach structural analysis. The words in choice A all contain the digraph "ck," those in choice C are homophones, and those in choice D are forms of matter, so are categorized by topic.

88. B. Mr. Oliver should model the rules of Standard American English, but be respectful of the students' regional dialect, choice B. Students should not be embarrassed or unwilling to speak in school. Therefore, correction methods, like those described in choices A and D, should not be utilized, as these may embarrass the students. Choice C, having them read a sentence to each other, is not a good choice, as the teacher cannot hear what the students are reading. By listening to a teacher's modeling of the correct rules of language, students will learn that Standard American English is expected at school, and that dialectical variations can be used in informal settings.

89. C. The teacher is doing this to explicitly teach her students that books have parts, choice C. Recognizing important parts of a book is considered a concept of print. Children need to know the parts of a book, and the terminology that is used to discuss books. Choice A, directionality of print, is incorrect, as the teacher is not working with text. Choice B is incorrect, as the teacher is not going through the book to preview the story. Choice D is incorrect; although the teacher shows the class the front and back of the book, that does not equate to the beginning and end of a story.

90. B. Readers' Theater, choice B, is helpful in building fluency. Fluency is built by purposeful re-reading, and when a teacher utilizes Readers' Theater in the classroom, students re-read to practice their performance. Choice A, popcorn reading, entails the teacher arbitrarily picking a student to read orally, and is considered ineffective. Partner reading (choice C), although incorrect, may be helpful, but it doesn't necessarily incorporate re-reading for practice. Choice D, cooperative learning, may not even involve reading.

Constructed-Response Model Answers

Before you begin writing an answer, you should review what is expected in order to obtain a score of 3 for your response. To paraphrase expectations,

- Clearly and directly answer all parts of the question.
- Show that you know reading content and understand it. Be accurate in that content.
- Write a strong explanation—support what you say.

Constructed-Response Question #1

Model Answer 1

The errors and self-corrections that the teacher noted on Katie's oral reading evidence one strength and one weakness. Katie's strength is that she is reading for meaning. Katie's weakness is that she is not reading through the word.

When analyzing Katie's strength, the teacher noted that, fortunately, the majority of her errors do not lead to semantic miscues, as what she reads does make sense. For instance, replacing "they" with "the duckies," "did not" with "didn't," and "ran" with "run" did not lead to any meaning miscues. Although Katie omitted the words "they" and "out," the sentence meaning did not change. In addition, Katie's self-correction of the word "following" shows she is self-monitoring for meaning.

Katie's weakness is not reading through the word. She read "they" as "the," "did not" as "didn't," "started" as "stard," "heard" as "hear," and "ran" as "run." Although Katie read the initial phonemes correctly, she made a miscue with either the medial sound or ending sound, which shows she is not focusing on the entire word. This is causing her to read with errors that could lead to incorrect comprehension of the text.

A goal for Katie would be to get her to focus on the entire word. Some word building techniques using longer words would be applicable. Since Katie missed the words "started" and "heard," some "r"-controlled vowel words should be included.

Model Answer 2

The teacher's coding of Katie's running record shows a strength and a weakness in word identification skills. Katie's strength is reading initial phonemes. Katie's weakness is an overreliance on context cues.

Katie shows that she is using phonics to decode the initial phonemes in unknown words. Katie read "they" as "the," "did not" as "didn't," "started" as "stard," "heard" as "hear," and "ran" as "run." In all of these words, the initial phoneme sound was correct. This is a strength for Katie, as she can be taught to look more closely at the medial and final phonemes to strengthen her decoding.

Katie's weakness is that she over-relies on semantic cues. Usually, using context cues to aid in word identification is an effective technique, but Katie is relying on context cues so much that she is omitting words and substituting them with words or phrases of similar meaning. Although it does not seem to change the meaning of the sentences in this particular reading, doing so could cause problems with comprehension in further readings.

A goal for Katie would be to focus on the visual aspects of words in the text. Katie needs to be told that she should be reading every word and not skipping words, as this may interfere with her comprehension. To be careful that Katie does not start reading word by word, some practice with unusual phrases would be appropriate.

Constructed-Response Question #2

Model Answer 1

Miss Canton needs to assess her students' reading levels as soon as possible if she wants to see optimal growth this year. She should begin the school year using big books as she has planned, but should have at least one assessment completed for all students in the first two weeks. This will enable her to place students in leveled groups preliminarily while she continues assessing in order to ensure they are placed properly. Once she has her groupings set, Miss Canton will be able to go to the book closet and find books at her students' instructional levels. Miss Canton will form three to four groups and meet with them daily in a guided reading format. She will continue to used shared reading in a read-aloud format as a vehicle to build vocabulary in her young students.

Technology will be continually used in the assessment of students. One of the assessments will be the schoolwide, computer-based assessment that aids teachers in placing students in instructional level groups. She will also give students a spelling inventory in order to form skills groups in areas of need. The results of the spelling inventory will be uploaded to the school's database so she can continue to update the data as she monitors progress.

Model Answer 2

Miss Canton appears to want to be a very effective teacher and she is on the right track. Using shared books with young children builds a community of readers and gives the students a common book to discuss at various times during the year. Miss Canton will need to use best practices as she does shared reading. Since she has students in her class who are still learning their letters, she needs to make sure she is explicitly teaching concepts of print as she reads. For a reader response, Miss Canton needs to differentiate to make sure all students' needs are being met. As she is using shared reading to begin the school year, Miss Canton needs to use multiple assessments to learn the students' instructional level for reading and their skills needs. She then needs to use flexible grouping procedures to group her students for reading and skills groups.

Once the students have been assessed, Miss Canton will use a variety of texts, enabling her students to be introduced to a variety of genres. She will also use software that allows students to read books on the same topic, but at various instructional levels. Since the students are reading about the same topic, Miss Canton can activate prior knowledge on a classwide basis, and build background as needed. The students who are still working on letters can be scaffolded through the voice activation on the software, and can listen to the book as the words are highlighted. For these students, Miss Canton will utilize apps that teach letters and letter sounds. She will also assess them on phonemic awareness for instruction if needed.

Constructed-Response Question #3

Model Answer 1

English Language Learners (ELLs) have a double challenge, as they are learning to speak English and to read it at the same time. As readers read, they construct meaning. If the words are new and not well known, trying to construct meaning without all the information is problematic and obviously interferes with comprehension. In the midst of all this new information, there are some word forms and phrases that are even more challenging for ELLs. Three specific types that can cause interruption in comprehension are idioms, multiple-meaning words, and homographs.

An idiom is a group of words that has an unexpected meaning. For example, an ELL student might read the sentence "Go fly a kite." and think that someone really expects the person to fly a kite, while most native English speakers have grown up hearing this phrase, which has nothing to do with a kite, but is a rather unpleasant way of telling someone to leave. Multiple-meaning words are words that have more than one meaning. Although many words have multiple meanings, there are some that can be especially confusing. For example, in math, a compass is used to draw circles, but in geography, a compass indicates direction orientation on a map. Finally, homographs can also be confusing. They too have multiple meanings and can also be pronounced differently, although they are spelled the same. For example, the word "minute" (as in a minute in time) is pronounced differently than "minute" (as in something that is small), yet for the reader, they look exactly the same.

When teaching difficult vocabulary to ELLs, the teacher must make sure that the students have multiple exposures to the word or phrase. One way of teaching idioms is to use current sayings. The idiom "May the Force be with you" may at least help ELLs understand the cultural context of idioms. Although some idioms can be taught through explicit instruction, most will need to be explained through close reading procedures. With multiple-meaning words and homographs, the definition taught should be the one that is used in the text being read. A new meaning can be taught when the word is used differently in another text. With homographs, if a different pronunciation is required, that needs to be directly explained.

Model Answer 2

English Language Learners (ELLs) need a lot of support to learn our language, as the English language can be very difficult. Three types of words or phrases that can be exceptionally difficult for ELLs are euphemisms, homonyms (or homophones), and acronyms. A euphemism is an expression that is substituted for something that is perhaps too harsh to say. An example would be instead of saying someone has died, a person might say "She passed away." Homonyms (or homophones) are words that sound the same, but are spelled differently and have different meanings, such as "hair" and "hare." Acronyms are words that are made from initials as in "radar" (radio detection and ranging) or remain in the initial form such as ASAP (as soon as possible). Radar could be defined as a regular word, but ASAP would need to be explained in more detail.

There are many ways to teach ELLs these confusing word types. First, the students would need to be taught one type at a time so as to not be confused, and numerous examples would need to be given. Homonyms are much more frequently used than euphemisms and acronyms, and should therefore be taught first. Euphemisms and acronyms are best taught within the context of the reading or speech. Homonyms could be explicitly taught, as they are encountered in the text or in a word study instructional unit in which the words are used in context. There are a number of apps that can be utilized to reinforce homonyms and their meanings. These apps are especially useful for ELLs because they often contain pictures, and visuals are effective tools for teaching ELLs.